THE CENTENNIAL BIOGRAPHY

ALBERT EINSTEIN

AN INTIMATE PORTRAIT

Bust of Einstein, sculpted by the author.

ALBERT EINSTEIN

AN INTIMATE PORTRAIT

by

Solomon Quasha

FOREST PUBLISHING COMPANY

Larchmont, New York

FIRST EDITION

Library of Congress Number: 79-57174
International Standard Book Number 0-9603978-0-9

The diagrams for Figures 1 through 6 were prepared by the author.

Book design by Alvin Schultzberg. Production supervision by The Town House Press, Spring Valley, New York.

Manufactured in the United States of America

FOREST PUBLISHING COMPANY
Larchmont, New York 10538

Dedicated to
Sam and Edith Quasha

"When for a moment he ceased to contemplate the interstellar spaces, he spoke sounder wisdom about war and peace than the practical men or the diplomats or the professors of political science; but they couldn't understand him any more than they could understand relativity."

The Christian Century,
March 18, 1931, p. 364.

"A greatness that has nothing to do with his scientific achievement."

Leopold Infeld,
American Scholar,
July 1947, p. 338.

"Concern for man himself must always constitute the chief objective of all technological effort . . . Never forget this when you are pondering over your diagrams and equations."

Albert Einstein

CONTENTS

LIST OF ILLUSTRATIONS

FOREWORD

During the latter part of his life Professor Einstein worked towards the establishment of a "unified field theory." He did so for many years and unsuccessfully, yet never with any loss of enthusiasm.

In his last illness he refused surgery "to artificially prolong life" (as he put it). He was satisfied and content even though he knew his final work had not been completed.

My association with this great man has taught me that a truly happy person, as he was, must strive to pursue his objectives and not give up. Yet one must also realize that we all function within our limitations which we must accept and not then become frustrated when certain goals remain beyond our reach.

Thomas Lee Bucky, M.D.

1

LIGHT CAUGHT BENDING, 1919

In the spring of 1919, with the war barely over, English scientists were busily engrossed with outfitting not one but two complete astronomical expeditions to test the gravitational theory, not of a fellow Britisher, but a physicist who was German.

During the war, German publications had been boycotted in France and the United States, so that the scientific communities of these countries had virtually no knowledge of German scientific advances. "But the British did not adopt this ostrichlike policy."[1] They kept their ears to the ground and their eyes and communication lines open to all that was happening in enemy countries in the spheres of science, technology and politics. Neutral Holland served both sides in a middleman capacity.

The man who single-handedly spearheaded the idea of the expeditions was Arthur Eddington, of the Royal Observatory. In 1915 he had read the German physicist's hypothesis, which included the theory: "As seen from the earth, certain fixed stars appear to be in the neighborhood of the sun, and are thus capable of observation during a total eclipse of the sun. At such times, these stars ought to appear to be displaced outwards from the sun . . . as compared with their apparent position in the sky when the sun is situated at another part of the heavens."[2] (Fig. 1). The physicist, a professor from the University of Berlin, predicted further that the angle of displacement would be approximately 1.75 degrees of arc.

This hypothesis was news to Eddington. Like every other astronomer and loyal Englishman he was an adherent of Newton's law of gravitation, which states in part, that light traveling in outer space travels in straight lines. The Berlin professor was, in fact, reconstructing the makeup of space. He said that "light from stars beyond the sun, when passing through the gravitational field of the sun and on their way to the earth, would be bent towards the sun."[3] But as seen from the earth the light would appear to be deflected outward from the sun.

Not a single scientific soul since the time of Newton had shown

1

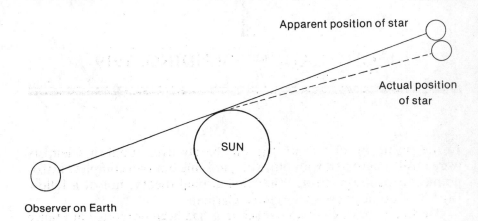

Figure 1. ". . . light from stars beyond the sun, when passing through the gravitational field of the sun and on their way to the earth, would be bent towards the sun." But as seen from the earth the light would appear to be deflected outward from the sun.

either the audacity or originality of thought to suggest a new theory of gravitation—a theory that in addition could be proved by observation. Just the same, reading Professor Albert Einstein's gravitational theory, the *General Theory of Relativity,* had convinced Eddington of its truth.

Eddington knew that despite Einstein's youth his theories were not to be lightly considered, no matter how they seemed to offend common sense. Einstein was the rising star of German science, with a reputation for scrupulous honesty. Previously, Einstein's 1905 *Special Theory of Relativity* had gained the attention of the scientific world because of its revolutionary departure from the precepts of classical science. Eddington saw that this new theory of gravitation was not just a generalization of the 1905 theory; it was an entirely new approach to gravity. Is light matter, as Einstein suggests? Can it be bent like matter by the sun's gravitational field?

Not content merely to acknowledge that Einstein had presented a new look at the universe, Eddington was impatient to get out into the field and check out the hypothesis for himself. He realized that Einstein's gravitational theory, if proved by observation, could account for the flaws in Newton's gravitational theory that cropped up uncomfortably now and then. They were bound to; no new gravitational theory had been advanced since Newton enunciated his back in the seventeenth century.

In his request to the astronomer royal, Sir Frank Dyson, Eddington, in 1916, asked for permission to test Einstein's theory using the approach Einstein himself had suggested in 1911: "As the fixed stars in the parts of the sky near the sun are visible during the total eclipses of the sun, this consequence of the theory may be compared with experience . . . . It would be a most desirable thing if astronomers would take up the question raised here."[4]

The essence of the question Eddington put to Dyson was this. Is it possible to detect an influence of gravitational fields on the propagation of light? Dyson, too, saw the unique possibilities. If proved, they would make Newton's gravity a special case of Einstein's new law. He therefore readily agreed to undertake the expeditions though funds were scarce and all departments were understaffed because of the manpower demands of the war.

A study of conditions showed that the total eclipse would occur in the vicinity of the equator, and that the sun would be favorably placed among a group of bright stars known as the Hyades. Two points of observation, Sobral in Brazil and Principe, an island off the west coast of Africa, were decided upon as the most favorable stations; that is, if war conditions allowed.

The Sobral expedition, headed by Dr. A.C. Crommelin and C. Davidson, was enthusiastically received by the Brazilian authorities. Dr. H. Morize, the Brazilian national astronomer, personally saw to arrangements for his English colleagues: an ample supply of water, the necessary labor with which to establish camp, and the grounds of the nearby "race course" where the equipment was set up.

The day of the eclipse, May 29, 1919, began unfavorably with early morning cloudiness, but the sky cleared making possible almost complete success with the telescopic photography. Davidson's telescope produced fifteen clear photographic images of the star group out of eighteen. Dr. Crommelin with a second lens secured seven successful plates out of eight.

Several thousand miles to the east, Eddington and his assistant, Mr. E.T. Cottingham, arrived at Principe on April 23 and immediately set up camp on the ten-mile-long, four-mile-wide island. They, too, were hospitably received and their host, Sr. Carneiro, made available the full facilities of his plantation for the purposes of solar research. "On the morning of the eclipse, the sky was completely cloudy, but about half an hour before totality we began to see glimpses of the sun's crescent through the clouds. We carried out our program exactly as arranged, and the sky must have been a little clearer towards the end of totality. Of the sixteen plates taken during the five minutes of totality the first ten showed no stars at all; of the latter plates two showed five stars each, from which a result could be obtained . . . . This result supports the figures obtained at Sobral."[5]

Crommelin and Davidson remained in Sobral until July when the same stars could be photographed in the night sky without the gravitational influence of the sun. This second series (the night series of photographs) was the crucial set of photographs; it gave a reference point, a point of comparison from which the eclipse photographs could be measured for the predicted difference of position of the stars as hypothesized by Einstein. According to Einstein's theory, the stars in the night sky would be shown to be closer to the sun than the same stars photographed during the eclipse. Because of unfavorable sky conditions, the Principe astronomers did not remain to take comparative photographs.

The plates from both locations were rushed to the Greenwich Observatory for precise measurement. The 1.75 degree of arc is so minute a measurement that making it has been compared to the task of trying to locate a single matchstick from a distance of half a mile. After months of painstaking calculations, the averaging out came to within decimal points of Einstein's prediction. The unbelievable proximity of Einstein's figures (which he had obtained with just paper and pen) to the observed figures came to be known as "one of the highest achievements of human thought."[6]

So momentous an occasion was this in the field of physics, astronomy and mathematics that Sir Frank Dyson convened the "Joint Eclipse" meeting of the Royal Society and the Royal Astronomical Society in London on November 6, 1919 to announce the results to the world: "After a careful study of the plates I am prepared to say that there can be no doubt that they confirm Einstein's prediction. A very definite result has been obtained that light is deflected in accordance with Einstein's law of gravitation." (*The Observatory*, November 6, 1919.)

The effect on the entire civilized world was electrifying. Einstein's photograph was flashed around the world to every city and town heralding his achievement. The time was ripe, perhaps, after the misery of the Great War, for victor and vanquished alike to turn to a man of peace, who had reached into the heavens and brought back a message to earth, be it all a scientific one.

The layman could not hope to understand the similarities of an "inertial" and a "gravitational" system as illustrated by Einstein in his "Principle of Equivalence," which is an essential part of the gravitational theory, but cartoonists, pulp magazine opportunists and hucksters played the novelty phase of the light-bending aspect of Einstein's gravitational theory to the hilt. For some reason Einstein caught on. He sold newspapers and magazines, in which often misrepresented versions of his theories were fed to an eager and curious public.

Scientific writers were at a loss to explain the theory within a two-column spread. It's questionable if they could have explained it with twenty columns at their disposal. It was thought that fewer than fifteen scientists in the entire world could follow the gravitational theory. But people were fascinated.

2

ORIGINS

Pauline Koch, Albert's mother, was born in Cannstatt, in 1858; his father, Hermann, in Buchau in 1847. Neither branch of the family can look back to their antecedents for a record of creative, intellectual, or academic achievements. Albert's forebears were tradespeople and semiprofessionals who had lived quietly, for hundreds of years, among the Protestant majority in the southwest corner of what is now the West German Federal Republic, in the Schwaben area of the Württemburg province. Whether offering a morning's greeting or engaging in the day's business, they were indistinguishable from their fellow Swabians, proud of their soft-spoken dialect, their slow-paced and easy-going manner, though by birth they were Jews. They never denied their heritage; they never flaunted it—nor did they practice it to any extent. They were loyal Swabians who benefited to a mild degree from the main occupation in the area, the growing of *Schillerwein* (a rosé), which because of the large amount of local consumption was rarely marketed in foreign lands.

Philipp Frank, Einstein's successor at the German University in Prague gives us a picture of the environment from which Einstein emerged:

> This background of southwestern Germany is very important in the understanding of Einstein's character. The Swabians merge almost imperceptibly with the French through the mediation of the neighboring Alsatians, and they are reflective, are practical in daily life, and participate joyfully in every kind of art and pleasure as well as in philosophical and religious speculations; but they are adverse to any kind of mechanical order. Their nature is different from that of the sober, practical Prussians, interested in order and domination, and from that of the earthy, merry, sometimes coarse Bavarians.
>
> The differences in the character of these people are quite evident from their dialects. The Swabians speech is melodic and flows like a rippling, murmuring brook, unlike that of the Germans of the ruling class of officers and officials, which sounds

6

like a bugle in a military camp. Neither is it like the cynical bleating of the Berliner, critical of everything in heaven or on earth, nor like the pompously precise literary German of the Pastors and professors.'

The peaceful Swabians had been forced to unite with the Prussians in 1870 to form one Germany. The south Germans had not been consulted regarding this merger; at that time neither the right to vote nor any semblance of a democratic system prevailed in any of the German states. South Germany had long been under the domination of the local princes and entirely subject to their whims, while the blatant northerners held the rural southerners in contempt.

The drive for German unification owes its direct origin to the battle of Jena in 1806. The Junker militarists, still smarting from the defeat by Napoleon at Jena were eager for retaliation against the French. (Prior to 1870, it was France that engaged Europe in bloody and costly wars in her attempts at European conquest and domination.)

Under Germany's first chancellorship, that of Count Otto von Bismarck, and under the rule of Kaiser Wilhelm I, German territorial expansion began. The Prussians felt the need for some form of buffer zone between the giant to their east and the adventuresome French in the west. Their first acquisition was Schleswig-Holstein, which was sliced off from Denmark in 1864. It was followed by the *Bruderkrieg,* the seven-weeks war against Austria in 1866. Then, in what must have been a very satisfying venture, they goaded the French into the Franco-Prussian War of 1870. It proved to be the only final and lasting (final and lasting for just a short period of time) victory the Germans were able to inflict upon their western enemy.

Because of incompetence in the higher echelons of her General Staff, it became impossible for France to mount an effective attack, though at the beginning she had ample opportunity and a decided advantage. The help she was promised from Austria, Italy and the princes of the southern German states was not forthcoming and France suffered a humiliating defeat, which cost her dearly in reparations.

The new found power of the North German Confederation paved the way for a united Germany, though under duress, and despite the obvious hatred between the north and the south. Bismarck was the embodiment of everything Prussian, demanding absolute obedience and unquestioning loyalty. "The great questions of the day", he proclaimed, "will not be decided by speeches and resolutions of majorities, but by blood and iron."

Hermann Einstein (1847–1902)   *Pauline Koch Einstein (1858–1920)*

It was against this background of recent wars and annexations, a new harsh order of things and the rekindling of the myth of German superiority that Pauline and Hermann were married, in the year 1876. They then settled in Ulm where Hermann managed a small electrochemical factory. On March 14, 1879 the marriage was blessed with the birth of their only son, Albert.

Ulm had been an important trading center from the third century on because of its location (at the junction of the Danube and Iller rivers). Also known as the "cathedral city," Ulm boasts a 258-foot church tower, said to be the tallest in Europe. And for those who find significance in coincidences—Ulm was the last home of Johannes Kepler, the renowned astronomer and mathematician. It was Kepler's law of planetary orbits that later became the basis on which Sir Isaac Newton developed his theory of gravitation.

The environment and daily life of the Einsteins and other Jews of Swabia were unlike those of their counterparts anywhere else in the world. "The life of the Jews in these districts was not similar to that in Berlin, where there was a class of rich, educated Jews, who themselves developed a specific variant of Berlin culture. There was none of this in the small Swabian towns. Here the Jews, like the other inhabitants, led a quiet life, associated with their natural environment, and were but little influenced by the nervous hustle and bustle of the metropolis.''[8]

The Einsteins did not attend synagogue services, not even during the high holy days, nor did they observe the Jewish dietary laws. Living amongst the Christian majority they were not the victims of a ghettoized existence, the demeaning lot of their fellow Jews in parts of eastern Europe. Swabia of the 1880s was the home of religious tolerance and enlightenment; Christians and Jews lived peacefully, side by side, with little or no friction. Religious differences did not enter everyday affairs. And had not the Nazis slaughtered those who were not of the master race, surely, in time, there would have been a peaceful assimilation of the Jew and German.

This liberal atmosphere, free from the persecution and restrictions that plagued the lives and stunted the hopes of Jews in other European countries, allowed the Einsteins the intellectual luxury of considering themselves freethinkers. They were good Germans who drank their beer and read their philosophers. Hermann was a kind, jovial and happy-go-lucky man, but not accomplished in any field. Pauline, a rather quiet, plain but capable hausfrau brought a love of music into the home and played the works of her favorite composers, Bach, Beethoven and Mozart on the family piano. The best qualities of both parents eventually rubbed off on their son, Hermann's good humor and Pauline's love of music.

Prosperity reigned in the larger cities of the newly-formed German empire as a result of the unusually large amount of reparations the victors had extracted from the vanquished. (Some estimates run as high as one billion dollars.) But, the financial benefits had not made themselves felt in the geographical area around Ulm, and certainly did not flow down to the average worker. Consequently, many young people migrated from the small cities to the larger ones to seek their fortune. And that's what the Einsteins did when Albert was one-year old. They packed their belongings and moved about sixty miles east, to the overwhelmingly Bavarian Catholic capital of Munich.

Near his new home, Hermann and his younger brother, Jake, established an electrochemical factory, Jake being somewhat of an engineer. The venture was successful from the start and the two Einstein families lived side by side, in modest comfort, only several hundred yards from the factory.

One year after they moved, a daughter, Maja was born to Hermann and Pauline. Maja was a laughing child and a constant com-

Birthplace of Albert Einstein, 20 Bahnhofstrasse, Ulm, Germany.

panion to her brother. Their close attachment and devotion to each other lasted their entire lives.

The Einsteins enjoyed good times—Sunday trips to the country in the summer, stopping at wayside inns for sausages, egg noodles, and big, red, mouth-watering radishes. They were sometimes joined by their Italian cousins and often by cousin Elsa and her family from nearby Hechingen, as they explored the wooded hills bounded on the southern horizon by the Swiss Alps. It was a warm family life that Albert experienced, in a happy home open to those in need and to many friends. The engineers from the plant would stop by occasionally after work for a songfest and a few steins of beer. Music, laughter and serenity blessed the Einstein fireside in those days.

Credit: Stadtarchiv, Ulm.

School in Ulm named for Einstein, 1972

3

CHILDHOOD

Unlike Mozart and other child wonders whose early accomplishments were extraordinary, Albert Einstein's start was notoriously slow. His development proceeded at a snail's pace when compared with that of other children his age, and his early years were a puzzling and sometimes discouraging time for his parents. They were worried because Albert started to talk comparatively late and they consulted a doctor because of it. Einstein remembered that he was not younger than three at the time.

His shyness, his lack of any obvious aptitude, and his inability to put on the usual cute, childish performances were looked upon by his relatives as a form of backwardness. His aloof, quiet and comtemplative ways soon discouraged his parents from expecting early signs of intellectual promise. They shook their heads sadly.

One day, however, the unexpected happened. Hermann gave his four-year-old son a pocket compass. Instead of playing with the compass the way most children would, Albert was excitably fascinated by the persistence of the needle in seeking magnetic north, no matter how it was held or how it was turned. He was mystified by what he later remembered to be some "outside force" inexplicably controlling the movement of the needle. (What had been considered empty space was actually filled with invisible forces.) In Einstein's words: "That this needle behaved in such a determined way did not at all fit into the nature of events. I can still remember—or at least believe I can remember—that this experience made a deep and lasting impression upon me. Something deeply hidden had to be behind things. What man sees before him from infancy causes no reaction of this kind; he is not surprised over the falling of bodies, concerning wind and rain, nor concerning the moon or about the fact that the moon does not fall down, nor the difference between living and non-living matter."[9]

This, his first encounter with the wonders of natural phenomena, it can now be said, was the first indication of a life-long journey on a path different from that of his fellow man and of an eternal all-consuming fascination with the mysteries of the universe.

Mention Einstein's name and people's immediate reaction is invariably "genius." Mathematician could almost cover it, philosopher perhaps, but physicist would be more like it, and then Zionist, pacifist and humanitarian. Because of such associations, when the subject of early schooling is brought up, people take it for granted that schoolwork must have been easy for Einstein. It wasn't. Einstein's student life was anything but a bed or roses—or time of achievement. In fact, his education in Munich was a terrifying experience at times.

He instinctively reacted against the compulsory nature of the educational process, especially when it required memorizing names and dates. The school system throughout the Germany of almost one hundred years ago adhered to the "obedience without question" method employed by the north Germans. When called upon to answer a teacher's question, the students were expected to leap from their seats and scream the answer at the top of their voices. Little wonder that Albert early developed an intense dislike for forced learning and regimentation.

His instinctive, inborn reaction against a disciplined, constituted authority, rather than proving a hindrance, served to awaken the curiosity that later developed into doubt and skepticism, providing him fresh vistas that were for the most part unseen by the conformist. He strayed further from the circle of a well-rounded childhood when he refused to engage in any form of competitive sports. He didn't plan it that way, but in essence he was somewhat of a loner, finding few friends in school with whom he had anything in common. If he seemed reluctant to form close friendships with his fellow students at the Catholic school in Munich, it wasn't because he was the only Jew in the class, but rather because of his shy, withdrawn and introspective personality.

Before the turn of the century, schools in Munich were administered by religious institutions, and since Catholicism dominated the geographical area, it also controlled the educational system. Albert's parents could have sent him far from home to a Jewish parochial school, but they were little inclined to insist upon a sound religious education for their son; they were quite content to have Albert mix with his neighbors.

Albert did receive some Jewish instruction, whether at home or at a special class at school is not clear from the scant reporting available. In any event, as Alexander Moszkowski noted, "It happened that he learned simultaneously the teachings of the Jewish as well as the Catholic Church; and he had extracted from them that which was common and conductive to a strengthening of faith and not what conflicted."[10] Later in life Einstein was to reject ritual, but retain the essence of religion.

Most people who came into contact with Albert found him rather dull. In the classrooms, his teachers were annoyed especially with his dreamy manner, which they interpreted as indifference, even snobbery. And when his concerned father anxiously asked his son's headmaster for an opinion as to the field Albert might best be suited, the response was that Albert would never accomplish anything. Lucius Bugbee adds to the legend: "Einstein was a dull and uninteresting boy. He did not have a retentive memory; lacking clearness and fluency in expressing himself."[11]

The Einsteins never quite gave up on their reluctant recluse. They tried music. This too became a form of coercion that he disliked; practicing was monotonous. "I took violin lessons from age six to fourteen, but had no luck with my teachers for whom music did not transcend mechanical practicing. I really began to learn when I was about thirteen years old, mainly after I had fallen in love with Mozart's sonatas. The attempt to reproduce to some extent their artistic content and their singular grace compelled me to improve my technique, which improvement I obtained from these sonatas without practicing systematically. I believe, on the whole, that love is a better teacher than sense of duty. With me, at least, it certainly was."[12]

Music became his second love, a respite from the isolation and complications in his whirling world of equations. More than the relaxation, Einstein enjoyed the continuity, the beauty, and the harmony. He found in music, especially in the music of Bach, Mozart, and Haydn, a unity that he also found in the construction of the universe. Throughout his adult life, wherever his many interests took him, he seldom traveled without his violin. Admitting to a pretty good amateur status Einstein often played with private chamber music groups for the sheer pleasure of it. He also performed publicly in trios and quartets in lecture halls and in palaces to raise money for the charities he supported.

The one type of music he really abhorred, if he would admit it to be music at all, was military band music. It was part of the Imperial German scene when Albert was growing up; the Junker generals seldom missed an opportunity to parade thousands of soldiers through the streets of Munich for the express purpose of reminding the citizenry of their military and cultural mission. Always accompanied by brass bands, the cavalry officers, with their exaggerated

Credit: Stadtarchiv, Ulm.

Gymnasium photograph, Munich, 1889. Einstein, at the age of ten, is third from the right in the front row. On close inspection, one sees that Albert is the only student wearing a smile.

bearing and the storm of marching boots over the cobblestones made up some of Albert's most distasteful memories. His revulsion from the military was pure instinct. He expressed this attitude very early in life. As he grew older and came to learn that the din of battle was far different from the din of cheering crowds, he adamantly spoke out against and consistently deplored the military way of settling differences. "The worst outcrop of herd life . . . the military system. That a man can take pleasure in marching in fours to the strain of a band is enough to make me despise him."[13]

Young Albert detested the obsequious manner of soldiers towards their officers and the outright flaunting by officers of their superiority. The power over life and death held by the generals was a responsibility he felt they had abused for centuries. "Conscription places the individual entirely at the mercy of military powers. It is a form of slavery. The people's unquestioning acceptance of this slavery illustrates its insidious effect."[14]

At the age of ten, Albert was transferred to the Luitpold Gymnasium (a secondary school that would prepare him for the university). His experiences at the Luitpold in no way modified the antipathy he had developed for regimented education. The teachers, as he saw

them, behaved like army sergeants, like automatons, not like concerned adult friends one could emulate and from whom one could
learn freely and willingly. Students lived in constant fear of the
teachers and rather than risk a teacher's anger and a possible whip-
ping, they behaved as submissively as possible. Years later, when Einstein reflected on this formative period in his life, he said: "It is bad
for a school to work with methods of fear, force and artificial
authority. They destroy the sincerity and self-confidence of the
pupils. They produce submissive persons."[15]

It was at school that Albert first became aware of the effect of
social and economic inequities, through the way the teachers treated
the students: the more prosperous the family, the better the treatment of the child of that family; the poorer the family, the harsher
the treatment. His sympathies for the less fortunate were beginning
to develop.

Rounding into his teens Albert still had not shown in the slightest
way evidence of being a "brain." He seemed to ignore most people
and most events. He was quite content to be absorbed in what to him
was his natural world. This absorption was in no way the result of a
psychological warp of personality; it was not a form of neurosis—nor
was it the result of rejection. And contrary to some claims, he never
had the symptoms of "dyslexia." The quietude he deferred to in his
formative years helped develop the unique individual who was later
characterized as "the conscience of the world."

Since neither friends nor relatives could penetrate or comprehend
that faraway look, they had no recourse but to leave him to his
private thoughts. *Biedemeier* (honest John), *Pater Langweil* (father
bore)—they nicknamed him for his dull honesty and lack of sparkle;
a "square" who wasn't really with it. He didn't lead; neither did he
follow. He simply "heard a different drummer." During his entire
lifetime no one could maintain a truly close relationship with Albert
Einstein for any given period of time. His physics, his science always
came before personal relationships.

My passionate interest in social justice and social responsibility
has always stood in curious contrast to a marked lack of desire
for direct association with men and women. I am a horse for a
single harness, not cut out for tandem or teamwork. I have never
belonged whole-heartedly to any country or state, to my circle of
friends, or even to my own family. These ties have always been
accompanied by a vague aloofness, and the wish to withdraw into
myself increases with the years. Such isolation is sometimes bit-

ter but I do not regret being cut off from the understanding and sympathy of other men. I lose something by it, to be sure, but I am compensated for it in being rendered independent of the customs, opinions and prejudices of others and am not tempted to rest my peace of mind upon shifting foundations.''[16]

Aside from his aversion to forced education, he saw that school for him was a waste of time and energy; having to study subjects simply to get good marks. Lacking interest, he seemingly daydreamed his way through school, ignoring most of his subjects. One class, however, conducted by a teacher named Ruess made Albert sit up, take notice and want to learn. This was the philosophy class, where Ruess demonstrated a unique ability at awakening individual thought in his students. Ruess's method provided the incentive for Albert's interest in the works of Schiller, Goethe and Shakespeare; and once Albert's curiosity was aroused, there was little anyone could do to curb it. In order to spend as much time as possible receiving instruction and guidance from Ruess, Albert purposely provoked punishment in Ruess's class, so he could be kept after class. He found Ruess's class an experience of pure joy, a complete contrast to the rote learning demanded of him by other instructors.

Years later when Einstein was a young and still poor professor in Zurich, he paid a nostalgic visit to his former gymnasium instructor on his way through Munich. Einstein glowed with fond memories of Ruess, but Ruess didn't even remember the name Einstein, nor could he figure out who the rather shabbily dressed figure standing in front of him might be. Though he greeted his former pupil courteously, Ruess probably thought the younger man had come by for a handout. After a brief but halting conversation Einstein realized that his good intentions in attempting to reawaken the student-teacher relationship, if only for a few minutes, were being regarded with suspicion. Disappointed and embarrassed, he retreated and left.

Albert's personal likes ran counter to what other youngsters found to be their natural inclinations, both in the classroom and on the playing field. He preferred to spend his time wondering about grass, trees, sky and the myriad marvels of nature we often ignore and take so much for granted. It was the beauty and harmony of the universe that he found infinitely more compelling than Latin, Greek or football.

What evolved from his religious training and his love of nature was a deep and devout religious feeling, which he manifested by composing religious themes on the family piano. Aside from criticizing his parents for not living up to the beliefs and customs of Judaism, his early "crusade" also led him to refuse to eat pork. In his own words, "Thus I came, despite the fact that I was the son of irreligious Jewish parents, to a deep religiosity."[17]

Hermann and Pauline were not very strict parents, and they welcomed this little revolt by their son. They were happy because of his involvement in religion, though not for religion's sake. They were so pleased that Albert had finally found the inner fortitude to assert himself that they accepted the criticism and waited to see what would follow.

Credit: Einstein archives

Brother and sister, Albert and Maja Einstein, at about fourteen and twelve years old, respectively.

4

EARLY INTERESTS

Jake Einstein, Albert's uncle, made a rather timely and perhaps the most important contribution to his nephew's development when he introduced him to the subject of mathematics. Uncle Jake didn't just plop a book down in front of Albert and demand that he read and understand. In order to acquaint the youngster with something that he considered of value, he developed a unique way of making the intricate study of mathematics interesting. Jake called it a "merry science." When the animal cannot be caught, we call it X temporarily, and continue to hunt it until it is bagged. Albert responded.

Remembering that the gyrating needle of the compass had been the first real wonder in his life experience. Einstein later recalled: "At the age of twelve I experienced a second wonder of a totally different nature; in a little book dealing with Euclidian plane geometry . . . the holy geometry book . . . This lucidity certainly made an indescribable impression upon me . . . .for example, I remember that an uncle told me the Pythagorean theorem before the holy geometry booklet had come into my hands. After much effort I succeeded in proving this theorem on the basis of the similarity of triangles."[18] The real wonder that this little pamphlet on geometry engendered later served as the vehicle by which he was propelled from dullard to genius. Perhaps, in the normal course of events his native ability would have surfaced at another period of his life, in another field, with like results, but that possibility must be considered remote. This awakening, at twelve, was the turning point in his life; it led him down the sparse and lonely but unique path to relativity.

Seeking knowledge on subjects that were not part of his school's curricula, he devoured every book and bit of scientific information Uncle Jake could dig up. So fast was he absorbing the basics of this new found religion that he soon outstripped even Jake's storehouse of information. Albert may have remained passive and uninvolved with what was taught at school, but when it came to mathematics and geometry, his unrelenting pursuit took on the passion of missionary zeal. As he himself put it: "I had a furious impulse to learn . . . . At the age of 12-16, I familiarized myself with the elements of mathematics together with the principles of differential and integral calculus. In doing so I had the good fortune of hitting on books which made the main thoughts stand out clearly and synoptically. This occupation was on the whole, truly fascinating . . . . I also had the good fortune of getting to know the essential results and methods of the entire field of the natural sciences in an excellent popular exposition, which limited itself throughout to qualitative aspects (Bernstein's People's Book on Natural Science, a work of 5 to 6 volumes) a work which I read with breathless attention."[19]

When Jake's well of scientific information ran dry and he no longer found it possible to cope the youngster's questions, he was relieved and eager to welcome as his replacement, a young medical student named Max Talmey. Talmey came to dine at the ample Einstein table by way of his brother, Dr. Bernard Talmey, a friend of the Einsteins. Max, at the time, was a student at the University of Munich, and it was a well-established custom for a Jewish family to share its table and hearth. Max became a weekly visitor. It didn't require many visits for him to recognize Albert's intellectual potential: "Extraordinary mentality was already evident in Albert Einstein when he was only a young boy. This I observed at close range through my association with him from his tenth to his fifteenth year . . . . whenever I came he delighted in showing me new problems from the book which he had solved in the preceding week . . . I found an exceptional intelligence which enabled him to discuss with a college graduate subjects far above the comprehension of children his own age."[20]

Anxious to watch and aid in the development of Albert's scientific bent, Talmey brought the most recently published scientific periodicals and books on geometry including Buchner's *Force and Matter* and Spiker's *Geometry*. But Talmey, too, was left behind: "Soon the flight of his mathematical genius was so high that I could no longer follow."[21] When Albert mastered everything in the books, Talmey in sheer desperation, hoping still to add fuel to Einstein's fire, turned the discussions to philosophy, especially Kant. At an age when most boys would be found out-of-doors playing games, Albert was secluded in his room reading and rereading Kant's *Critique of Pure Reason*. Talmey observed: "At that time he was still a child, only thirteen years old, yet Kant's works, incomprehensible to ordinary mortals seemed clear to him . . . . Albert was seldom in the company of boys his own age . . . . I never saw Albert reading any light literature . . . . He usually held himself aloof, absorbed in books on

Dr. Max Talmey

mathematics, physics, and philosophy. His recreation he found mainly in music.''[21]

While concentrating heavily on physics, mathematics and philosophy at home on his own time, Albert neglected history, biology and languages, barely receiving passing grades. What made matters worse, as a result of obtaining a superior knowledge in the subjects of his choice, he became a source of irritation to his teachers, who were ill-equipped by their own limited education to answer the technical questions Albert asked. The embarrassment this curious situation caused in front of the other students only helped estrange Albert further from his teachers. The teachers, who defensively considered his unanswerable questions calculated effrontery, predicted that "Einstein would never come to any good." Dogmatic pedagogy and strict requirements for obedience had been discouraging enough for Albert; in addition, the subjects in which he was most interested were not even taught at the school. That made attending school pure drudgery.

The difficulties at school did not affect his intellectual progress as much, however, as the conflict that arose within him because of the reading he did at home. Scientific truths are based on proven scientific experiments. Their sound reasoning seemed at variance with Albert's other passion, fundamental religion. "Through the reading of popular scientific books I soon reached the conviction that much in the stories of the Bible could not be true. The consequence was a positively fanatic orgy of free-thinking, coupled with the impression that youth is intentionally being deceived by the State through lies; it was a crushing impression. Suspicion of every kind of authority grew out of this experience, a skeptical attitude towards the convictions which were alive in any special environment—an attitude which has never again left me."[22]

Albert resented the fact that religious instruction was compulsory and forcibly imposed on him by the State, from the outside. He felt that personal human values should be accumulated through one's own life experience and not through indoctrination with the dogma of others. The outcome was the suspicion of all accepted principles, scientific as well as religious, that he never abandoned throughout his school years and later in life. He learned to rely on his own intuition and to place less credence in the written word regardless of the subject or source. The "crushing impression" created only a short pause in Albert's search for the ultimate and universal truth; his disillusion with organized religion merely shunted to another track the vehicle with which Einstein was to drive an opening wedge into the revered, redoubtable, and heretofore unquestioned principles of classical science. From this time on, he began to question where for centuries most had slavishly accepted and few had inquired.

Albert's young mind was now more receptive than ever to revolutionary concepts, freethinking, and unbridled imagination. He continued his voracious reading at home, including the works of Buddha, Spinoza, Schopenhauer, Confucius, Socrates and Aristotle. But his greatest rewards still came from studying mathematics, physics and the holy geometry book. His thoughts now traveled through the far reaches of the universe, wondering what it would be like hurtling through space alongside a beam of light at the speed of 186,000 miles per second.

5

ITALIAN SOJOURN

"He was a dark-haired, brown-eyed boy belonging, just as his near kin, to the brunette type," and still, more often than not, deep in thought, shy, and unusually slow in answering questions. Albert still seemed to measure every word painstakingly before uttering a syllable, and was reluctant to take part in routine, everyday conversation.

Poppa Hermann was proud of his son's scientific bent. For one thing, it showed that the youngster was following in his family's footsteps, and for another, that at least in the field of engineering, or any allied field, Albert's lack of communicative skill would not stand in the way of his providing a living for himself. But Frau Einstein quietly hoped her son would someday become a professor.

Hermann was concerned about his son's future for another reason. In the last few years the factory had suffered financial reverses and would be forced to shut down. And worse yet, the cheerful home with its middle-class comforts was to be sold. Despite this financial setback, Hermann's perennial enthusiasm was not to be dimmed. He traveled south to confer with the well-to-do Milan relatives, who agreed to help him set up another plant; but this factory would be established in Italy where the family could maintain a watchful presence. Not that they didn't trust cousin Hermann; it was just that he had a reputation of being somewhat of a bon vivant and they had to protect their investment. So, the Munich Einsteins packed up and moved to Pavia, on the outskirts of Milan; all except Albert, who was to remain behind to finish his schooling.

For the next six months, Albert's lone existence became progressively less bearable. Bewildered by the necessity of having to leave the only home he had ever known and live among strangers in a boarding house; despairing because of the loneliness he suffered with the sudden departure of his family; on his own, facing the gray, inhospitable city alone, everyday, with few friends as solace . . . with all these intolerable conditions crowding in on the hapless youth, he decided that the situation was no longer one he could continue to endure. He then took matters into his own hands. For the first time in his young life he was compelled by these unacceptable circumstances to use his own initiative. Happily, he found he was equal to the task.

His decision became final and irrevocable when his family wrote glowingly of the warm Italian sun and of the carefree people and their laughter, which stood out in marked contrast to the cold, austere nature of his countrymen. He decided he would leave school and leave Germany. Obviously, there was a better and happier life to live, elsewhere. As it turned out, it was one of the best moves he ever made; and in his lifetime he was to make several.

Albert came to the conclusion that if he was to effect his escape with the least amount of disruption to all concerned, he would have to put a twofold scheme of some devious means into play. First, he would have to fake a nervous, exhausted state; and second, he would have to obtain from his school a certificate attesting to his unusually high level of scientific achievement, so that at a later date he could present this paper to a university in lieu of a graduation certificate. Einstein literally became a high school "drop-out" long before dropping out became popular.

The medical paper indicating a change of climate as being essential for the improvement of his health was not difficult to obtain from the friendly and sympathetic family doctor. In his quest for the certificate in mathematics, he found an ally where he least expected one, in the person of his mathematics teacher, who, he discovered, would be delighted at Albert's departure, since it would bring to an end the classroom embarrassment.

Armed with his violin, some books, a couple of small carrying bags, and two very important certificates, the 15-year-old traveler boarded the next train for Milan. It didn't occur to him as the train speeded through the snow-peaked mountains of Switzerland that he would return to this beautiful land to complete his education. What did occur to him and what was uppermost in his mind, so far as the immediate future was concerned, was his determination to renounce his German citizenship and his equally strong decision to leave the Jewish community. There emerged from Germany, unnoticed by his fellow passengers, a youth whose early beliefs had been jostled about, but who now stood firmly convinced that religion was archaic and patriotism merely another reason for senseless murder.

His quiet and pensive manner veiled an uncompromising obstinacy, which had parried the thrust of forced education and permitted the young Einstein to filter from the system the material that suited his needs. What he liked he absorbed; what he thought useless, he ignored. Had he not been born in a country so hysterically steeped in the military mystique, he might not have developed such an early revulsion against the military system. Even as a tender youth he understood how cruel a burden was imposed upon the citizens of individual nations, having to defend with their lives the artificial, man-made national boundaries to which their respective governments were stupidly committed. "I don't want to be the citizen of any country. I think if you are a citizen you are made to do things that are wrong. You are forced to go into the Army, you must fight in wars and maim and kill other men—men you don't even know. I don't believe in wars, or in armies or in countries that make war on other countries. I think war is the greatest crime that there is on Earth. I would rather go to jail for the rest of my life, I would rather be torn to pieces than to be a soldier for as much as a single day." Young Einstein's distaste for war and nationalism were not the temporary rhetoric of an idealistic youth; he felt the same way his entire life.

In Milan, in the year 1894, the Einstein parents were faced with a "fait accompli" and were helpless to do anything but accept their son into their new surroundings. This was his first in a lifetime of rebellions against authority. He remained a rebel throughout his life; in his career, his social behavior and his disdain for material comforts. This was for him his natural way, not an affectation.

Having rejoined his family, Albert frolicked for the next six months or so, warming to the climate and scenery of northern Italy. He hiked the Appenine mountains, waded their glistening streams, and responded in kind to the friendliness and laughter of the people. The happiness he encountered and the flowering that followed can best be compared to the release of a young plant from the shadows into the sunlight. In Italy he met young people his own age with whom he developed an instant rapport. It was evident that the more relaxed way of life was responsible, in a large measure, for his ability to relate to his new friends more easily than to his schoolmates back in Munich.

Albert's sojourn in Italy brought him other benefits as well. He picked up remarkably in his ability to speak the Italian language (his difficulty with languages before this has been well documented). The company of open and friendly people made it possible for him to shed inhibitions and reveal a dormant sense of humor. His new trademark was a honking laugh, with his head thrown back. Visiting museums and art galleries throughout northern Italy, Albert gloried in his newfound freedom. At the same time, his social antennae were not asleep, and he marked well the sharp contrast between the harsh German temperament and the happy attitude of the Italians. He noted particularly that in Italy he never heard the word *verboten.*

There was no hint yet that in ten years from the time of the Italian interlude, a young Einstein would be publishing a series of revolutionary papers that would present a radically new look at the universe, the scope of which remains unequaled in the annals of man and the scientific ramifications of which have not as yet been fully ascertained to this day.

Too soon the holiday came to an end. Hermann Einstein had talked around the subject, uncomfortably, several times. And though previous attempts had ended in failure,he was finally able to sit his son down and convey to him the bad news: the factory in Pavia was having no greater success than the one in Munich; the family fortunes were once again at a low ebb. Therefore, it was most imperative, at this time, that Albert seriously consider his future and somehow find the means to support himself. Since his natural abilities pointed to a career in either engineering or one of the other sciences, after further consultations the family was once again asked to come to the financial rescue. They responded favorably as before, and volunteered to provide one hundred francs (approximately $25.00) per month for Albert's university education. This generous endowment was made both from a sense of family obligation and a long-standing respect for education, not from any precognition of Albert's intellectual potential.

No one who knew Albert in those days can be faulted for not predicting a brilliant future for this young man whose thoughts dwelt somewhere in the clouds. Living seemingly in a world apart, he showed no driving ambition or competitive spirit. His highest hope appeared to be that some time after graduation he would teach science, a pursuit that would allow him ample time to contemplate the universe. Everyone agreed that teaching would indeed be a fitting profession for the dreamy youth. Later in life Einstein related his thoughts during this period.

> Out yonder there was this huge world, which exists independently of us human beings and which stands before us like a great, eternal riddle, at least partially accessible to our inspection and thinking. The contemplation of this world beckoned like a liberation, and I soon noticed that many a man whom I had learned to esteem and to admire had found inner freedom and security in devoted occupation with it. The mental grasp of this

extrapersonal world within the frame of the given possibilities swam as the highest aim, half-consciously and half-unconsciously before my mind's eye. Similarly motivated men of the present and of the past, as well as the insights which they had achieved, were the friends which could not be lost. The road to this paradise was not as comfortable and alluring as the road to the religious; but it has proved itself as trustworthy, and I have never regretted having chosen it.[23]

From this point on, his future was clear; he had set his stride. The universe, translated in terms of geometry and mathematics was a world in which he could plant his faith firmly without fear that it would be swept away. He had experienced and rejected religious dogma and the slogans of narrow-minded patriotism in Germany. Now the slate was clean. His mind was free, unencumbered by prejudices and misguided loyalties, to roam from the far reaches of outer-galactic space to the innermost, hidden, unseen and unexplored world of the atom.

In the year 1895, the two most honored and most sought after centers for scientific studies were located in Germany—Göttengin and Berlin. Despite the prestige attached to these enclaves of scientific learning, Albert refused to return to German soil. Conveniently situated, however, between Italy and Germany, the peaceful and democratic country of Switzerland proudly boasted a highly respected candidate of its own, The Swiss Federal Institute of Technology (Eidgenossiche Technische Hochschule). Furthermore, the ETH was located in Zurich, a center of culture, and a haven for Europe's exiled radicals, with a German-speaking population.

Then only sixteen years old, Albert headed north to Zurich, armed only with Hermann's approval and his own certificate in mathematics. His father had promised to make an application for him to become a Swiss citizen; since he was still a minor, it fell to Hermann to arrange the switch in citizenship.

When he arrived at the ETH where the average age of the applicants was eighteen, he took the necessary entrance examinations. Unfortunately, he failed most of them because of his lack of interest in languages, zoology and botany. But his remarkable showing in mathematics and related subjects did not go unnoticed by the rector, Doktor Albert Herzog. Recognizing Albert's ability, Herzog recommended he make up his failed subjects by attending the Kantonschule at Aarau, a school some twenty miles west of Zurich.

Failing the examinations was sufficiently discouraging, but the thought of returning to the rigors and discipline of a gymnasium was a most disheartening blow to one whose mind was beginning to develop serious questions regarding the structure of the universe. He had thought that his torturous phase of his school life was behind him. From a practical and inescapable point of view, however, he had no other alternative. He hadn't finished high school, he possessed no skills, and his only interest was science. With the future picture of himself as a physics teacher still in mind, he put his pride in his pocket, acted on Herzog's suggestion, and moved to Aarau.

6

EDUCATION IN SWITZERLAND

At the Kantonschule in Aarau, Albert was astonished to encounter, for the first time in his life, a never-before-heard-of liberal attitude on the part of the teachers; rote or forced learning had no place in these classrooms. Here at last was a school where the instructors were helpful and understanding, providing an environment that was conducive to learning. This new method of education, though entirely unexpected, proved to be a thoroughly enjoyable experience for Albert. And once under the influence of this positive approach to learning, he became more communicative, shed more of his protective shyness, gave up more of his predilection for solitude, and eventually lost his distaste for school.

In Aarau he met the friendly Professor Jost Winteler, who invited Albert to room at his home and join his own seven lively children. Winteler's daughter, Anna and son, Paul, were to form a long and lasting friendship with the young Einstein. One of the happy results of the ongoing friendship was the later marriage of Paul Winteler to Albert's sister, Maja. The bright and happy daily comings and goings of the Winteler home, the musical concerts they attended, the hikes through the surrounding hills and mountains, these rekindled the still warm memories of his own upbringing.

During the pleasurable year at Aarau, he also learned of the relaxing rewards of sailing, at which he was to spend many a lonely but thought-filled hour. Einstein seldom let an opportunity slip by to go sailing—away from the persistent reporters and bothersome visitors —whether on the Havel near Potsdam or Carnegie Lake on the campus of Princeton University. When asked later in life why he had taken up sailing to the exclusion of other hobbies, Einstein replied, "because it required the least amount of physical exertion." The best description of Einstein, the sailor, was written by Antonina Vallentin, a personal friend of Elsa Einstein during the Berlin days.

> You had to see Einstein in a small skiff to be able to judge the strength of the roots which attached him to a primitive life. Barefoot or in sandals, his white ducks baggy at the knees, sagging at the hips, his broad chest molded in an old pull-over or a

faded swimming suit, his powerful neck bare, reddened by the sun and wind, his leonine head with its aura of long hair standing on end, he stood swaying gently to the rocking of the boat as though nailed to the deck and at one with the sail he maneuvered. The low horizon enlarged him out of proportion. The sun beat down on his screwed-up eyes, his face grimaced under the biting of the wind, his hair was tousled and the muscles of his arms were knotted like cords. He tugged at the sail, shouting something at me, and his mouth formed an O. The wind carried away his words. He looked so pagan, so healthily animal, that he seemed to have loomed up from the heart of the elements, from the age of the sea-gods or pirates. In fact, he looked anything else than a scientist.[24]

Albert was completely captivated by the beauty and hospitality of the small democratic country, which while requiring military service remained the least threatening and most peaceful of nations. Perhaps here in Switzerland, he would find the quiet contentment he was seeking. Perhaps here in Switzerland, he would live peaceably and teach for the rest of his life. But it wasn't as easy as all that; the profession of teacher in Switzerland, required civil service status, which in turn required Swiss citizenship, a privilege not dispensed quickly, freely or arbitrarily. Towards this goal he saved twenty of the one hundred francs he was receiving each month from his relatives and waited patiently to attain his majority. At the moment he was not the citizen of any country.

In the year at Aarau, Albert broadened his horizons through a growing love for people, a healthier respect for teachers, a deepening awareness of the mysteries of nature, and a firmed-up resolve to become a physics teacher. The examples of Jost Winteler and of his physics teacher, August Tuchschmid, helped.

During that joyful year, he also fulfilled the requirements necessary to reapply to the ETH in Zurich. This time his application was accepted without question and he was admitted as a full-time student. Before long he was meeting with students and professors from other lands, drawn, as he had been, by the reputation of the ETH.

Among the acquaintances Albert made at the ETH, three had the most influence on his life during his university days and for a long time thereafter. The first was a brilliant mathematician in his own right, Marcel Grossmann, a Swiss, without whose help Einstein might have remained the obscure, high-school physics teacher his critical self-image had settled for. It was Grossmann who early detected Einstein's incisiveness of mind and remarkable ability at cutting away the extraneous matter and getting to the heart of a problem. Grossmann, like Max Talmey before him, sensed the makings of a genius.

His second friend was Friedrich Adler, the son of Viktor Adler, the leader of the Austrian Socialist Party. The elder Adler, in his zeal as an active socialist had run afoul the laws of the autocratic, Austro-Hungarian Empire, and as a consequence had spent some time in prison. Aside from Friedrich's interest in physics and philosophy, Viktor Adler had another purpose in sending his son to the Swiss school—to keep him out of political trouble. Friedrich, like his father, was an uncompromising and militant idealist. In his determination to alleviate human suffering and exploitation and eventually bring about a universal peace he had joined the ranks of the pacifists. Einstein was easily accepting of the pacifist cause, and the two pacifists talked far into many a night about the evils of war. They concluded that pacifists must work towards someday establishing an international organization whose duties would include arbitrating differences between antagonists without resorting to senseless war, "the ultimate in human exploitation." Einstein's peaceful world could only be put into effect by a world government. "With all my heart I believe that the world's present system of sovereign nations can lead only to barbarism, war, and inhumanity, and that only world law can assure progress toward a civilized, peaceful humanity."[25] Adler's unique and somewhat bizarre contribution to world peace was his dramatic assassination of the Austrian prime minister, Karl von Sturgkh, during the First World War.

The third and perhaps most important friend Albert found at the ETH was a dark-haired, quiet, Serbian girl from Novi Sad, Hungary. Mileva Maric was her name and her devotion to and interest in science matched even Einstein's. They obviously had more in common than a shared desire for a scientific education, for they were more often than not found together, reading, studying, and talking. Mileva had hoped to teach mathematics in Switzerland too, rather than return to Hungary where her people were a minority and suffered from a lack of civil rights.

Mileva was the perfect sounding board for Albert's newly-forming theories; a serious, sometimes moody, but also a practical and decisive counterbalance to Einstein's lack of discipline, disregard for personal habits, and preoccupation with matters other than the daily routine.

There was money for only an occasional restaurant meal; other times it was potluck for Albert, cooking his own meager fare in his sparsely appointed room. And sometimes nourishment was forgotten when he was deeply engrossed in his own research. This youthful neglect had its painful effect; for many years afterward Einstein was to suffer from recurring stomach trouble. "But, it was the nourishment of the mind and not the satisfaction of the stomach which continued to engross Einstein."[26] He neglected his clothing and eating habits, but he did take on a few tutoring jobs that made it possible for him to attend a musical concert or two high up in the cheap seats.

Albert's fruitful year at Aarau had whetted his appetite for further study. Now at the ETH his scientific development was proceeding faster than his schoolmates' thanks to the extracurricular reading he found necessary in order to keep abreast of the latest findings in science. In his *Autobiographical Notes,* Einstein said of these school days: "At the age of 17, I entered the Polytechnic Institute of Zurich as a student of mathematics and physics. There I had excellent teachers (for example, Hurwitz, Minkowski), so that I really could have gotten a sound mathematical education. However, I worked most of the time in the physical laboratory, fascinated by the direct contact with experience. The balance of the time I used in the main in order to study at home the works of Kirchhoff, Helmholtz, Hertz . . . . The most fascinating subject at the time I was a student was Maxwell's theory (electrodynamics)."[27]

Through his continual reading, day and night, Einstein came to some profound conclusions that set him apart not only from his contemporaries but also from the "classicists." He agreed with Ernst Mach's rejection of Newton's theory of absolute space and time. "It was Ernst Mach who, in his *History of Mechanics,* shook the dogmatic faith in classical mechanics which physicists saw for a century as a firm and final foundation for all physics. This book exercised a profound influence upon me in this regard while I was a student. I see Mach's greatness in his incorruptible skepticism and independence."[28] But he also found an area of disagreement. In Einstein's opinion, general laws (phenomena) are tested by everyday laboratory experience, "but owe their origin to the inventive faculty of the human mind."[29] Mach, on the other hand, would not be dislodged from the notion that the general laws of physics are only summaries of "experimental results."

Mach was one of the few scientists in the latter half of the nineteenth century who found fault with the construction of the Newtonian-Galilean universe, and who felt that the time was long past due for a reevaluation of the construction of the universe. The winds of

Credit: AIP, ETH Bibliotheck

The Physical Institute of the Zurich Polytechnic; Zurich, circa 1900.

scientific revolution were beginning to gather, but most professors had long ago donned their earmuffs and blinders and were not listening or watching. When Max Planck was a student in 1874 and was trying to decide which field—music, philology or physics to pursue, he was advised by one of his professors that nothing essentially new remained to be discovered in physics. Perhaps not all professors voiced the same opinion, but the number was in the majority.

At the ETH Einstein's healthy skepticism towards accepted scientific principles made no more friends for him among the faculty than it had made at the Luitpold gymnasium. Again by constant questioning he incurred the enmity of the professors. Some professors were clearly envious of his unaccepting, forever inquisitive mind; others were simply incapable of thinking beyond the level of their own scientific knowledge, which they had ceased increasing with the appointment to their posts. For the latter group, Newton had said it all, for all time, and they would allow no adding to or improving upon. This is not to question their honesty or integrity as scientists; they taught principles that they believed to be valid and true. The few skeptics among them had not developed a sufficient library of recent discoveries from which to teach; they used only the approved texts which were invariably based on Newtonian mechanics. The professors were helpless prisoners of the accepted, provable dogma. But not Einstein; he automatically questioned the assumptions that most scientists took for granted.

In the middle of the nineteenth century, James Clerk Maxwell had introduced the "electromagnetic field" theory, an outgrowth of Michael Faraday's discoveries in electricity and magnetism. Later, Henrik Antoon Lorentz and Ernest Rutherford attempted to explain the behavior of electrons (the electron theory was regarded as heresy at most universities) and in the year 1900 Max Planck had just read (somewhat uneasily) his paper on the quantum theory. Such was the material Einstein was busily absorbing in his spare time. The world of the whirling electron had no meaning for most scientists; they believed in the indestructibility of the atom. Without observable or laboratory proof they would not concede the existence of this often hinted at microscopic world. The electron theory was not even included in the curriculum of the ETH, so that Einstein was obliged to instruct himself. Meanwhile, the conservatives among teaching physicists were finding it increasingly difficult to keep propping up Newtonian classical physics, which had remained essentially unchanged for the past two hundred years. Einstein saw as his mission a directing of his skepticism into an uncompromising search for the truth in the universe.

Ernst Mach

James Clerk Maxwell

The professors at the ETH were not oblivious to Einstein's obvious brilliance (begrudgingly conceded by some) and encouraged him to believe that he would be appointed to an assistant professorship (Privatdozent), a nonpaying, lecturing position, upon graduation. A position of this kind would be the ideal situation for Albert; it offered the use of the university's facilities and further study in an academic environment. The only fee obtainable, however, would be left to the generosity of the students. The uncertainty of a livelihood would not have been an obstacle; he had become accustomed to the frugality necessitated by a student's life. His lifelong disdain for material comforts freed him from the everyday pursuits of his fellow man. "Even when I was a fairly precocious young man, the nothingness of the hopes and strivings which chases most men relentlessly through life came to my consciousness with considerable vitality. Moreover, I soon discovered the cruelty of that chase, which in those years was much more covered up by hypocrisy and glittering words than is the case today. By the mere existence of his stomach everyone was condemned to participate in that chase. Moreover it was possible to satisfy the stomach by such participation, but not man so far as he is a thinking and feeling being."[30] Each adventure among his fellow man only fortified his desire to shrink away from the cruel and violent "civilization" he encountered. Albert wished to take no part in it, save only for sitting quietly in his own corner, studiously doing his work. And he was satisfied that the requirements of his university work would not interfere with his investigations of the mysteries of the universe.

The unworldly near-graduate, continuing on his own path, his mind occupied with his own theories on how God had created the universe, placed reliance on the half-smiles and promises of those who had assured him of a position on the faculty. But first the reality of final exams had to be faced. Albert's earlier decision to deemphasize mathematics in favor of physics had left him deficient in the former. "The fact that I neglected mathematics to a certain extent had its cause not merely in my stronger interest in the natural sciences than in mathematics but also in the following strange experience. I saw that mathematics was split up into numerous specialties, each of which could easily absorb the short life time granted to us . . . . and it was not clear to me as a student that the approach to a more profound knowledge of the basic principles of physics is tied up with the most intricate mathematical methods. This dawned on me only gradually after years of independent scientific work."[34] Obviously, the Privatdozent position would ultimately be dependent upon his showing in the finals. Realizing his predicament, he appealed to his friend, Marcel Grossmann, who had never missed a lecture and had transcribed his notes accurately and neatly. Together with Mileva, Grossmann crammed months of mathematics into Albert's head in the space of two weeks. Needless to say, he passed his exams, achieving a 4.91 out of a possible 6.00.

Reminiscing about these exams, Einstein recalled: "One had to cram all this stuff into one's mind for the examinations whether one liked it or not. This coercion had such a deterring effect upon me after I passed the final examination, I found the consideration of any scientific problems distasteful to me for an entire year."[32]

Time did not soften Einstein's distaste for and opposition to the forced feeding method of education . . . . to the attitude that "we know what's best for you, so just listen and learn." According to Einstein the teacher's influence should be based on other than authoritarian dictates: " Give into the power of the teacher the fewest possible coercive measures, so that the only source of the pupil's respect for the teacher is the human and intellectual qualities of the latter."[33] He continued to criticize. "It is nothing short of a miracle that modern methods of instruction have not entirely strangled the holy curiosity of inquiry; for this delicate little plant, aside from stimulation stands mainly in need of freedom; without this it goes to wreck and to ruin without fail. It is a very grave mistake to think that the enjoyment of seeing and searching can be promoted by means of coercion and a sense of duty.[34]

Before graduation, he was finally able to take care of a matter that had been of major concern to him for the past four years, Swiss citizenship. Having paid his dues, which he had saved painstakingly year by year, he now stood before the board of inquiry. The fact that Zurich was heavily German-speaking had no effect on the attitude of the examiners. They peppered the applicant with a series of searching and hostile questions, intended only to temporarily frighten the young man, whose only desire in life it seemed was to write down some equations in a peaceful land. Finally, the board decided he was perfectly harmless and signed the necessary papers granting Swiss citizenship to Albert Einstein. And now, for the first time in five years, Einstein was no longer a "stateless person."

7

PATENT OFFICE, 1905

Albert Einstein could look back with satisfaction over the five years from 1895 to 1900 as a period of widening experiences, deepening insights, and more important, a period of vast accomplishments. The greater self-esteem and the buoyant self-confidence born of these accomplishments were not enough to hide his boyish shyness altogether, however. Einstein in his twenty-first year, at the turn of the century, was still an unsophisticated country boy, wondering what equations God had used to create the universe.

At this juncture of his life Albert thought he could look forward with justifiable optimism to a secure life at the university, in peaceful contemplation of the universe. He was a new citizen of a country he had come to love, soon to be married and perhaps thereafter to raise his own family. Such were his happy thoughts and enviable prospects. After graduation, however, the promise of a happy, well-planned future disappeared; he was not appointed to the often-promised post. His disappointment was bitter; the blow to his self-confidence was staggering but temporary. Try as he would, he could not understand the unforeseen turn of events. Was he not as qualified as he was given to believe? He was determined to find the answer. But these were human equations he was attempting to deal with and did not necessarily follow from one logical step to the next. He made the rounds of the professors, and they all managed to put him off without a satisfactory explanation. Even those who had been friendly, could only at the very best recommend alternatives. How had he offended them? Could it have anything to do with his sometimes annoying brilliance? Friends suggested the reason could have been that he was a Jew.

Einstein could forgive jealousy as a motive for not placing a candidate in a university post, but he could not accept the accident of race or nationality as the criterion. Should one not expect freedom from bigotry among the most honored, the best educated, the highest on the intellectual level—the college professors? Or do professors succumb to the same hate patterns that rule those who cannot be expected to know better? Considering that Einstein had rejected organized religion, his being of Jewish origin was obviously more important to the university than it was to him.

An equally plausible reason for not having been given the post was his newly-acquired Swiss citizenship. It was commonly known that the native-born Swiss felt only contempt for the "paper Swiss", particularly if one showed a unique talent and could outshine them, and especially if one were a Jew. If indeed academic bigotry, politics, or race were the deciding factors, rather than proven ability, then Einstein felt sorry for them, for they would never be able to approach their academic responsibilities with honesty and a sense of justice. Aside from his own disappointement, Albert from then on could well imagine the difficulties facing his fellow Jews in the less-than-democratic countries of eastern Europe. The obstacles on the road to an education and to eventual employment must be infinitely more difficult and discouraging for them.

Einstein's real troubles now began. Upon graduation, the sum of one hundred francs per month his relatives had so bountifully forwarded for five years, stopped; no more trips to the post office for rent and food money. The near poverty level of his existence dropped still lower; he was almost penniless. Fortunately, he was able to obtain a few tutoring jobs, which kept him from starving. With all the difficulties in his path, Einstein never set aside his work in physics. He completed a paper on "Capillarity," which was published by the bible of the scientific world, the *Annalen der Physik*.

Though later in life Einstein looked back recalling "Capillarity" as worthless, at the time he thought its content important enough to have sent a copy to the famous professor of chemistry at the University of Leipzig, Wilhelm Ostwald. Capillarity had to do with the reason a liquid in a glass or cup when stirred by a spoon revolves faster in the center than on the periphery. Albert never heard from Ostwald in response to his first letter of inquiry for a post at Leipzig, nor did he hear after a second desperate appeal. It is somehow ironic that after reading Einstein's paper on the "Brownian Movement" published in 1905 in the *Annalen der Physik,* Ostwald, one of the last of the diehards, became convinced of the molecular theory, and of the atomic structure of matter as well. Later, Einstein and Ostwald met in scientific circles and became friends. It was typical of Einstein never to have mentioned the 1901 letter to Ostwald.

Despite job uncertainty, Einstein continued to write. His next paper "Method of Determination of Molecular Dimensions" was written for his PhD. and was submitted to the University of Zurich. After initial rejection, it was accepted when Einstein deleted a line or two. This paper, too, was published in the *Annalen*—in 1905.

Though he felt he was amply qualified, his hopes of obtaining a university post were fast waning. He and Mileva had to postpone the marriage because of his lack of prospects. Again Einstein turned to Marcel Grossmann for help. Grossmann had been appointed as an assistant mathematics instructor at the ETH. Having no influence at the university Marcel appealed to his father. The senior Grossmann, it seems, had among his old acquaintances, a former colleague who held the post of Direktor at the Swiss Patent Office in Bern. An appointment was arranged and Einstein traveled to Bern to be interviewed by Direktor Haller. Haller was sufficiently interested in the young applicant to stretch a normal interview into an intensive two-hour discusssion. He pointed out Einstein's shortcomings, to which the latter readily agreed, but for the most part, he was impressed with Einstein's scientific knowledge, especially his familiarity with the new "electromagnetic field theory." So favorably impressed was he that he suggested Einstein apply for a vacancy that was coming up, when the advertisement appeared in the local newspaper.

To keep himself eating, Einstein accepted a temporary position at a technical school in Winterthur, a town some fifteen miles northeast of Zurich. The job involved substituting for a teacher who had been called to fulfill his military obligations. It was Einstein's first taste of teaching, and he soon learned that humor is both a necessary ingredient and a helpful tool in dealing with a class of unruly youngsters.

Following Winterthur, he obtained a position at a grammar school in Schaffhausen, north of Zurich on the German border. Here his charges were two children who had been considered difficult and hard to handle. Left in his care, they seemed to respond in a cooperative manner—so much so, that Einstein was encouraged to believe he could accomplish more with the youngsters if they were left entirely in his care. But, when he asked for complete freedom with the education of the boys, he was looked upon as a usurper and was fired.

Back in Bern in December of 1901, the long-awaited advertisement for engineer, second class appeared in the newspaper, and Einstein applied. Despite competition for the job, he was accepted. The appointment was delayed several months, however, and he had to advertise for tutoring jobs again. One of these "ads" was answered by Maurice Solovine, a Roumanian student who wanted to be tutored in physics. The lessons turned far afield from their original intent, and when Einstein invited his friend, Conrad Habicht, to take part in the discussions, the "Olympia Academy" was born. The academy consisted of the three young men, who in the full flush of their self-righteous and youthful optimism felt free to dissect or defend any theory, philosophy, political entity, or economic system; any person, place, or thing. The discussions reflected, in spirit, the radical thinking alive in Switzerland at that time. They were serious; they were fun. They were quiet discussions; they were boisterous. Above all, they were an honest exchange of ideas that led to a broadening of concepts. All tutoring fees were forgotten. Though the life of the academy continued only some two years in Bern, the participants having thereafter gone their separate ways, Solovine to Paris and Habicht to Schaffhausen, the three remained friends and corresponded for many years.

With the arrival of the summer of 1902 Einstein settled down to his long-awaited "cobbler's job." Steady employment and a week's pay, albeit meager, finally brought some measure of order and stability into his life. Later he often suggested to young assistants or beginning theoreticians the taking on of a cobbler's or lighthouse keeper's job, one that would not cramp the mind with too much thinking during the day and allow ample time in the evening for scientific thought. Einstein believed that if one had talent, it should not be flushed out in scientific over-production. His own six-day schedule gave him evenings and Sundays for his theories. His mind now was seemingly at ease, but just beneath the surface was a simmering volcano almost ready to erupt.

At the office he required little instruction in how to determine the validity of a new patent application. More often than not, after evaluating the day's new inventions, he went to work on his own inventions, which took the form of papers with strange equations, strategically placed in various desk drawers to escape detection. He had to risk being found out, by Haller; his mind was a frenzy of new theories about to burst upon an unexpecting and unprepared scientific world.

A few months into this happy state, and Einstein was to suffer the greatest single loss of his entire life. On October 10, 1902, at the age of fifty-five, Hermann Einstein died. He had been a rather unique inspiration to Albert. If we were to measure Hermann Einstein's life by the material goods he had amassed, or by the great changes he had caused to come into being, or by the amount of power he was able to wield, he would be considered a failure by anyone's standards. It was not as a great achiever that the son remembered his father, but as an "extremely friendly, mild, patient, charming and good man." He felt the loss profoundly for a long time. After the funeral, Albert remained in Italy comforting his mother and sister and renewing his acquaintance with some of the old books he had left behind a few short years before.

Several months later, in 1903, he and Mileva were married in Switzerland. Solovine and Habicht were witnesses, but his family did not approve and did not attend. There was neither time nor money for a honeymoon; the newlyweds found a suitable apartment at 49 Kramgasse, near the Aar River, in the Kirchenfeld section of Bern and moved in.

Despite the many hours Einstein devoted both to his job and theories, he still managed to find time to host an occasional evening of conversation and chamber music. The host usually played second violin, and Mileva, after getting the discussions going, would remain quietly in the background.

> She was somewhat older than he. Despite her Greek Orthodox background she was a free-thinker and progressive in her ideas, like most of the Serb students. By nature she was reserved, and did not possess to any great degree the ability to get into intimate and pleasant contact with her environment. Einstein's very different personality as manifested in the naturalness of his bearing and the interesting character of his conversation, often made her uneasy. There was something blunt and stern about her character. For Einstein, life with her was not always a source of peace and happiness. When he wanted to discuss with her his ideas, which came to him in great abundance, her response was so slight that he was often unable to decide whether or not she was interested.[35]

A year passed and in 1904 the Einstein's were the proud parents of a son, whom they named Hans Albert. The wizard of physics and mathematics, the discoverer of new worlds, some may be surprised to learn, turned out to be the average garden-variety father. His greatest pleasure and proudest moments came with wheeling the baby carriage through the streets of Bern. But, so far away were his thoughts of his soon-to-be-emerging theories that he would wander, oblivious to direction, sometimes losing his way. Einstein remembered these years as his happiest, when everyone found him to be both amusing and a delight to talk with. Parental duties aside, the product of his life's thinking was coming to a head, reaching a point of fruition. Newtonian mechanics was about to fall because Einstein wanted to discover the "way things really are."

In the same year, Michelangelo Besso, an Italian engineer and

Mileva and Albert, circa 1903.

friend of Einstein's Zurich days, joined him as an employee at the Patent Office. Promptly, Besso was welcomed to the ranks of the

Olympia Academy. Whether at the office or walking home or sitting in a café sipping coffee, where Einstein plagued his friends with his foul-smelling cigars, these radicals without a cause would constantly expound on theories of light and motion, inserting a postulate here and rejecting a premise there. Fortunately, Besso turned out to be a good listener at a time when Einstein was on fire with the "truth" and it needed a good airing and a good listening to. Besso patiently heard Einstein out, pointing out flaws and setting thoughts in a different direction. As a consequence of his devotion in helping to understand these new concepts, Einstein dedicated his Special Theory of Relativity to Besso. At the very end of his paper, Einstein wrote, "In conclusion I wish to say that in working at the problem here dealt with I have had the loyal assistance of my friend and colleague M. Besso, and that I am indebted to him for several valuable suggestions."[36] The special theory is also known under the title of "The Electrodynamics of Moving Bodies."

Mileva Einstein was not unaware of the importance of the statements her husband was about to release. Her own knowledge of mathematics gave her some insight into the secrets in the microscopic world of the atom and in the vastness of macroscopic outer space that her Albert was about to reveal. She had a hand in correlating and helping to keep order amid the outpourings that sounded strange even to her trained ears. She also had to cope with her husband's ups and downs—elation when the equations fit and frustration when he felt his theories were falling apart. For the six-week period prior to his completion of the papers, Einstein was hopelessly and compulsively in the clutches of a furious effort to put down on paper the language—not of a new universe, but of a world extant, yet heretofore undiscovered.

David Reichenstein later noted:

It is strange how productive a certain span of Einstein's life was. Not only a particular theory of relativity but also a great number of other fundamental publications bear the date 1905:

1. The Electrodynamics of Moving Bodies.
2. Does the Inertia Of A Body Depend Upon Its Energy Content?
3. Law Of The Brownian Movement—On The Movement Of Small Particles Suspended In A Stationery Liquid According To The Molecular Kinetic Theory Of Induction.
4. On A Heuristic Viewpoint Concerning The Production And Transformation Of Light—The Photoelectric Effect.

5. Method Of Determination Of Molecular Dimensions.

In addition, the events in his life followed an extraordinary sequence:

Married at the age of twenty-four in 1903;
A father at twenty-five in 1904;
Publication of his five papers at the age of twenty-six in 1905.[37]

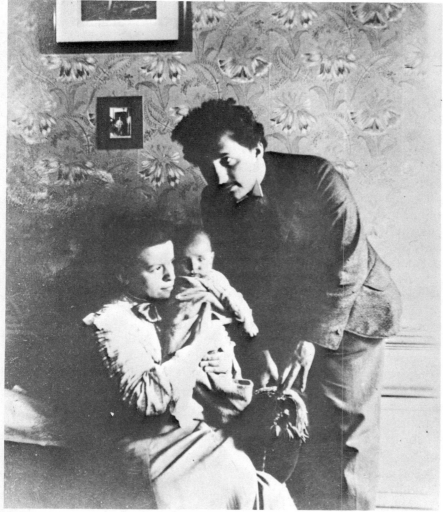

Credit: Einstein Archives

Mileva and Albert Einstein, 1904, with newborn son, Hans Albert.

Without the benefit of laboratory experiments, without the use of microscopes or telescopes, without the beneficial atmosphere of an academic community, but merely using pen and paper he issued some of the most revolutionary and significant statements regarding phenomena in the history of mankind. What is more astonishing—and it demonstrates the breadth of his grasp—is the fact that each of the five papers published in the *Annalen der Physik* pertained to a different subject.

Einstein's monumental works stem from his philosophy, which is grounded in the belief in the order and harmony of the universe; cause and effect and predictibility. Many times he would be heard to say that, "God does not play dice with the universe." Einstein's goal was to be able to see the universe as it really is, not as we see it, or hear it, or feel it with our limited and imperfect five senses. He did not believe that mother nature hid her secrets guardedly, parceling them out piecemeal. He believed rather that man is an isolated prisoner of his own senses, excluded from seeing the realities of the universe as they really exist, by his inability to perceive the invisible phenomena all around him in the form of cosmic rays, gamma rays, ultraviolet rays, x rays, infrared rays, television signals, and ultrahigh frequency radio waves. The only rays we consciously experience are light of a certain wavelength and sound waves of limited frequencies. In other words, in the spectrum of known radiation, man's reasoning powers and senses of sight, touch, smell, taste and hearing detect only a fraction of the phenomena that exists all around us. And if we choose to believe only what we can perceive with all our senses, we will learn but little of the unseen yet ever-present realities.

The example of the common dog whistle, which makes no impression on the human ear, points up our rather limited ability to pick up certain sound waves. The human eye is equally deficient, in that it is sensitive only to, and therefore can only see, the narrow band of light (radiation that is emitted from the sun) that falls between the wavelengths of .00007 centimeters and .00004 centimeters. What this amounts to is that we can see less than ten percent of the known radiation around us. And since we are thus restricted by our limited vision from seeing the realities in existence around us every moment of our lives, awake or asleep, what we can perceive is of necessity distorted, limited, and hardly the true picture of the reality that actually exists.

The world around us would take on added dimensions and would appear totally different if humans were given the ability to perceive some of the x rays or gamma rays the way we see light rays and hear

Patent examiner Einstein in Bern, circa 1905.

some sound waves. We can feel heat from most sources of light, but, by and large, we are unaware of most of what is going on around us. We have only to examine the operation of our own radios and television sets to understand one type of radiation taking place virtually right under our noses and throughout the universe, unseen and unde-tected until transformed by mechanical means to the human visual and auditory level. Einstein accepted human limitations. ''The world as we see it is only the world as *we* see it. Others may see it differently. Perhaps it isn't the true world at all.'' He was convinced, however, that the universe was not conceived and put together in a helter-skelter fashion by some accident. One of his most often quoted sayings, now chiseled over a fireplace on the campus of Princeton University expresses his belief in a benevolent and consistent God:

"Raffinert is der herr Gott, aber boshaft is er nicht.'' [*Trans.—* "God is subtle, but he is not malicious.'']

"Pythagoras, Copernicus, Galileo, Kepler, Newton—each achieved a milestone in the progress of the human race through the misty morning of knowledge. Einstein took the tree of knowledge fostered by these pioneers, pruned away much of the deadwood which was hindering further growth and transplanted the whole tree in a new and specially rich field, in which to take root and to expand in new directions toward a fuller understanding of our amazing Universe.''[38]

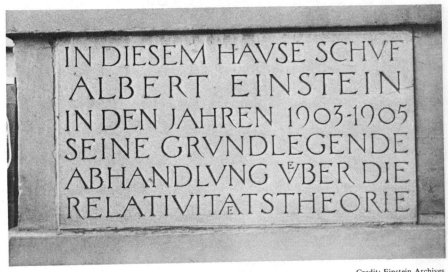

Credit: Einstein Archives

Plaque in front of apartment building where the Einsteins lived in Bern.

8

INTRODUCTION TO SPECIAL RELATIVITY

From the time of earliest recorded history, and before that, among astronomers and other observers, it was firmly believed that the earth was at the center of the universe and that the sun and stars revolve around the earth. This is known as the geocentric theory. It seemed a logical conclusion; it was, after all, what their observations told them was true. And even today, if we were to rely completely on our senses when we look up into the heavens and try to find some order among the countless billions of bits of matter floating around, it would seem logical to conclude that the sun does indeed traverse the earth, and that the reverse is not true. Doesn't everyone refer to the appearance of the sun in the eastern sky in the morning as "sunrise" and the disappearance of the sun below the western horizon in the evening as "sunset"? Don't these terms sunrise and sunset suggest that the sun is in actual motion around the earth? When studying natural phenomena, however, we cannot rely only on our given senses, or on common sense, or on logic in the search for the true scheme of things; all our intelligence provides only a partial glimpse of what actually exists.

If we left it to our senses to define the workings of the universe, then we would never believe that the earth is speeding around the sun at some 66,000 miles per hour. Our limited native abilities have not been the only drawbacks to finding real and scientific truths. Superstition, too, has fogged the road to discovery. Even as recently as five hundred years ago, sailors feared voyaging too far from home port lest they sail off the edge of the flat earth. Sailors, especially navigators, should have been the first to discover that the earth was round, or at least spherical in shape. When they left port and sailed away from the dock, they could see less and less of the buildings of the port as the distance between ship and dock grew, until they could see only the tops of the buildings and then nothing.

It remained for a monk, Nicolaus Copernicus (Niklas Koppernigk), born in Torun, Poland in 1473 to describe our earth as traveling around a stationary sun. He said, "We revolve around the sun like any other planet." To the established Church, which he served, this was heresy and he was subsequently silenced by the threat of religious persecution; his theories on the construction of the solar system were not published until he was near death.

It was not without some difficulty that the thought that the earth does not occupy the center of the universe gained acceptance. One of Copernicus's followers, Giordano Bruno, suggested that the sun was just another star, simply one among many, and not very large at that when compared to some of the real giants in the sky. For his fearless and illuminating pronouncements, Bruno was burned at the stake; he would not recant. It is doubtful if the Inquisitors would have been interested in knowing that while our sun is the nearest star to earth, with a generous diameter of some 864,000 miles compared to earth's 7,900, it is far from being among the big ones in the sky (just as Bruno said). The sun may seem huge when compared to earth, but the star Antares in the constellation Scorpio has a diameter nearly three hundred times that of our sun—a fact that has hardly any bearing on our life here on earth, but it does emphasize the relative insignificance of our tiny planet in the larger view of the universe.

The blessings of life are precariously contingent upon the amount of solar radiation emitted by the sun. If the solar radiation were to change by only a small fraction, we would either freeze or fry to death. But our sun, while it may not be one of the biggest stars in the heavens, suits our earth just fine. It is a very stable sun and should go on radiating evenly for billions of years to come.

Established religion had much to lose from the dissemination of the theory that the earth was not the center of the universe. The Church could not allow people to be persuaded that the earth moves around the sun lest the story in the Old Testament of Joshua commanding the sun to stand still be questioned. "If the book of Joshua and the Old Testament cannot be relied upon then people may soon begin to distrust the New Testament. If that happens, what will become of the foundation of the Church? In other words, an astronomical theory endangered the entire structure of the Holy Catholic Church."[39] Therefore, all theories contrary to the geocentric theory of the structure of the universe had to be suppressed and their advocates silenced by the threat of, or by punishment itself.

Copernicus had put the pieces in their correct places, but it remained for Johannes Kepler (1571-1630) to describe the true path of the earth around the sun. Kepler found that the earth traveled an elliptical path (not a circular path) around the sun and that a planet moves faster when near the sun and slower when further away. As Einstein explained: "Kepler first of all determined the true motion of the earth in planetary space. Since the earth itself may be used as a point for triangulation at any time, he was able to determine the true motions of the other planets from his observations. Kepler's life-work was possible only once he succeeded in freeing himself of the intellectual and religious traditions into which he was born."[40]

Later, Galileo (1564–1642), confirmed that Copernicus was right when he said that the earth travels around the sun. One of the first to employ the use of a telescope, Galileo discovered the moons of Jupiter. He was destined to struggle through a career of unique discoveries, and many attempts were made to stifle his genius. He was the first to conduct experiments with "falling bodies." Galileo found that if two objects such as a billiard ball and a ping-pong ball were allowed to fall from the same height at the same time, in a vacuum, both would fall at the same speed.

Galileo, too, was a victim of the narrow thinking and confining policies of the Church. The reward for his contributions to the forward progress of man and to science was to be tried by the Inquisition and forced to denounce his own theories. For daring to pronounce the truth, he was kept under house arrest for the remainder of his life.

Perhaps the most productive mind capable of original thought up until the twentieth century was encased in the frail and sickly body of Isaac Newton (1642-1727). Newton developed differential and integral calculus and described the propagation of light as corpuscular (discontinuous). He pioneered the mechanical view of the universe in his laws of motion, inertia and acceleration insofar as the speeds are known here on earth. Through his gravitational theory, Newton explained how the solar system functioned. His scientific findings were astounding for their time and dominated scientific thinking for two hundred years.

In the latter part of the nineteenth century, however, doubt of Newton's infallibility began to create chinks in the walls of his long-respected classical mechanics. A host of curious investigators from Faraday, Maxwell, Young, Fresnel, Mach, and Hertz to Planck and Einstein found glaring and unavoidable exceptions to classical mechanics. Speeds never before encountered by the Newtonian classicists showed the time-honored principles of "absolute space and absolute time" to be obsolete. Two thousand year old Euclidian geometry did not take into consideration the curvature of space and late investigations discovered that the invisible "electron" was whirling around in its orbit with a speed almost that of light.

It was on the shoulders of the scientists named above that Einstein stood when he made his contributions through his revolutionary views on time, space, mass, energy, the motion of bodies, and the amazing speed of light.

If our planet were the only physical body existing in space, we would have no way of knowing whether we were in motion or not. There must be another body, a rigid body to which to refer. Einstein says that motion is a relative state; unless there is some system of reference to which it may be compared, it is meaningless to speak of the motion of a single body. Lucius Bugbee demonstrated the relativity of motion for the layman this way: "Here is a vessel sailing west and on its deck a passenger walking east. Is he really moving or standing still? It depends upon your point of view. If you happen to be a fellow passenger on the same vessel it will appear to you that he is moving, but if you are standing on the shore while the vessel passes by, he will seem to be standing still and marking time."[41]

Position, point of view, these are the differences that make things relative. Einstein illustrates:

> I stand at the window of a railway carriage which is travelling uniformly, and drop a stone on the embankment, without throwing it. Then disregarding the influence of the air resistance, I see the stone descend in a straight line. A pedestrian who observes the misdeed from the footpath notices that the stone falls to earth in a parabolic curve. I now ask: Do the 'positions' traversed by the stone lie 'in reality' on a straight line or on a parabola? . . . . We are in a position to say: The stone traverses a straight line relative to a system of co-ordinates rigidly attached to the carriage, but relative to a system of co-ordinates rigidly attached to the ground (embankment) it describes a parabola. With the aid of this example it is clearly seen that there is no such thing as an independently existing trajectory, but only a trajectory relative to a particular body of reference. (Fig. 2)[42]

High above the surface of the earth, if we were to have the use of a giant telescope at some point out in space we could check relativity of motion for ourselves. The method would be to zero that telescope in on a very tall building somewhere on earth just as someone drops a small cannonball from the top of the building. The observers on earth *know* that the cannonball fell straight down to the street below in a matter of seconds. But, the observer with his eye glued to the telescope, from somewhere out in space, seeing the action from a different point of view, would describe seeing the cannonball travel in a parabola. Those on earth saw the cannonball fall in a straight line; those out in space saw the cannonball move in an arc. Which is the

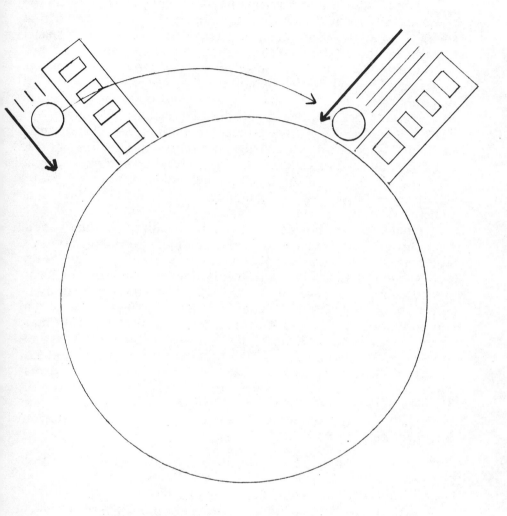

Figure 2. "There is no such thing as an independently existing trajectory . . ."

real truth? Well, both are true statements. Whether you saw the cannonball move in an arc or straight down depends on your position relative to the action. Einstein said: "The paths of moving objects vary in relation to the position of the observer."

If we were to make further use of this telescope and again focus it in on our planet, we would see things that might astound us. Viewing the northern hemisphere, we would see its inhabitants, two-legged as well as four, standing and moving in an upright position. When the telescope was focused in on the equator, however, we would find similar beings, great and small, perfectly able to stand out in space, sideways, without falling off the earth, with no apparent difficulty or discomfort. And when we looked in on the natives living on the under part of the globe, they would seemingly possess the greatest of magical powers, for they would be able to hang on to the sphere with their feet attached and their heads dangling off downwards into the space below. An airplane flying under the south pole would appear to be flying upside down, whereas the pilot thinks he is flying right side up. The point is that in space there is actually no up or down, no east, no west, no north or south. There are only positions of bodies relative to each other—the sun, moon, a star, or any other body that punctuates space.

To natives of the poles and the equator the direction "up" would be in three different directions. Stars and other celestial phenomena, while they are viewed as being *up above* the northern hemisphere are also *up above* when viewed from locations in the southern hemisphere. Bodies in space are located all around the earth, in every direction, not only in the sky above Alaska or Lithuania, but also in the sky above Florida and Australia. So, at this juncture, we must begin to rethink the meaning of some of the common, everyday language that has meaning only if we intend to remain earthbound. Hereafter, when we speak of space, we should keep in mind that down is not south, but somewhere towards the center of the earth. Up does not mean north, but merely indicates an area away from the center of the earth. And what of the blue sky that can be viewed from any location on earth?

> On clear winter days when all the dust and soot have been washed out of the air by snow, the sky shows its own true color, a pure clear blue. On high mountains, above the vapours which rise from forests and human settlements, it is still more beautiful darker blue. The higher we rise, the less air do we have overhead, and the darker is the blue of the sky. If we could get up above the atmosphere, the sky, even when the sun is shining, would without doubt appear as black as it does at night. The sky is not the crystal sphere which the ancients imagined; the appearance of a blue vault is an illusion, and as there is nothing up there but air, the blue must be the colour of the air. That is why we are interested in it. We want to know how a transparent substance like air can appear so brightly coloured. Why is it blue rather than any other colour?[43]

9

THE PHENOMENON OF LIGHT

A study of, or even a familiarization with, any of Einstein's theories requires an introduction to the subject of light—its speed and propagation. The phenomenon of light is one that is sorely under-understood by the public and scientists alike. What it is made of eludes us; how it travels is unknown; and the unanswered mysteries of light and its propagation have been the subject of speculation by astronomers, physicists and philosophers ever since man first looked up at the sun, moon and stars and wondered.

We see light from many sources in the daily routine of our lives. We use it to illuminate our dark corners. The light and warmth from the sun make it possible for everything to grow, make life itself possible. But, just what is light? Where does it come from? How does it spread its rays? These questions are still largely unanswered today. All we have are theories, yet unproved, that physicists have been able to partially agree on.

It's safe to assume that everyone understands that original light comes from our sun, moon, and stars. But nowadays, when we flip a wall switch we get instantaneous light; and yet, through observation we find that light is not instantaneous, that it takes time for light to travel from place to place. As an example, it takes some eight minutes of our earth time for the light from the sun to travel the ninety-three million miles between the sun and earth. It may come as a shock to some, but as we view the sun we see it as it was approximately eight minutes ago. And when we view a beautiful sunset, remember that the action actually took place some eight minutes earlier. Since light travels at a great but limited velocity, the light we see from the stars way off in the distant heavens may have been traveling for centuries before they become visible to us. Some of these stars may have disintegrated and disappeared eons ago, yet we may still be seeing their light. Other stars may have been born millions of years ago, and they may be so distant that we have not yet received their light and we therefore are unaware of their existence.

In the year 1675, Olaf Römer, a Danish astronomer, determined that light does travel and calculated its speed at 186,284 miles per second, which translates into 11,177,040 miles per minute, 670,622,400 miles per hour; in one year's time, light will travel some 5,874,652,204,000 miles. The distance which light will travel in one year is called a "light-year." For convenience, it is much simpler to work with the rounded off figure of 186,000 miles per second.

When we speak of the speed of light, we are referring to a tremendous speed. In our everyday experiences, here on earth, we need not be concerned with this speed. But, when we begin to move away from the relatively slow speeds encountered on earth, and check out the traveling time from earth to the moon, we have a basis for comparison. For instance, light's speed is so fast that it gets to the moon and back in the time span of a little over two seconds, whereas astronauts, traveling in their space ships take over five days (some 432,000 seconds) to accomplish the same mission.

In 1905, Einstein made two seemingly simple statements regarding light: "The speed of light is constant," and "light never fails to maintain its speed regardless of its source." The scientific community paid absolutely no attention to what Einstein was saying, until he added a couple of lines more. These were the lines: "The speed of light is the fastest known phenomenon in the universe"; and, "the speed of light is a limiting speed", meaning that *nothing* can travel as fast or faster than light in the entire universe. Then a few eyebrows were raised; it was unbelievable. No one had ever said things like this before. Controversy followed.

Whether light is propagated (transmitted) in a series of discontinuous particles, as in the blast of machine-gun bullets, or in undulatory waves, as in a series of ocean waves, has been a point of divergent views from as far back as the fifth century B.C. In ancient Greece, Democritus, who was also considered the first "atomist," developed the particle theory of light, which says in effect, that light emanating from its source is a series of discontinuous particles. Many centuries later, Newton referred to the same phenomenon as "corpuscular," which means the same thing.

Soon however, the "particle" theory was being challenged. It was challenged first by Newton's contemporary, Christian Huygens, who concluded that light emanated from its source in undulating waves. To this day, light is often designated as "light waves." Later, Thomas Young in England and August Fresnel in France presented laboratory proof backing Huygens undulatory-wave theory. James Clerk Maxwell, one of Einstein's heroes, whose equations first described the "electromagnetic field" theory, concurred with the findings of Huygens, Young and Fresnel. And with all this accumulated evidence gainsaying the particle theory of Democritus and Newton, that theory was about to fall into disrepute. Except with

Einstein. Einstein concluded, in his elaboration of Planck's quantum theory, that light is emitted in separate "light quanta." In the final analysis, if a definitive statement can be made regarding the propagation of light, most physicists would agree that light seems to have a dual nature, wave under some laboratory conditions, and in other experiments, particle. Planck unwittingly, but Einstein knowingly, saved the particle theory from extinction.

In the 1880s it fell to the inventive genius of Heinrich Hertz, experimenting with the data handed down from Faraday and Maxwell, to produce physically what we now know as radio waves. Hertz expressed his confidence in the wave theory of light when he addressed the Heidelberg Conference of 1899. "Doubt as to these things is no longer possible, a disproof of these conceptions is unthinkable for the physicist. The wave theory of light is humanly speaking, a certainty." But the experiments of Planck and the postulates of Einstein led to conflicting and different conclusions: not back to either the corpuscular or wave theories, but rather to a melding of the two, corpuscular and wave. As Hans Reichenbach puts it: "It is the same type of conceptual progress, from thesis, by way of antithesis, to synthesis, that we found in the development from the Ptolemaic view of the world, through the Copernican, to the Einsteinian, which we have now to describe as the progress from the emission theory, through the wave theory to the quantum theory of light."[44]

Though not regarded as such at the time, one of the most exacting, far-reaching, and significant experiments concerning light was performed in the year 1887, when Einstein was but a boy, by Albert Abraham Michelson. Michelson, who was born in Poland in 1852 and educated at The United States Naval Academy was professor of physics at the Case School of Applied Science in Cleveland, Ohio and had invented the interferometer. The interferometer was so refined an instrument that it could measure minute angles to within one millionth of an inch. (Tribute is due the machine mechanics of the day, who were able to turn out very sophisticated experimental equipment at the designer's request. The symbiotic relationship between experimenter and builder should be given great emphasis, for the former simply could not function without the latter.) Michelson, incidentally, was the first American to be awarded the Nobel Prize for physics. His lifelong and burning desire was to be able to measure the speed of the earth through the legendary "ether" and with it the speed of the entire solar system through space. This ambition he shared with a colleague, E.E. Morley, a professor of chemistry at nearby Western Reserve University.

For hundreds of years it was theorized that this invisible "ether," which no one could see or smell or hear or touch or discern in any manner, was the invisible medium by which light was conveyed throughout the universe. Scientists assumed that since sound required a medium, the molecules in the atmosphere, by which to transmit sound vibrations, that the transmission of light operated on the same principle; that the ether was to light what the atmosphere was to sound. Despite the lack of proof, the ether theory carried and gained full acceptance. Otherwise, "It would be inconceivable that bodies exist at a great distance from each other without some connecting medium. It is inconceivable that light can reach us from the sun or stars without such a medium."[45]

The ether theory became a catchall for any questionable phenomenon; ether was thought to permeate the entire universe, occupying every nook and cranny to infinity and every empty spot between atoms. Not even the vacuum created in the common light bulb was immune from the presence of the all-pervasive ether. According to the ether theory the only way for light to pass from the filament to the glass and then on out, was its conveyance by the "luminiferous ether." Despite all these imposed attributes, no observable or experimental proof of the ether's existence was forthcoming; not an atom of its makeup was ever detected. Yet, the greatest scientific minds through several centuries allowed themselves to be convinced that this nebulous permeation shouldered the responsibility for guiding the billions of lights throughout the universe. "The only sure thing that the physicists seemed to know about the ether was the result of an experiment of Armand Fizeau, a French physicist who demonstrated that the ether, if it exists, must be in an absolute state of repose; that is, not being dragged about by the Earth in its translation."[46] That was good news for Michelson; his experiment was based on just that, a stationary ether.

The interferometer, which consisted of a hollow pipe at right angles to another like hollow pipe, could measure the speed of light in the direction of the earth's rotation (west to east) as opposed to the speed of light reflected across the ether stream (north-south). The time lag that Michelson and Morley expected to show between the speed of light in the two different directions would show the degree to which the ether retarded the velocity of light. (It was assumed that the light would be retarded by the ether much as a boat moving upstream is retarded by the current.) Theoretically, the beam of light that crosses the ether-stream (north-south) should be slowed by the stationary ether the same speed that the earth orbits the sun, somewhere in the vicinity of twenty miles per second. Therefore, the interferometer should show that the speed of light through the ether-stream (north-south) measures 186,264 miles per second and the speed of light unopposed by the ether should register at the exact speed of light, 186,284 miles per second.

The experiment proceeded as follows:

> He flashed a single pencil of light at the juncture of the two pipes. He arranged (by the use of mirrors) for the ray of light to divide, one part going up one pipe and back again, and the other up the other pipe and back again. Thus one ray went in the direction of the Earth . . . . and back, while the other (ray) went *across* the ether stream and back. He naturally expected that it should take longer down-stream and back than cross-stream and back. But to his astonishment, both rays came back at the same instant. He could not understand it (nor could the other scientists). Why did it not take longer to go down-stream and back than across and back?[47]

Michelson's Interferometer

Michelson performed the experiment countless times through the ensuing years, but the findings were always the same: *no difference in the speed of light in either direction*. This conclusion infuriated Michelson, because it was not the answer he was seeking. Nevertheless, he persevered—again and again, changing the material makeup of the pipes, changing the size of the pipes, using more elaborate mirror combinations, changing the physical location of the experiment. Yet he was never able to square the actual with the expected results. Michelson then moved on to Chicago, while Morley continued experimenting along with Professor Dayton C. Miller, with the same hope of determining the "ethereal drift." Miller's bright idea of moving the equipment to Mount Wilson in California came a cropper when it was found that "no good measures could be made" because of the varying densities of the open air. He returned to the midwest. This time, still utilizing Michelson's interferometer principle, Morley and Miller constructed an interferometer of steel in the form of a Greek cross, with each arm fourteen feet in length. Weighing some 1,900 pounds, "the whole apparatus is floated in a trough containing 800 pounds of mercury" supplemented by eighteen mirrors inside the steel arms to reflect the light in different directions.

Obviously no task was too difficult for the ether classisists to perform to keep from denying its existence. Despite their tenacious dedication and devotion to the ether theory, even this elaborate experiment was a failure. *There was no difference in the speed of light in either direction.* The obvious conclusion, which the scientists were hard put to explain—and accept—was that the velocity of light is not affected by the mythical ether or by the motion of the earth. Some scientists remained stubbornly loyal to the ether concept, criticizing the interferometer; others found the ether unpredictable; still others toyed with the ancient notion that the earth did, after all, stand still. After years of trying to find non-existsnt answers, the experiment was considered a failure. But according to Einstein, Michelson continued the experiments until the end of his life and never got it wrong. Among others, Reinhart Wetzel of the City College of New York supported Einstein: "The theory of relativity says that Michelson's experiment, far from being negative as Michelson thought, was exactly what was to be expected. How could an ether drift be established when the ether had no physical existence." (Science, October 3, 1913, page 472.)

When Einstein took into account the propagation of light and its speed, he conducted no experiments, nor did he allow the preconceived idea of a mythical ether to become a factor in his pursuit of the physical realities of light. Einstein simply chose to ignore the ether, since in his view, "not mentioning the ether simply removes it from consideration in the propagation of light." It was as simple as that; Einstein banished the ether.

This methodology was typical of Einstein's almost simplistic approach to any scientific problem and consistent with his inquisitive personality. His acquired skepticism and his reluctance to rely on previously accepted premises made it possible for him to start his investigations with a clean slate. He accepted no theory as "gospel." He saw clearly that it was not necessary to rely on a mythical, scientific crutch with which to prop up a weak postulate. This freedom in attitude left him unhampered in his investigations by the dusty dogma of bygone centuries. He could explore the scientific spectrum, less inhibited, and with more options open to him. The skies that had opened for him remained clouded to others. When Einstein, in his special theory of relativity, stated that "from whatever source, whether in movement or standing still, the speed of light (in a vacuum) is constant, it never varies, it cannot be added to or subtracted from," the theory had actually been proved by Michelson and Morley some twenty years before, without their being aware of it. And yet, "The Michelson-Morley experiment was not Einstein's basis for the Theory of Relativity. It did not play a determinative role in his thinking."[48]

"Einstein scoffed at the idea that Nature had planned a well-organized conspiracy to prevent mere man from prying too closely into her innermost secrets. To him, the famous Michelson-Morley test, instead of being proof of such a conspiracy, was simply an expression of a law of Nature which scientists had failed to grasp. The more he pondered the problem, the more he become convinced that man had been duped by his own senses, and that a radical reorganization of our imaginative picture of the universe was needed if we were to have a truer understanding of Nature and her forces."[49]

Einstein's theory of the constant, limiting speed of light ran contrary to Newtonian mechanics, which assumed that if you kept adding power (energy) to force a body (any mass) to move from its normal state of inertia, with sufficient power a body or particle of matter could be forced beyond the speed of light. Philipp Frank states Einstein's premise this way: "Mass does increase with velocity in such a way that as the velocity becomes very great, the mass also becomes very great. A given force will produce smaller and smaller change in the actual velocity as it approaches the speed of light. For this reason no body or particle can ever actually attain the velocity of light, no matter how great a force acts on it or for how long a time."[50] Stated another way, if you exploded all the atoms in the universe and harnessed all the energy therefrom, you still will not have derived sufficient power to push any body of matter, whatever the size beyond the speed of light.

Einstein's theories were not immume from the criticisms of adversaries. Many were openly critical of his mass-energy theory until it was proved by the explosion of the first atomic bomb. In a more amusing vein, commentators have singled out the constant speed of light theory as the target of their wit:

> "There was a young lady named Bright
> Whose speed was far faster than light;
>   She set out one day
>   In a relative way
> And returned home the previous night."

Others have wandered into a world of pure fantasy. "If a man were projected out into space with a speed exceeding that of light, as long as he is able to view happenings on the Earth, he would see history unfolding itself, reversely. Actually, as he travels away from the Earth, faster than the speed of light, he would at each stage of his journey be overtaking the light reflected from earlier and earlier events."[51] So far as we know today, this kind of thing will never happen since it is impossible for any moving body in the universe, to exceed or even match the velocity of light.

The speed of sound, which is much slower than light, is more easily grasped by the average person. We all understand that the proverbial tree falling in the forest, where there is no human or animal ear to discern (catch) the air vibrations given off by the falling tree, will emit no sound. The vibrations of the air, caused by the tree hitting the ground, without a receiver to transform them into what we know as sound, would simply dissipate in time and never be converted to sound. We may never be able to travel at the speed of light, but with sound it's another story. "If a person were to travel on this Earth at the rate of thirteen miles per minute, which is approximately the speed of sound, and a gun were fired at the point and instant of his outset, the sound would remain in his ears as an accompanying roar, because the air vibrations, traveling precisely at his speed, would naturally keep him continuous company, allowing, of course, for their natural destruction through interfering forces. If, however, this traveler's velocity were to exceed thirteen miles per minute, the sound of an explosion taking place a moment after his departure, however powerful, would never reach him, and for him the sound would not exist."[52]

Now, back to light. The Dutch astronomer, Willem de Sitter, made a startling revelation in the wake of Einstein's statement on the constancy of the speed of light. It seems that there is a phenomenon out in space not unlike our earth's gravitational relationship to our moon. It is called the double star or binary star system, a condition of space where two stars revolve around each other. In their orbits, de Sitter found, these binary stars travel towards and then away from the earth. And the light from these stars, whether they are advancing towards or retreating from the earth, would reach the earth at the same velocity. Since the speed of the nearer star is always greater than the speed of the receding star, one would expect that the speed of the light emanating from the nearer star would exceed the speed of light emanating from the receding star. But de Sitter found that light from both stars reaches the earth at the same speed and thus confirmed Einstein's prediction that the speed of light is constant whether in movement or at rest.

Einstein never lost his almost religious wonder at the construction of the universe, as one by one he removed layer after layer of heretofore unexplored, unknown phenomena. Most of us take the complicated workings of our entire universe for granted and go about our daily business without much thought to the extremely precarious balance our universe functions on, but Einstein reverently marveled. "The sense of the mysterious is the noblest emotion that a man can have . . . that person who cannot stand in awe, rapt in wonderment at the marvels of the Universe which we only dimly see, that person's eyes are closed and he is as good as dead. To know that that which is impenetrable to us really exists, manifesting itself in the highest wisdom and most radiant beauty which we with all our dull senses can only partially grasp, that knowledge of the mysterious is the basis of all religion and in that sense only, I belong to the most devoutly religious of men."[53]

Einstein next turned to examining another time-tested, evergreen of the scientific community, a principle accepted since the time of Galileo, "addition of velocities." Newton felt the principle worthy of mention and saw it as an obvious observation. And for Newton's time and beyond, when its application was limited to the speeds of an earthbound existence, it remained true. This "obvious observation" held that if one is walking forward in the aisle of a bus (or other moving vehicle) at the rate of two miles per hour, and the vehicle itself is in the same forward motion at forty miles an hour, it should be obvious to the traveler and any observer standing on the sidewalk as the bus goes by, that the traveler is moving forward, relative to the sidewalk, at forty-two miles an hour. Einstein said that this was all well and good for the bus and passenger, but where the speed of light is concerned, the principle falls apart. Here is where the common sense addition of velocity theory disappears. If the driver of the same bus, which we know is traveling forward at the speed of forty miles an hour, suddenly switched his headlights on, we would expect, if we follow the addition of velocity principle, that the speed of the vehicle would be added to the speed of light to give us a forward speed for the speed of light equal to a total of the two speeds. We find, however, according to Einstein that contrary to the addition of velocity principle, we do not add the vehicle's speed to the speed of the light emanating from the headlights to derive the speed of the traveling vehicle's light. Einstein said that if you add any velocity less than the speed of light *to* the speed of light, it will *equal* the speed of light. According to Einstein's statement, the speed of light shining forward from the vehicle in motion remains the same as if the vehicle were not in motion, 186,000 miles per second, no more, no less. Einstein proved that addition of velocity does not apply to the phenomenon of light; that light from whatever source, whether in motion or not, travels at a fixed velocity.

The speed of light, as the limiting speed in the universe, is also the basic measuring unit of the universe. If we want to measure a distance in our living room, we use a ruler or yardstick. To measure the distance across a continent, we use the speed of a vehicle multiplied by the number of hours the trip takes. But if we want to measure the distance between two points in the vastness of space we use the light year; the distance light traveling at 186,000 miles per second travels in one year. That distance is 5,878,000,000,000 miles.

Excluding our sun, the nearest star to our planet is Alpha Centauri, which is approximately twenty-five trillion miles or some four and a half light years from our earth. Since it takes the light from Alpha Centauri four and a half years to reach us, we are actually seeing Alpha Centauri as it appeared four and a half years ago. If Alpha Centauri suddenly dissolved for some unknown reason, today, at this very instant, earth time, we would not know of the event until the light from that star ceased to shine in the night sky some four and a half years from today. All the other stars in the sky are further from the earth than Alpha Centauri. Some are hundreds, others are thousands, and still countless others are many millions and billions of light-years away from earth. Consequently, we are viewing them as they appeared that many hundreds, thousands, millions and billions of years ago. We are seeing the stars not as they are today; we are actually looking back in time and seeing things as they were.

Proceeding outside our own Milky Way galaxy we can now observe our galactic neighbor, the Andromeda galaxy, which is estimated to be some 2,500,000 light-years distant from the earth. This means that we are seeing Andromeda and receiving signals from it as it existed 2,500,000 years ago. The light Andromeda is sending out now, at this very instant, will not reach our sight for another 2,500,000 years. Like Alpha Centauri, if Andromeda suddenly exploded today, earth time, we would not see it or detect it, even with the most sophisticated of today's telescopic or radio receiving equipment for 2,500,000 years. To get some idea of just how vast space is, multiply 2,500,000 by 5,878,000,000,000. The product will be the enormous distance in miles between earth and Andromeda. Please remember that Andromeda is one of our nearest neighbors in the universe. Some of the outlying galaxies are so distant that the light from their stars began traveling in our direction before the earth was formed—which makes our planetary system one of the youngest in the universe.

10

THE BROWNIAN MOVEMENT, THE PHOTOELECTRIC EFFECT

One of the lesser known of the five papers Albert Einstein published in 1905 was entitled, "On the Motion Of Small Particles Suspended In A Stationary Liquid According To The Molecular Theory of Heat." The length of the title begs the more simply stated "Theory of the Brownian Movement."

At the beginning of the twentieth century the construction and makeup of a molecule was by no means an agreed upon fact. The theory of the destructibility or the indestructibility of the atom was a matter of individual thinking; neither one could be proved. And so we had reputable scientists on both sides of the question.

Going back almost a century—Robert Brown, a Scottish botanist, was among the early investigators into the realm of the molecule. In 1827, he observed with the aid of a microscope that minute particles (some $\frac{1}{5000}$ of an inch) of pollen when suspended in water moved in an uncontrolled and zigzag manner without any obvious, outside stimulus. His conclusions, as stated in the *Philosophical Magazine* of 1828 was that "these motions arose neither from the currents in the fluids, nor from the gradual evaporation, but belonged to the particles itself."

When Einstein investigated the motion of tiny objects suspended in liquids, he approached the problem from a statistical point of view. He had never read of Brown's earlier experiments. Einstein found that molecular agitation is increased by heat and the ceaseless motions of the particles (pollen) was due to the bombardment to which they were subjected by the heat-stimulated molecules of the liquid. He stated that "an exact determination of actual atomic dimensions is now possible." He used this movement of particles to formulate into verifiable equations the number of molecules per unit volume in a given mass.

Jeremy Bernstein pointed out the great implications in this seemingly simple approach by Einstein: "The main strength of Einstein's approach to the theory of Brownian motion is its quantitative character. It is one thing to argue, as has been done, that the Brownian motion had something to do with molecular motion, but it is another thing to make quantitative predictions as to what will happen . . . . Einstein predicted that, at room temperature in water, a Brownian particle will diffuse an average of something like a ten thousandth of a centimeter in one second.''[55]

In 1908, Jean Baptiste Perrin (1870-1942) a French physical chemist, received the Nobel Prize in physics for his verification of Einstein's Brownian motion equations.

Max Born, later an Einstein colleague in Berlin, and an especially close friend commented that, "I think that these investigations by Einstein (Brownian motion) have done more than any other work to convince physicists of the reality of atoms and molecules, of the kinetic theory of heat, and of the fundamental part of probability in the natural laws."

Another paper, more widely known in the field of physics for the reason that it won for Einstein the Nobel Prize, was on a "Heuristic Viewpoint Concerning the Production and Transformation of Light— The Photoelectric Effect." Einstein's quantum law was based on, complementary to, and developed beyond Max Planck's quantum theory.

At the beginning of the century, Einstein ws not the only genius to set tongues wagging and heads shaking. Planck preceded him; he was the first to jolt the scientific establishment. Unlike Einstein, however, Planck himself didn't really plan to rearrange scientific thinking; he had no such revolutionary designs. He thought of his work as being involved in a routine problem of physics and expected to find answers within the framework of the knowledge then existant.

Planck's youthful brilliance had won him an assistantship to the great Professor Gustav Kirchhoff at the University of Berlin. After Kirchhoff's death Planck was appointed to the physics chair. While examining the possibility of stating in mathematical form the equation for "heated bodies," Planck found that the light from these heated bodies was radiated as a result of "oscillation of atoms." His investigations were limited to the emission and absorption of light and not concerned with the properties of light rays per se. Planck remained a traditionalist, holding firm to the ancient ether theory and the wave theory of light.

Upon further investigation, Planck found to his displeasure that the light emitted from heated bodies was propagated in successive, separate, and distinctive packets of energy he called "quanta." The finding was both puzzling and disquieting to Planck because he was forced to admit that his quanta were discontinuous, and he was hard put to square this conclusion with the fact that he also stood by the continuous wave theory of light. The quantum theory, translated into everyday language, means that light, when likened to water released by a tap, would be emitted in one-ounce drops and not in a full stream. This seemed an unlikely conclusion as well as a ridiculous concept. The finding offended "common sense" and ran counter to labora tory experiments conducted by Faraday, Young, Fresnel and Max well, all of whom favored the undulatory-wave theory of the emission of light.

Planck, himself, was unwilling to accept his own premise; never theless his equations were proof enough that it worked—each quan tum contained a definite amount of energy. Although he read his paper on quantum theory to the German Physical Society and even had it published in the *Annalen der Physik,* no one took notice or ever mentioned it. It just lay there on the printed page, gathering dust and waiting to be forgotten. If the scientific community had an opin ion of Planck's work, one way or the other, they were conspicuously noncommital by their silence. And Planck, dissatisfied with his own work, spent the next several years trying to solve the problem within the concept of the wave theory.

During the years from 1900 to 1905, however, while the hierarchy of sciencedom ignored Planck's "quanta," one mind was busily devouring this latest blast at the vulnerable walls of classical physics. Albert Einstein alone appreciated the originality and significance of Planck's work. Since Einstein did not feel bound by the barrier of classical physics, he could even see beyond Planck's theory. As a matter of record, he went several steps further (which Planck frowned upon) by postulating that *all* light, every form of energy, whether the source be heat, x rays, gamma rays, or other forms of light that the human apparatus can or cannot detect, actually travels through space in separate and discontinuous quanta; that light is composed of in dividual particles or grains of energy called light photons. In this work, Einstein was influenced by other revolutionary theories, par ticularly Maxwell's electromagnetic field equations, Wien's law of distribution of radiation, and Lorentz's electron theory.

Einstein went on to relate the quantum theory to another phe nomenon, namely the photoelectric effect, first discovered by Heinrich Hertz in 1887. Several years before Planck's original quan tum theory appeared in print, Philip Lenard, a leading German phys icist, but later a vehemently outspoken Nazi, began experimenting with the photoelectric effect. Lenard, who was also a staunch believer in the wave theory of light, could not understand why when an ultraviolet light was shone on a metal plate, electrons were thrown from the plate singly and individually. According to the Maxwellian wave theory, this should not have happened. The wave theory expected that all electrons in the path of the untraviolet light should have been swept away in one fell swoop.

Lenard discovered two other effects that further confused his thinking: when ultraviolet light, which is a high-frequency color, is shone onto a metal plate, electrons of high energy will be ejected from the metal plate. And when a low frequency light, such as red, is shone onto the metal plate, the same number of electrons will be ejected, but with less vehemence. In other words, the higher the frequency of the light, the higher the speed at which the electrons are ejected from the plate. Then when we bring the source of light closer to the metal plate, there would be a proportionate increase in the number of electrons ejected from the plate.

Einstein helped solve Lenard's predicament but received only paranoid villification and anti-Jewish spoutings from Lenard in the years following World War I.

In his own investigations on the photoelectric effect, Einstein said that since photons are light, composed of grains of energy, and when one photon, as it emanates from the light source, hits an electron in the metal plate, the action is similar to one billiard ball striking another. The one photon ejects just one electron from the metal plate. He further found that the velocity with which each electron flies from the metal plate is proportional to the energy content of the original photon that strikes it. The expulsion of an electron occurs only when it has absorbed a whole quantum of radiation. An electron that absorbs a violet photon (high frequency) is expelled at a greater speed than one absorbing a red photon (low frequency).

The photoelectric effect, using Einstein's light photon theory, later found its application in television and medicine, in the treatment of cancer, tuberculosis and polio. Einstein's equations for the photoelectric effect were later proved by the precise laboratory experiments performed by Robert Millikan, of the California Institute of Technology. For his experiments and findings in this field, Millikan received the Nobel Prize for physics in 1928. Einstein received the Nobel Prize for physics for his work on the photoelectric effect for the year 1921.

Einstein had found order and harmony in the movement of the billions of bits of matter speeding through the vast reaches of space. He was certain that for each effect there is a cause that must be determined by way of either individual thought, observation or laboratory experiments. Einstein's physics was firmly rooted in causality—where action can be measured and predicted.

The unpredictability of the flow of electrons (later stated by Werner Heisenberg in 1927 as the principle of uncertainty) was the reason Einstein later abandoned the disordered world of the electron and the quantum theory. For the last thirty years of his life, his scientific thrust was focused on formulating a common ground theory, a theory whose equations would link the electromagnetic world of the microscopic atom with the gravitational world of macroscopic outer space—the unified field theory. He published several papers on the subject in the ensuing years, and though he himself was never satisfied with his findings, never gave up the search. As he often marveled, "what is incomprehensible about the universe is, that it is comprehensible." His mission was to quantify, to prove by mathematical equations or, as the Marquis Pierre LaPlace had written in 1825, "to embrace into a single formula the movements of the largest bodies in the universe and those of the lightest atom."

Einstein expressed his doubts about the quantum theory in a 1926 letter to Max Born. "Quantum mechanics demands serious attention. But an inner voice tells me that this is not the 'true Jacob.' The theory accomplished a lot, but it does not bring us close to the secret of the 'Old One.' In any case, I am convinced 'He Does Not Play Dice.'"[57]

Max Born was perhaps better qualified than most to comment on Einstein's theories, (he later developed his own atomic theory); nevertheless, he had his differences with the master in the theoretical field and said so.

> One of the most remarkable volumes in the whole of scientific literature seems to me Vol. 17 (4th series) of *Annalen der Physik,* 1905. It contains three papers by Einstein, each dealing with a different subject, and each today acknowledged to be a masterpiece, the source of a new branch of physics. These three subjects, in order of pages, are: theory of photons, Brownian motion, and relativity . . . . In my opinion he would be one of the greatest theoretical physicists of all times even if he had not written a single line on relativity . . . . He has seen more clearly than anyone before him the statistical background of the laws of physics and he was a pioneer in the struggle of conquering the wilderness of quantum phenomena. Yet, later when out of his own work a synthesis of statistical and quantum principles

emerged which seemed acceptable to almost all physicists he kept himself aloof and skeptical. Many of us regard this as a tragedy for him as he gropes his way in loneliness and for us, who miss our leader and standard bearer.[58]

While Einstein had come to reject some of his own work, Planck was slowly beginning to acknowledge the possibility of its accuracy. Years later Planck admitted: "I now know for a fact that the elementary quantum of action played a far more significant part in physics than I had originally been inclined to suspect."[59]

11

THE ELECTRODYNAMICS OF MOVING BODIES, MASS–ENERGY

Albert Einstein "abolished the ether" as Sir Arthur Eddington put it. He also placed a speed limit on the universe, excorsized energy from matter (theoretically, of course), forbade "simultaneous events" to ever appear in space again, wedded time and space forever, and kneaded the centuries old Euclidian, three-dimensional world into the new staple of twentieth century physics, the four-dimensional world.

The special theory of relativity is many-sided, and contributions to its structure come from a number of sources. In the nineteenth century investigations that had a bearing on relativity were made by Michael Faraday and James Clerk Maxwell, when they examined "electromagnetic waves;" by Ludwig Boltzmann with his work on gasses; by Ernest Rutherford on the atom; Henrik Antoon Lorentz, the electron; Max Planck, quanta—Henri Poincaré dared a limited relativity. But it remained for Einstein to remove these separate theories from the timid hands of the classisists and to expose to scrutiny and sometimes ridicule a revolution in thought.

What a weird idea that in the direction of the motion, all objects shorten—which means that at half the speed of light a rocket ship would become shorter, its windows narrower, its clocks slower, its occupants thinner. Equally "ridiculous" was the mass/energy theory. As one Viennese professor reacted, "It takes one's breath away to think of what might happen in a town if the dormant energy of a single brick were to be set free, say in the form of an explosion. This, however, will never happen."

Even today we cannot expect to see the world as Einstein saw it, though we can and do understand some of his basic premises. For the most part, it must be left to succeeding generations, after much simplification and education to understand the Einsteinian world. "What is staggering to us, will be simple for our grandchildren."[60]

To whatever heights Einstein's thoughts soared, however far-reaching his discovery of existing natural phenomena, he humbly acknowledged that to him there was allowed only a partial glimpse. "The truths we discover are only fragmentary. We see relative motions, but we cannot actually see the world as it really is. We will never be able to see the big picture. After all, the world as we see it, is only the world as we see it.''

Newton too, realized that he stood but on the threshold of a greater knowledge. ''I do not know what I may appear to the world, but to myself I seem to have been only like a boy playing on the seashore, and diverting myself in now and then finding a smoother pebble or a prettier shell than ordinary, whilst the great ocean of truth lay all undiscovered before me.''[61]

Under the title ''The Electrodynamics Of Moving Bodies'' Einstein gives the essence of his special theory of relativity. But don't let the title scare you; all it really does is to relate what happens when a vehicle or a body is in motion; What happens to the vehicle, to the occupant, to time; at very fast speeds.

To understand the theory, let's begin by agreeing that ''simultaneous events'' are events that are happening at the same exact time; like two horses in a photofinish. Also, a factory whistle blowing and the hands of a clock reaching 5:00 PM can be simultaneous.

Newton said that ''two simultaneous events in one system are simultaneous in a system moving uniformly relative to the first.'' That made sense until Einstein introduced the element of the speed of light. He found that where the speed of light is concerned, a whole new way of thinking is required. Now, let's understand that the sun setting on a beautiful summer evening and our timepiece striking 8:30 PM are not simultaneous events. They may have seemed to have taken place simultaneously, but the physical reality is that the sun actually set some eight minutes earlier, and, as we already know, it took eight minutes of earth time for the rays of the sun to reach us here on earth. Another example: looking up into the heavens, but this time beyond our local planetary system, we see light rays from two stars whose individual distances from earth are many and a different number of light years. Merely seeing them at the same time does not mean that the light rays from both stars began their journey to the earth at the same time. The moments when they respectively produced observable light may be millions of years apart. They may appear as simultaneous events to us, as we view them from the earth, but in the larger view they are not. When we are looking at the stars we must recognize the fact that we are seeing them as they were at different times. Hence, according to Einstein, we must set up a different time zone for each one. Each star, or any other body occupying space, has its own calendar, its own clocks, and its own time. And no two of them are the same. And they are all different from our time here on earth.

It wasn't Einstein's intention to prove Newton's theory of simultaneity wrong. He merely pointed out its limiting aspect when he stated, in effect, that two events simultaneous to the observer at rest are *not* seen as simultaneous to the moving observer, where the speed of light is concerned. The following is Einstein's own example of the relativity of seemingly simultaneous events:

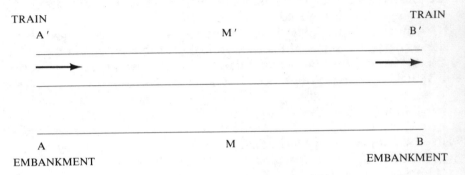

TRAIN   TRAIN
A′   M′   B′

A   M   B
EMBANKMENT   EMBANKMENT

Place an observer on the embankment beside the railroad track, "at the mid-point M of the distance AB. This observer should be supplied with an arrangement (e.g. two mirrors inclined at 90°) which allows him visually to observe both places A and B at the same time. . . . We suppose a very long train traveling along the rails with a uniform velocity in the direction indicated in the above illustration. . . . Are two events, the two strokes of lightning, A and B, which are simultaneous with reference to the railway embankment also simultaneous relatively to the train? We shall show directly that the answer must be in the negative.

When we say that the lightning strokes A and B are simultaneous with respect to the embankment, we mean: the rays of light emitted at the places A and B where the lightning occurs, meet each other at the mid-point M of the length A—B of the embankment. But the events A and B also correspond to positions A′ and B′ on the traveling train. Let M′ be the mid-point of the distance A′—B′ on the traveling train. Just when the flashes of lightning (as judged from the embankment) occur, this point M′ naturally coincides with the point M, but it moves towards the right in the diagram with the velocity of the train. If an observer sitting in the position M′ in the train did not possess this velocity, then he would remain permanently at M, and the light rays emitted by the flashes of lightning A and B would reach him simultaneously, i.e. they would meet just where he is situated.

Now in reality, the observer, with his own mirror arrangement, sitting in the position M ' in the train is hastening towards the beam of light coming from B ', whilst he is riding on ahead of the beam of light coming from A '. Hence the observer (on the train) will see the beam of light emitted from B ' earlier then he will see that emitted from A '. Observers who take the railway train as their reference-body must therefore come to the conclusion that the lightning flash B ' took place earlier than the lightning flash A '. We thus arrive at the important result: Events which are simultaneous with reference to the embankment are not simultaneous with respect to the train, and vice versa (relativity of simultaneity). Every reference body has its own particular time; unless we are told the reference-body to which the statement of time refers, there is no meaning in a statement of the time of an event.

New before the advent of the theory of relativity it had always been assumed in physics that the statement of time had an absolute significance, i.e. that it is independent of the state of motion of the body of reference. But we have just seen that this assumption is incompatible with the most natural definition of simultaneity . . . according to the foregoing considerations, the time required by a particular occurrence with respect to the train must not be considered equal to the duration of the same occurrence as judged from the embankment.''[62]

It may be difficult to digest, but Einstein has just shown that a second of time in the train is not equal to a second of time on the embankment. If you are looking for that fine line that separates Newtonian classicism from Einsteinian relativity, it is best illustrated in the above example. Einstein showed that time flows differently in a moving vehicle than time at rest.

If we fly a clock (vehicle in motion) from London to San Francisco at five hundred miles an hour, the slowdown of the clock will hardly be noticeable or for that matter, measureable. But boost the speed of the vehicle to half that of light, and a clock or a heartbeat will be slowed by fifteen percent. Other body functions will also be slowed. The traveler in the vehicle will not notice this slowdown because his watch or clock will also slow down. Only the outside observer can detect the difference. The traveler in the vehicle also will not know that his vehicle has shortened, has contracted in size, and seems to the stationary observer shorter in motion than when standing still. Now, if two vehicles are traveling in uniform motion, beside each other, at very high speed, then the traveler in the first vehicle will notice the second vehicle contracting, but not his own. And of course, the same holds true for the traveler in the second vehicle.

The "twin paradox" is a hypothetical speculation growing out of Einstein's premise that time and heartbeats are slower in a moving vehicle; that aging is slowed. It says, that if a man traveled out into space at or near the speed of light, for a period of two years (as measured by him in his vehicle), he would find on his return to earth that the earth had aged two hundred years. He will have aged but two years, but his twin who remained on earth aged two hundred. If the twin paradox appears a bit far-fetched to you, check out an experiment that took place in October 1971. At that time, Assistant Professor Joseph Hafele of Washington University in Saint Louis, Missouri, teamed up with physicist-astronomer, Richard Keating, of the United States Naval Observatory. "In an attempt to throw some empirical light on the question of whether macroscopic clocks record time in accordance with the conventional interpretation of Einstein's relativity theory, four cesium beam atomic clocks (which gain or lose only one second in some thirty thousand years) were flown around the world on commercial jet flights, first eastward, then westward. Then Hafele and Keating compared the time they recorded by the reference atomic time scale at the U.S. Naval Observatory. As was expected from theoretical predictions, the flying clocks lost time (aged slower) during the eastward trip and gained time (aged faster) during the westward trip."[63] The findings were in "good" agreement with predictions of conventional relativity theory.

We should not fear contradiction if we say that the common household "yardstick" measures thirty-six inches in length when it is in a state of rest. That statement, however, can be questioned right from the beginning before we go any further, because nothing is in a state of rest in this universe. Everything is in motion and moving in several directions at the same time. But, that's another matter for another time. Just for the sake of this discussion, let's agree that at rest, relative to our planet, the yardstick measures thirty-six inches. If we place the yardstick in an automobile traveling sixty miles an hour, its length will be reduced to 0.99999999998 of a yard. The car will also shrink. However, the shrinkage will be such a small amount that no one will notice. However, if we raise the speed of the vehicle to eighty-seven percent of the speed of light, then the stick will be half its original length. And at the speed of light, the entire stick, while re-

Left, Joseph Hafele of Washington University, St. Louis and Richard Keating of the Naval Observatory in Washington, D.C. pose with two cesium atomic clocks prior to taking off on a round-the-world flight in which they will test Einstein's theory of relativity.
October 4, 1971

taining dimensions of height and width, would measure "no length" —but no object can attain the speed of light, according to Einstein.

Just to keep the record straight, the above measurements and percentages are made on the basis of the yardstick's length relative to our earth while it is traveling some twenty miles per second around the sun. If we were to measure the yardstick in relation to some other point in our galaxy that is traveling faster than our planetary system, its length would be entirely different from the length we perceive it to be here on earth. The yardstick, depending on the system you relate it to, has different lengths. What is the true length? Is its earth length the correct one? Or is its Jupiter length the true one? The fact is, there is no one true length; there is just a relative length. The length of any object depends on the system you relate it to, the speed at which it is traveling. And that holds true for everything here on earth. Everything is its present size and shape only relative to our earth and its speed.

We not only depend on other matter in the universe for our time system, but we also use other matter for a point of reference to calculate our motion. What this means is that without other bodies scattered throughout the huge void, we would have no way of knowing whether or not the earth is in motion. Only by studying the positions and motions of other bits of matter in space can we know at what rate we are traveling and in what direction—relatively speaking, that is. Relatively, because we only know the direction we are traveling relative to other bodies; we may never know in what direction we are moving relative to outer-galactic space. According to astronomers, we have been traveling as we are now for at least four billion years, and we really don't know where we are headed. Is space indeed infinite? Are we going around in gigantic circles? Will we ever see the "big picture"?

Scientists had set aside certain unquestioned areas that were to remain sacrosanct and untouchable to the questing mind of man. One such area was the gravitational theory of Newton; another, the concept of time. Aristotle had said, "There is one single and invariable time." Aristotle's time had survived unscathed down through the ages, even through the Newtonian revolution of thought. Newton was more emphatic in not wishing to disturb the workings of the "great giant clock" that presided over the entire universe. He said: "Absolute, true and mathematical time, taken in itself and without relation to any material object, flows uniformly of its own nature . . . . Time flows equably without relation to anything external." In other words, according to Newton, time in and of itself exists, whether or not there are bodies or matter scattered throughout the huge void. He was quite emphatic. "Time flowed on . . . . has its own existence independent of the bodies of the universe . . . . Time, like space should exist even if the bodies and other phenomena disappeared, and by another name is called Duration. Absolute space, on the other hand, independent by its own nature of any relation to external objects remains always unchangeable and immovable."

Einstein came to a different conclusion regarding the inviolable time. Time, he suggested, is, after all, only the measurement we have devised here on earth to fix the positions of bodies, primarily that of our planet in relation to the sun; without objects out in space (notably the sun) with which to measure time, time would cease to exist.

We divide the daily rotation of our planet on its axis into twenty-four convenient hours. Each hour of time, in reality, corresponds to fifteen degrees of the three hundred and sixty degrees the earth rotates in that same twenty-four hour period. All clocks, sundials, and any other method of telling time here on earth have been geared to the earth's daily rotation. *Our* time is calculated in relation to *our* solar system. Other planets, or other bits of floating matter existing in other solar systems, traveling at speeds different from that of earth, would each have a time different from ours here on earth. But if there were no sun, moon, stars and other matter, there would be no "fixed point" in space from which we could reckon the earth's motion and come up with a time system. Time, therefore, without other matter in the universe, would not be measureable; would not exist.

Space, by itself, also has no reality. It is a huge void, an emptiness. And as in the case of time, if there were no matter such as planets, suns and nebulae, cluttering up the area, there would be *no space*. Time is not possible without the matter that makes up space. But once matter (more than one body of matter) exists, time and space are automatic and exist interdependently in a space-time continuum. Einstein said "time is simply another dimension of space." And this other dimension of space is called the fourth dimension (the other dimensions we already know as height, length and width.)

If we were to measure the length of a floor, that's a one-dimensional measurement. To determine the size of a parcel of land, we measure its length and width; that's two dimensional. To construct a room we must know the three dimensions of height, length and width. But if we try to locate an airplane in flight, our information must include the three dimensions of space—altitude, latitude and longitude—plus the fourth dimension of space, time. As Professor J.S. Ames explains in his article entitled, "Einstein's Law Of Gravitation," "All four coordinates are necessary; we never observe an event except at a certain time, and we never observe an instant of time except with reference to space."[64]

Einstein did not originate entirely the thinking that led to the space-time continuum. As he himself explained to an enthusiastic public, inadvertently crediting him with every creation except the original one: "It is a widespread error that the Special Theory of Relativity is supposed to have, to a certain extent, first discovered, or at any rate, newly introduced, the four dimensionality of the physical continuum. This, of course, is not the case. Classical mechanics, too, is based on the four-dimensional continuum of space and time, ... But, classical mechanics does not consider the four-dimensional point of view *as necessary* . . . . The Special Theory, on the other hand, creates a formal dependence between the way in which the spatial co-ordinates on the one hand, and the temporal co-ordinates, on the other *have* to enter into the natural laws."[65]

Time, as we experience it here on earth, is called "local time" or "terrestrial time". That means that our earth day of twenty-four hours and our earth year of three hundred sixty-five days do not apply to any other body in our solar system or perhaps for that matter, to any other body in the entire universe; unless sometime in the future we should locate another body out in space, circumnavigating its sun in exactly the same orbit and at the same speed, and rotating on its axis in the same exact time that the earth does.

It may be difficult to imagine all the motion that is continually taking place throughout the universe. Every bit of matter in space is constantly in motion (nothing is standing still) and all these billions of bodies (large and minute) are traveling at different speeds. Each has its own individual time. "There is no such thing as a universally equal time, with seconds, minutes or hours everywhere alike."

Major changes in living schedules would have to be made if we were to inhabit another planet. For instance, Mercury, the planet nearest the sun, at an average distance of thirty-six million miles (its orbit is a football-shaped ellipse) turns on its axis once every fifty-eight of our earth days. Yet, its orbit around the sun consumes only eighty-eight of our earth days. Together, they make for a very fast year, but an awfully long day.

Venus, next in proximity to the sun, at an average distance of some sixty-seven million miles, has a day that lasts some 247 of our earth days, but, a year of only 224 of our earth days. The Venus day then is longer than its year. It would be a strange existence, if Venus were at all habitable; the day would consist of 123½ earth days of continual sunshine followed by an equal period of darkness.

Voyaging from the inner to the outer circle of planets, we find Jupiter, the largest planet in our solar system, orbiting the sun some 483 million miles away. Jupiter's day is very short, about ten of our earth hours; that's very fast spinning for a mass whose diameter is 86,800 miles compared to earth's 7,926. Jupiter is so large that all the other planets in our solar system could fit within its boundaries. The days may go fast on Jupiter, but the years pass very slowly; each is some eleven and three quarters of our earth years. It should now be fairly evident that absolute Newtonian time cannot possibly apply to the entire universe. And that's precisely Einstein's point.

As was mentioned previously, the earth is traveling in several directions at the same time. First, the earth rotates on its axis once every twenty-four hours at a speed of a little over one thousand miles per hour. At the very same time it is also engaged in orbiting the sun, once every three hundred and sixty-five days at a speed of some twenty miles per second. Our entire solar system, including the sun and all the planets and their respective moons, is in movement within the confines of our "local star system" at thirteen miles per second. The local star system, in turn, is moving within our Milky Way galaxy at two hundred miles per second. Now, the Milky Way, as a complete unit, is drifting off in some unknown direction at about one hundred miles per second. Recently, it was discovered that our galaxy travels in the company of other galaxies that make up a "cluster" of about twenty galaxies. All these bodies are traveling in different directions, all at the same time. And no one has the faintest idea of where all this travel is leading us to. How vast can this universe be, if all this movement continues without any body of matter bumping up against a wall of some kind? All these vast distances have been negotiated, all these speeds have been maintained without the occurrence of some natural disaster for many billions of years. And astronomers tell us that we never occupy the same space more than just the one time.

Can you believe that distant galaxies are receding away from our galaxy at the speed of *ninety thousand miles per second;* that is, half the speed of light? Correction. They *were* receding some millions of years ago, since it takes millions, if not billions of years for their light to reach us here on earth. Since light and radio signals (which also travel at the speed of light), that we receive now were sent out millions and billions of years ago, the big question is, where are these galaxies now, at this very instant? The two hundred inch telescope at Mount Palomar has picked up quasars traveling at one hundred-fifty thousand miles per second. Some astronomers wouldn't at all be surprised if other galaxies are receding from our galaxy at the speed of light. If so, then we'll never know about it since we haven't devised any system that can project radio signals faster than the speed of light, the speed required to catch up with the fast-moving galaxies. Einstein says this is impossible. If Einstein is right, we will never know of their existence.

It took Einstein only three pages to lay the groundwork for atomic energy. First, he determined that mass (any mass) has energy and gave his paper the title: "Does The Inertia Of A Body Depend Upon Its Energy Content?" After writing the technical part, he suggested a method of testing: "It is not impossible that with bodies whose energy content is variable to a high degree (e.g. radium salts) the theory may be put to the test."[66] Indulgent colleagues and smirking detractors wanted to know how he could be so sure that enough energy was bottled up in a single grain of sand to run a ship across the Atlantic Ocean, since he hadn't performed any laboratory experiments to prove his thesis. Einstein countered that if a rich man had never spent any of his money, no one would know he was rich. It's the same with matter. If none of the energy is visible or detectable, it's existence cannot be ascertained.

Einstein had more to offer than the adroitness of a clever analogy. In his 1905 paper, Einstein shows that he had developed the theory of the "equivalence of mass and energy" to the point where he could account for the tiny amount of mass needed to produce a tremendous amount of energy when he wrote the following equation:

$$M = \frac{E}{C^2}$$

Stated simply, the equation says: Energy has mass and mass has energy. "If a body gives off energy E, in the form of radiation, it's mass, M, diminishes by EC² (C being the speed of light)."

The Einstein mass-energy relationship theory answered one of science's most frustrating questions, how the sun had been able to radiate so much energy for so long a time. Scientists knew that if the sun were a huge lump of coal its energy would have been used up long ago, leaving the earth a cold, lifeless waste. In Einstein's equations they found the reason the sun has been emitting light and radiant heat, continually, for billions of years and why it will continue to do so for billions of years to come. We have been blessed with a very stable sun. It follows Einstein's equations, using a very small amount of matter and converting it into a huge amount of energy.

Coaxing energy from a source proved to be a bit more complicated than simply sending an atom "out" to the neighborhood "atom-smasher" at 9:00 a.m. and having it ready by 3:00 p.m. Even Einstein had his doubts. He knew the energy was hiding, but as time went by even Einstein grew more skeptical as to the early feasibility of converting a mass into energy. "At present there is not the slightest indication of when this energy will be obtainable, or whether it will be obtainable at all. For it would presuppose a disintegration of the atom effected at will—a shattering of the atom. And up to the present there is scarcely a sign that this will be possible. We observe atomic disintegration only where Nature herself presents it, as in the case of radium, the activity of which depends upon the continual explosive decomposition of its atom. Nevertheless, we can only establish the presence of this process, but cannot produce it; Science in its present state makes it appear almost impossible that we shall ever succeed in so doing.'' Even as late as 1934, when war clouds were again gathering over the European continent, Einstein was still a skeptic. Yet, at the same time, cyclotrons were being built in Germany, England, Denmark, and the United States. The extent of the experimenters' progress during the twenties and early thirties was not fully appreciated by Einstein until in early 1939, when Niels Bohr rushed over from Denmark with the news that Lise Meitner and her nephew, Otto Frisch, had indeed split the atom and measured the energy given off.

It took several years after the 1905 publication for the physicists, scientists, and philosophers of his native Germany to note and truly appreciate the enlightening theories of the original mind dwelling among them. But it remained for a foreign power, the United States of America, to secretly transport complicated scientific equipment to a barren waste in the western state of New Mexico, near an out-of-the-way town called Alamogordo, to prove Einstein's mass-energy theory by exploding the first atomic bomb on the morning of July 16, 1945, some thirty-eight years after his equation,

$$E = MC^2$$

first saw the printed page.

12

ZURICH

The first reaction to young Einstein's 1905 papers came not from the scientific community, not from his colleagues, but from a totally unexpected quarter. The first reaction was neither critical nor scientific. It was a physical reaction felt by the author himself. The intense concentration he had brought to bear for a full six weeks prior to publication left him suffering from complete exhaustion. The ordeal —the infinite care necessitated by the revolutionary nature of his heretofore unheard-of theories—left him physically drained and confined to his bed for several weeks.

Mileva had helped in the preparation, where she could. Although not a theoretical scientist, she understood and appreciated her husband's creations. She was very proud of him. A "beautiful piece of work" she called it. When his recovery was complete, Einstein, the civil servant, resumed his position at the Bern Patent Office. This responsibility he carried out punctiliously while he waited for some sort of response from his publications. Wait he did, but none came, at least not right away.

Publication in the respected Annalen der Physik usually generates follow-up papers from scientists working in the same or allied fields. But the usual practice didn't hold true for Einstein's papers. The principal reason was that Einstein had offended common sense; his papers did not contain the "usual" investigative work. Learned professors may have read Einstein's papers, but showed by not reacting that they were not impressed. Or, perhaps they were loath to shout "revolution" when their profession, prestige, and salary depended on keeping a lid on classical concepts.

The two who did react positively and with encouraging warmth were to become lifelong friends of the young German-born Swiss. They were Max Planck of Berlin and Henrik Antoon Lorentz of Leiden. These two, now as then, were and are two of the greatest names in the field of physics. Both had made their names in the field and could offer encouragement to Einstein despite their reluctance to clasp Einstein, scientifically, to their bosom.

Relativity gradually did gain acceptance, despite the constant Einstein detractors. His one-time assistant at Princeton, Leopold Infeld, remembers the period after the 1905 publication this way: "My friend Professor Loria told me his teacher Professor Witkowski in Cracow read Einstein's paper and exclaimed to Loria, 'A new Copernicus has been born: Read Einstein's paper.' Later when Loria met Max Born at a physics meeting he told him about Einstein and asked Born if he had read the paper. It turned out that neither Born nor anyone else there had heard about Einstein. They went to the library, took from the bookshelves the seventeenth volume of *Annalen der Physik* and started to read Einstein's article. Immediately Born realized its greatness and also the necessity for formal generalizations. Later, Born's own work on relativity theory became one of the most important early contributions to the field of science."[68]

Einstein had neither the time nor the inclination to sit idly by nervously hoping for approval. His mind, looking at mathematical conclusions as anything but conclusions, leapt ahead to the next implication of relativity. To him, every theory, proven or otherwise, was a stepping-stone to a greater truth, but never the final and unalterable declaration of what exists. For he believed, and science now agrees, that we will never reach a stage where we can make the statement that we can ever know the workings of the entire universe; we can never see the big picture. He believed that the most any investigator could do was to lift only partially a corner of the curtain of truth.

Einstein continued to develop his mass-energy theory until, in 1907, he could determine the amount of energy that the mass times the speed of light squared could produce. Then and only then could he write the most famous equation in history: $E = MC^2$.

When consideration of his work became unavoidable, it was often accompanied by abuse and ridicule. The academicians were extremely skeptical of theories promulgated by an obscure clerk in a patent office and in no way connected with a university. What papers had he written before? Where was his laboratory proof? No laboratory proof? Never conducted experiments? Then it's all rubbish. But Einstein was oblivious to the negativism; his mind was elsewhere.

The Patent Office was an ideal setup for Einstein. Examining patent applications came easy to him. At home, he made up games and built toys with which to amuse Hans Albert. Soon he became quite proficient at balancing a book, smoking a cigar, and rocking the bassinet, all at the same time, thus winning approval from his wife. He was quite content in his work, in his marriage, and in the role of husband and father, as long as he could squeeze in some time for physics.

This idyllic home scene was in danger of being disrupted, however; forces were at work behind the scenes in far-off places. There were those, principally the hierarchy of the University of Zurich, who were determined that the Einstein family should no longer remain in provincial Bern but should move to intellectual Zurich. They conspired to tempt the civil servant away from his Patent Office by offering him a position at the university; comprehension, disapproval or approval of his theories were not factors to be considered. They had concluded that they could no longer allow a mind that ranged from the outer reaches of galactic space to the innermost workings of the atom to continue to languish in the unfertile surroundings of a patent office. The man obviously should be occupying a physics chair at a university, whether his theories made sense or not.

Professorships, then, were usually attained at the end of a career, as a reward for years of rather menial lectures, first as *Privatdozent,* then as assistant professor (when and where available) and if one lived long enough, had written more papers, and acquired more prestige, the door to professordom would perhaps be opened. Often it was a matter of survival. To start the ball rolling, Professor Alfred Kleiner, a physicist himself, and first known to Einstein when Einstein submitted his doctoral thesis, "Method Of Determination Of Molecular Dimensions", back in 1903, was sent to encourage the Bernese civil servant to accept the *Privatdozent* position at the University of Zurich.

Einstein would have welcomed the opportunity of working in an academic atmosphere with other scientists, but the conditions attached to Kleiner's proposal forced him to turn it down. It was purely a matter of economics. The *Privatdozent* is not salaried by the university, so that his income would depend on the number and the generosity of the students he could attract to his lectures. The university is obligated only to provide facilities, not pay. He would gain in experience, but he might starve for his dedication. Einstein would have had to give up his job in Bern and move back to Zurich for a position with no income. A persistent Kleiner then suggested he apply instead to the nearby University of Bern for the same position, since Zurich wanted him to get some lecturing experience; then perhaps he could be brought into Zurich for a better position.

Obtaining the position at Bern presented no problem, financial or otherwise. He could work at the university in the evening. The addition of the lectures to his daily schedule, however, did eat into the time he had allotted for his creative period, the hours after work and Sundays.

Giving lectures from a prescribed textbook was not and never would become Einstein's style. He had rebelled against boring lectures in his own school days by not attending. It was not done for effect or to defy authority; it was his natural reaction to conventional methods and thinking. Following his bent, at the University of Bern, he departed from the text and spoke extemporaneously on subjects he himself found of interest. His lectures became friendly and informal discussions. Actually, the way the classes were conducted didn't matter very much; Einstein wasn't able to attract more than two or three students. Kleiner sat in on one of these informal performances and made his displeasure known to Einstein, complaining that it was far below the level of competence he had expected; that Einstein's notes were not organized, that he didn't know how to conduct a class. Einstein bridled at Kleiner's criticism and protested in turn that he didn't insist on being a professor at the University of Zurich.

While Zurich was trying to figure out how to deal with this rare bird of unconventional ways, interest was expressed in another academic area. Einstein accepted an invitation to speak at the 1908 Physics Congress, to be convened in Salzburg, Austria. This was his first opportunity to come into contact with the world's leading physicists. At Salzburg he could look forward to discourse with fellow physicists on matters of mutual interest, an exchange that could only prove beneficial to him; he had not conferred with physicists in the eight years since his graduation. Excited, Einstein prepared his best material, the special theory and the phenomenon of light. On this occasion his notes were meticulous, for he was to address the "great masters and leaders of science whose names are mentioned only with respect."[69]

Reactions to his lectures were mixed. Some scientists who listened intently had long felt that Newton's reign would be impossible to maintain much longer and saw in Einstein's radical approach their vehicle for loosening the stranglehold of classical mechanics. Others, stormed out of the conference hall, horrified at the thought of a moving vehicle shortening its length.

The reportage of the Salzburg Conference by scientific publications was not wasted on the University of Zurich. Their previous efforts to land Einstein had been rather lukewarm. But after reading that the young rebel had gained the interest and attention of the great and revered Lorentz, they could dally no longer. They swung their recruiting system into high gear and through Kleiner offered Einstein the Associate Professorship in physics. The offer found Einstein prepared to accept without further deliberation.

Again a hitch developed. It seems that during their period of indecision the post had been offered to Friedrich Adler, the same Adler who had been Einstein's close friend and classmate at the ETH. Adler's appointment had been favored for political reasons, since the board at Zurich was generally sympathetic to the philosophy of the Austrian Socialist Party. How now to extricate themselves from the embarrassing position of having offered the same position to two men? Einstein was not aware of the double offer, but Adler was. And it was only his integrity that saved an otherwise perplexed group of men from their double-dealing. When Adler heard that his old friend Einstein had also been offered the post, he addressed the board as follows: "If it is possible to obtain a man like Einstein for our University, it would be absurd to appoint me. I must quite frankly say that my ability as a research physicist does not bear even the slightest comparison to Einstein's. Such an opportunity to obtain a man who can benefit us so much by raising the general level of the University should not be lost because of political considerations."[70]

13

BEGINNINGS OF GRAVITATIONAL THEORY

Not yet thirty, Associate Professor Einstein, looked forward to the give and take of scientific discussions with students and professors. The eight years in Bern had softened his attitude towards faculty frailties. With the disappointing experience of 1900 far behind him, he was determined to approach his new position, unprejudiced. He was fully aware, however, of two distasteful aspects of the life of a university faculty member—lecturing, and the inevitable faculty gossip, which he hoped to avoid. He would attempt to put up with the mandatory lectures by introducing his own material. And the faculty games of numbers—the number of papers published, the number of doctoral students, the number of speaking engagements— the ego trips, and the self-glorification he left to others.

First came a welcoming-home feast and a period of getting reacquainted with old friends including Grossmann, Besso, the Wintelers, and especially sister Maja. And then the Einsteins settled in, among friends and family in a city they all loved. The Einsteins were fully content with every aspect of the move, except one, the financial. Professor Einstein's pay was to be the same as patent examiner Einstein's. This didn't bother the professor at all—so far as his needs were concerned; he was never interested in amassing money. What made the difference was the financial responsibilities in Zurich, which were greater than those in Bern. In Bern, he was not expected to dress for occasions. In Zurich, it was obligatory. In Bern, he could go "bohemian." In Zurich, he couldn't. A professor was expected to dress better than a civil servant. They felt the financial crunch so, they were forced to take in student boarders. Assessing his financial malady in Zurich, Einstein remarked quizzically, "In my relativity theory I set up a clock at every point in space, but in reality I find it difficult to provide even one clock in my room."[71]

As late as the year 1909 Einstein's 1905 special theory of relativity had won woefully few adherents. True, Planck and Lorentz gave it grudging breathing space; but, it fell to a figure in Einstein's past to emerge and to champion his former pupil's thesis. Herman Minkowski, Einstein's professor at the ETH had since received an appointment to the University of Gottingen, the mathematics capital of Germany, where he first came upon Einstein's papers. A believer from the first reading, Minkowski, began his lecture "Space and Time" with these words: "The views of space and time which I wish to lay before you have sprung from the soil of experimental physics, and therein lies their strength. They are radical. Henceforth space by itself, and time by itself, are doomed to fade away into mere shadows, and only a kind of union of the two will preserve an independent reality."[72] At a later date, Charles Proteus Steinmetz, lecturing on "The Four-Dimensional Time-Space of Minkowski," said in part: "We have always known that this world of ours is in reality four-dimensional—that is, every point event in the world is given four numerical values, data, coordinates or dimensions, whatever we may call them, three dimensions in space and one dimension in time. But because in the physics before Einstein space and time were always independent of each other, we never realized this or found any object or advantage in considering the world as four-dimensional, but always considered the point events as three-dimensional in space and one-dimensional in time, treating time and space as separate and incompatible entities. The relativity theory, by interrelating space and time, thus changes our entire world conception."[73]

Minkowski was more surprised than most that the special theory was created by his former pupil. He remembered his student Einstein as a "lazy dog," an appellation he felt was apt because the latter had attended his lectures infrequently. Minkowski's further development of Einstein's theories helped gain them wider acceptance. Tragically though, Minkowski died shortly thereafter and did not live to see the development of the relativity theory.

In July 1910, a year after their return to Zurich, the Einsteins second son, Edward, was born. And again, the proud poppa could be seen maneuvering a baby carriage through familiar streets that suddenly lost their familiarity in competition with his growing concentration of thought. Einstein knew no rest from investigating the mysteries of the universe. And he also knew no rest from the growing legion of scientists and students who were now becoming interested in his thinking. He was soon to become the oracle of the new physics, and he attracted scientists from allied fields as well. One such scientist was David Reichenstein, himself a professor of physical chemistry. Reichenstein was introduced to Einstein by a mutual friend during a physics colloquium, where new papers were read and discussed. Reichenstein recalled that "His low calm voice, his deep thoughtful eyes, which did not seem at all teacherish, and his cordiality surprised me."[74]

After the weekly colloquiums the men would often repair to the local cafe for refreshments. Once, Reichenstein recounts, Einstein begged off going to the cafe because it was washday for his wife and he had promised to take care of the baby. Reichenstein gives us this account of Einstein's relationship to his colleagues and students.

As far as I am personally concerned, I was constantly aware of Einstein's superiority to me. Of course I had my own scientific problems, my own hypotheses and theories, and already in early life felt myself an independent investigator. But when working over my problems I often came into contact with strange fields adjoining physical chemistry, and there for the first time, a doubt arose in me as to whether my hypotheses were not in opposition to already firmly established achievements in these adjoining fields. Here Einstein was marvelous. Often a half hour discussion was enough to clear up the whole matter. I frequently fell into a state of intellectual bondage towards him. This was all the more remarkable as *I* had always been the independent one, the leader of research among my coworkers in the field of physical chemistry and already while I was an assistant in Leipzig, was the stimulating advisor of my Leipzig professor.

To understand this excessive influence of Einstein over me and some other young research workers who were then closely connected with him, one must take into account the fact that Einstein's critical remarks, his objection to a respective train of thought often came unexpectedly during a walk or in the cafe, in the midst of a quite different, unimportant conversation. Often his objection came in the form of a joke or in a jesting tone. His joking, his good humor, his wit, were beyond description. It must be taken into consideration that it was not a case of relations between pupil and teacher. They were much more intimate, more friendly . . . Of course we also poked fun and laughed, but the conversation did not overstep a certain limit. With us, who were really only a few years younger than himself, he was much more free and unconstrained. The feeling of a social distance between us who were assistants and himself, was at that time unknown to him . . . His delicious, almost child-like, unconstraint, his frank, open nature, together with his intellectual superiority, never failed to affect us."[75]

As Einstein's fame spread and his influence grew, interest in him reached out in all directions beyond the Alps, particularly to Prague.

News was conveyed back to him that he was one of the two scientists being considered for the post of professor of experimental physics at the German University there. Prague's interest in Einstein was centered on his former pro-Machian principles, for Ernst Mach had long ago occupied the physics chair at that university. Anton Lampa, who now held the physics chair, backed the choice of Einstein over Professor Gustav Jaumann of the Technical Institute at Brno. Lampa's preference was based partly on a recommendation made by Planck, who wrote that if Einstein's theory should prove correct, as he expected it would be, then he (Einstein) would be considered the Copernicus of the twentieth century. Jaumann, too, had been pro-Machian to the extent that he disdained the microscopic world of the atom. Einstein, on the other hand, fully accepted the notion that atoms are made up of still smaller building blocks. Jaumann eventually backed out of the competition complaining that "I will have nothing to do with a university that chases after modernity and does not appreciate true merit."[76]

Einstein had been quite happy in Zurich and so had his wife and children; they were just becoming comfortable and felt no desire or need to relocate. If the Einsteins were to be uprooted after only two years in Zurich, it would have to be prompted by an overwhelming offer, one that could not be refused. Gypsies they were not, and a serene family life required stability. Mileva felt this, and when her husband disclosed the details of the offer to her, she asked him to reject it. She was content in Zurich, she argued. And if her husband cared to look ahead for a higher position sometime in the future, this, she felt he could easily accomplish within the boundaries of Switzerland. Besides, the Prague post called for an experimental physicist and Albert was a theoretical physicist. His tools were pad and paper and a blackboard. Experimental physicists worked in laboratories, and Einstein had hardly seen the inside of a laboratory since college. Perhaps the most salient reason for Mileva's opposition was the location, Prague. Prague was a major city in the polygot Austro-Hungarian Empire. The many obstinate ethnic groupings within its borders were each in turn dissatisfied with the authoritarian dictates of old Emperor Franz Josef and yearned for autonomy. The people from whom Mileva stemmed, the Serbs, were among the most vocal dissidents and proved to be the most troublesome. The Emperor, on the other hand, was all too often placed in the unenviable position of decision-maker, and, unerringly, when trying to please one group, he inadvertently displeased another. It was becoming more and more obvious that one patchwork quilt could not contain the nationalistic aspirations of Czechs, Slovaks, Croats, Serbs, Magyars, and Germans. A redefining of the geographical lines was in the offing, and as history corroborates, this event was not long in coming.

Mileva presented her husband with good reasons and forceful arguments for remaining where they were. But she found him stubbornly inclined toward a change. He had heard of the huge, magnificent library, with its priceless, ancient European volumes and he was impressed. He may have reasoned that a professorship now in Prague was worth two in the future. Perhaps the best persuader was the provision that he would be allowed to lecture less. Then, too, his pay was to be doubled, and for the first time in their lives they would be able to afford the luxury of electric lights. The final determination, however, was made on the basis of the conditions that would best advance his work. Einstein opted in favor of Prague over the protestations of his wife.

Before arrangements could be completed Einstein was obliged to fill out a questionnaire prepared by the Austro-Hungarian government. It presented no difficulty to speak of, but one question seemed rather annoying. The applicant was asked to state his religion. Relics of medieval thinking still pervaded the monarchical system, at the insistence of the Emperor himself. In Switzerland citizenship was required for civil service employees; in Austro-Hungary, adherence to an accepted religion was made mandatory for university employees, supposedly as a surety for the high moral character of the employee. Einstein chuckled and entered the word "Mosaic" which was commonly understood to signify Judaism. Many an agnostic has been relieved to learn that the obligation of stating a religious preference did not necessarily entail the practice thereof.

Einstein's brief stay in Prague marked the beginning of his attempts to formulate his new gravitational theory. He was fortunate in this regard in having met there, George Pick, a mathematician. Ever since his days at the ETH, when he chose to concentrate on physics to the neglect of mathematics, Einstein found that his lack of fluency in mathematics hampered him in the development of his theories. Theories can be arrived at by means of physics, but they have to be expessed in the language of mathematics. Pick proved helpful by recommending to Einstein that he examine the "absolute differential calculus" of Gregorio Ricci and Tullio Levi-Civita. Pick and Einstein discussed Mach a good deal; Pick had been Mach's assistant when he was a young man. Philipp Frank relates that "Einstein liked to hear Pick reminisce about Mach, and Pick was particularly fond of repeating statements by Mach that could be interpreted as anticipating Einstein's theories."[77] Pick was a good violinist, too, and paved the way for Einstein into Prague's musicale world. Tragically for Pick, because he was a Jew, he died at the age of eighty in one of Hitler's extermination camps.

The city of Prague was divided ethnically among Germans, Czechs, and Jews. The Germans and the Czechs, comprising the numerically superior groups, showed only contempt for each other, a contempt often leading to open hostility. The only way the Jews could survive battering by the two antagonistic groups was to mediate between them. The chasm was so sharply divisive that it led in 1888 to a two-way split of the University of Prague; one part was then called the German University of Prague, and the other, the Czech University of Prague. With even the intellectuals party to the absurd double-edged hostility, the arrangement pleased both groups and kept the hatred simmering. So complete was the cleavage that contact or interchange on matters of mutual university interest was impossible. "Even professors of the same subject had no personal contact and it frequently happened that two chemistry professors from Prague would meet for the first time at an international congress in Chicago."[78]

Some Jews catered to and imitated the Germans. The more liberal sympathized with the Czechs. A third group, whom Einstein had met among the artists and writers of Prague, looked beyond the immediate struggle on the continent Europe and the ghetto mentality in which the Jew was inextricably enmeshed towards the promise of Zionism; a national homeland in Palestine for the oppressed Jews. Zionism taught that the immediate need of the Jew was to develop along his own lines, independent of the guns and persecution of the ever-present majority, in the land of his ancestors, in his own land.

Talk of patriotic fervor and nationalistic boundaries found no fertile soil in the thinking of Einstein. He was an internationalist, unimpressed with the immediacy of the Zionist cause at this particular time. His thinking was directed elsewhere, almost to the exclusion of earthly matters.

Prague was where Einstein developed his first serious approach to the problem of gravitation. The year was 1911 and his paper was entitled, "On the Influence Of Gravitation On The Propagation Of Light." Einstein wrote: "In a memoir published four years ago (*Jahrbuch fur Radioakt und Elektronik 4, 1907*), I tried to answer the question whether the propagation of light is influenced by gravitation. I return to this theme because my previous presentation of the subject does not satisfy me, and for a stronger reason, because I now see that one of the most important consequences of my former treatment is capable of being tested experimentally. For it follows from the theory here to be brought forward, that rays of light passing close to the Sun, are deflected by its gravitational field, so that the angular distance between the Sun and a fixed star appearing near it is apparently increased by nearly a second of arc.''[79]

Not only did Einstein suggest a fundamental change in the thinking on light and gravity, he also directed astronomers on how to verify it. ''As the fixed stars in the parts of the sky near the Sun are visible during the total eclipse of the Sun, this consequence of the theory may be compared with experience . . . It would be a most desirable thing if astronomers would take up the question whether it is possible with the equipment at present available to detect an influence of gravitational fields on the propagation of light.''[80]

Again, Einstein did not conduct experiments, nor did he consult with astronomers or even peak through a telescope to reach his conclusions. His method, that of the theoretical physicist, was the thought experiment, the intuitive theory. Einstein maintained that in addition to the impressions we receive from everyday experiences and the conclusions we reach in the laboratory, another ingredient indispensable to discovery is intuition, original intuitive thought. ''A theory'' he said, ''can be checked by experiment, but there is no path that leads from experiment to a theory that has not yet been established.''[81]

One interested reader of Einstein's gravitational theory was Erwin Finlay-Freundlich, a Scottish-German, whose work in astronomy brought him to the University of Berlin Observatory in Potsdam. Freundlich's exploring mind saw the possibility that Einstein's premise might lead to a different interpretation of the way the universe functions. Both for the furtherance of science and his own curiosity he was eager to be the first to observe the ''Einstein deflection.'' Freundlich thereupon initiated a correspondence with Einstein about the possibility of photographing the next solar eclipse. Einstein, in turn, encouraged his Berlin colleague in this undertaking. Freundlich's enthusiasm for the gravitational theory so convinced his Berlin colleagues that plans were made for an astronomical expedition to photograph the sun's rim at the time of the next solar eclipse, which would take place in August of 1914. Evidently advancing technology in the field of photography had placed in their hands equipment adequate for the expedition. But the astronomers calculations could not have arrived at a more fateful location for observation, the Russian Crimea. They determined that the area of totality, when the eclipsed sun would be observable for the longest period of time, would be at its maximum at that particular geographical location. At the same time, as scientists oblivious to political matters, they were hardly aware of the powerful military buildup taking place in middle Europe, in their own backyard.

Einstein was destined not to remain long in Prague, for as soon as he had moved from Zurich, feelers were out from several universities in Europe hoping to win him to their respective staffs. In response to one particular invitation, the Einsteins spent the better part of a month visiting with Lorentz at the University of Leiden, in Holland. Einstein's respect for Lorentz knew no bounds: "He's a miracle—a living work of art." To the young Einstein, the older man was the master; the greatest and noblest man of our time. "His never failing kindness and generosity and his sense of justice, coupled with a sure and intuitive understanding of people and human affairs, made him a leader in any sphere he entered."[82]

Despite his high opinion of Lorentz, Einstein regretfully turned down the offer that was forthcoming from Leiden at Lorentz's own request. Instead, he now was considering an offer from the university from which he had been graduated, the ETH. This matter needed the most careful consideration because the ETH included a full professorship as well as reduced lecturing time in its offer, then this wandering from university to university had to come to a stop, and he was concerned for the welfare of his wife and children. Mileva's delight at the prospect of leaving Prague was predictable. Zurich was and always would be her favorite city. In Zurich, Serbs were not treated as second-class citizens, the way they were in Prague—though as the wife of a professor she personally was held in respect. It was enough that she had been raised under the autocratic rule of the Austro-Hungarian Empire. She wanted to spare her children that dubious privilege. But before the question could be resolved, Einstein was called to another conference.

14

PROFESSOR AT ETH

The Belgian industrialist, Ernest Solvay, underwrote the cost of the conference in Brussels in 1911 that bears his name, the Solvay Conference, but the conference itself was pulled together through the organizational ability of Walther Nernst, a Berlin University professor of physics and chemistry. It was Max Planck, Nernst's colleague in Berlin, who prevailed upon Nernst to include an invitation to Einstein among those Nernst was sending to key scientists throughout Europe.

Solvay had made his fortune in the production and sale of chemicals and had his own pet ideas he wanted the world's leading physicists and chemists to explore. He was willing to pay heavily for that privilege. Realizing that his guests could not be expected to take up and evaluate Solvay's theories without prior study, Nernst convinced Solvay that the conference would best be served by having the invited scientists read papers they had prepared in their own fields of work. In this way, the Solvay Conference would become the instrument by which the work of the foremost scientists of the time would become known. Nernst spared none of Solvay's money. He invited, in addition to Planck and Einstein, Ernest Rutherford and Sir James Jeans from England; Henrik Lorentz and Kammerlingh-Onnes from Holland; and a host from France including Marie Curie, Henri Poincare, Louis de Broglie, Paul Langevin, and Jean Baptiste Perrin. Franz Hasenohrl, as well as Einstein represented Austro-Hungary.

Responsibility for conducting the proceedings was assigned to Professor Lorentz. The thirty-two year old Einstein observed with reverence the mental agility of the kind Dutch scientist, switching languages easily to accommodate all guests, and juggling egos in his sensitive role as chairman of the conference. Einstein's increasing admiration for Lorentz, bordering on adulation, continued at the conference. "Whatever came from this supreme mind was as lucid and beautiful as a good work of art and was presented with such facility and ease as I have never experienced in anybody else . . . . Never did he give the impression of domineering, always of serving and helping."[83]

Lorentz, too, gained from the meeting of the scientific minds; he developed a lifelong admiration for the astuteness with which the young "Turk" carried his genius. Regarding theory, Lorentz was not so easily convinced. As late as 1922, in an address at the California Institute of Technology, Lorentz was unwilling to make the complete break with the ether theory, but was gradually giving way. Lorentz said: "As to the ether . . . . though the concept of it has certain advantages, it must be admitted that if Einstein had maintained it he certainly would not have given us his theory, and so we are grateful to him for not having gone along old-fashioned roads."[84]

Marie Curie also won Einstein's respect and admiration. "Her strength, her purity of will, her austerity toward herself, her objectivity, her incorruptible judgment—all these were of a kind seldom found in a single individual."[85]

In 1899, when Marie and Pierre Curie isolated the element

1911, Brussels, The Solvay Conference at the Hotel Metropole. Standing left to right: Goldschmidt, Planck, Rubens, Sommerfeld, Lindemann, De Broglie, Knudson, Hasenöhrl, Hostelet, Herzen, Jeans, Rutherford, Kamerlingh Onnes, Einstein, Langevin, Seated: left to right: Nernst, Brillouin, Solvay, Lorentz, Warburg, Perrin, Wien, Mme. Curie, Poincaré.

radium, their work was considered monumental because of its beneficial and therapeutic application in the saving of many lives. Unfortunately, Pierre did not live to see the life-saving results of their work; he fell victim to a truck accident and died in Paris in 1906. In his wife's words: "He had the faith of those who open new ways."[85] Of working in science, Madame Curie said: "A great discovery does not leap completely achieved from the brain of the scientists . . . . it is the fruit of accumulated preliminary work. Between the days of fecund productivity are inserted days of uncertainty when nothing seems to succeed, and when even matter itself seems hostile; and it is then that one must hold out against discouragement."[86]

Marie Curie was most impressed by Einstein's lucidity in the paper he read on specific heats. This presentation marked his acceptance as one of Europe's leading physicists. Future conferences found the name Einstein featured as one of the chief attractions.

Immediately after the conference, in the fall of 1911 he was again approached as Lorentz was about to retire from his chair in Leiden. The University at Utrecht also wanted him for their faculty. And a heavy money offer had come from the University of Vienna. All these and a few others, he turned down in favor of the tentative offer from the ETH. Again, the Swiss proved cautious. Though he was surely in great demand, the board of trustees wanted further assurances about his qualifications. They sought out the opinions of both Marie Curie and Henri Poincaré. Both responded positively. Marie Curie wrote back:

> I much admire the work which M. Einstein has published on matters concerning modern theoretical physics. I think, moreover, that mathematical physicists are at one in considering his work as being in the first rank. At Brussels, where I took part in a scientific conference attended by M. Einstein, I was able to appreciate the clearness of his mind, the shrewdness with which he marshaled his facts, and the depth of his knowledge. If one takes into consideration the fact that M. Einstein is still very young, one is justified in basing great hopes on him and in seeing in him one of the leading theoreticians of the future. I think that a scientific institution which gave M. Einstein the means of work which he wants, by appointing him to a chair in the conditions he merits, could only be greatly honored by such a decision and would certainly render a great service to science."[88]

This was heady stuff for a former small-town boy who a few short years back could foresee only service as a teacher in some rural community as his life's work. Poincaré's letter was equally laudatory:

> Herr Einstein is one of the most original minds that I have ever
> met. In spite of his youth he already occupies a very honourable
> position among the foremost savants of his time. What we marvel
> at in him, above all, is the ease with which he adjusts himself to
> new conceptions and draws all possible deductions from them.
> He does not cling tightly to classical principles, but sees all con-
> ceivable possibilities when he is confronted with a physical prob-
> lem. In his mind this becomes transformed into an anticipation
> of new phenomena that may someday be verified in actual expe-
> rience . . . . The future will give more and more proofs of the
> merit of Herr Einstein, and the University that succeeds in at-
> taching him to itself may be certain that it will derive honour
> from its connexion with the young master."[89]

Aside from the glowing recommendations from Curie and Poincaré,
the ETH board was being nudged from yet another side. From the
day he left, Marcel Grossmann and Einstein's other confederates in
Zurich had been plotting measures to return him to the city they
knew he loved. It was again "old-home" week, especially since his
mother had come north from Italy and was now living with Maja and
her husband, Paul Winteler. The Einsteins hoped they could now
relax among friends and family and settle down to watch their children grow. But, soon it became evident that moving back to Zurich
would not solve the difficulties between husband and wife. Ironically,
the greater the tribute paid to her husband, the farther the wife
retreated into her dark moods. The more the invitations poured in
from near and far, the more the relationship slipped away.

Hans Albert was now eight years old, and Edward, three. Hans
showed proficiency at the piano and Edward also learned fast. Einstein enjoyed most teaching his sons the peaceful pleasures of sailing.
The facilities were at hand, the sparkling waters of the Zurichsee,
under the bright sun hovering over the Alps. He thoroughly enjoyed
the company of his sons. In a 1951 interview, Hans Albert remi-
nisced: "I remember he would tell us stories—he often played his
violin in an effort to make us quiet. But I also recall my mother saying that even the loudest baby crying didn't seem to disturb father.
He could go on with his work completely impervious to noise."[90]
Hans also remembered the times when their behavior became completely intolerable and a fatherly spanking was forthcoming.

When the newness of being back again in Zurich wore off and he
could finally get back to work, Einstein met with Grossmann as often

as his schedule would allow, in an effort to find mathematical answers to his gravitational questions. Grossmann, by now, had attained a full professorship and possessed some knowledge of curved-space geometry as propounded by Bernhard Riemann and Karl Gauss.

His 1907 paper was not satisfactory by his own admission, and Einstein felt that his 1911 paper was also not fully developed. With Grossmann's know-how as an aid, he again continued his search, using a new approach, in the first serious challenge to Newton's gravitational theory in two hundred years. Einstein later wrote of this particular phase of his work, that the path was more arduous than had been expected because it was in contradiction to Euclid's geometry.

Grossmann could help with the new geometry, but only after the original concept had been developed by Einstein. As Madame Curie suggested, these intuitive thoughts were not bolts out of the blue, the product of some magical, invisible power from on high working through the searcher's brain and onto the printed page. It was hard work, to drag seemingly reluctant truths out from behind eons of ignorance. It was hard work, wrong answers, sweat, and more hard work. Einstein, it is said, owes as much to his uncompromising obstinacy as to his original ideas. Through the years, Einstein had repeatedly insisted that he did not possess any sort of extraordinary powers. He honestly could never fathom why so much fuss was made by the public over a man who did not consider his brain outstanding. He considered himself merely more stubborn and more passionate about physics than most men . . . . he felt he had no particular talent, just extremely inquisitive.

Einstein had hypothesized in 1907 that light had weight, albeit an infinitesimal amount. If this premise proved to be correct, then light could be considered as having the same properties as matter and subject to the same effects; and therefore light is matter. Matter, in turn, would be subject to the effects of a gravitational field. Then he looked up into the heavens to the largest gravitational field in our solar system, the sun. Next came the inescapable conclusion that light from a star beyond the sun, as it passes through the gravitational field of the sun, on its way to the observer on earth, would be bent towards the sun. Visually, the path of the light ray is drawn inward toward the sun. But, an observer on earth looking back up the ray of light would see the star as though it were moved outward from the sun.

The displacement or deflection would then place a star in a different position in the sky than the one which we observe. This really is mind-boggling; it means that the star or stars under observation are not physically in the position in the heavens that our eyes and telescopes perceive them to be.

The implications of such a theory were simply too explosive to contemplate. And it soundly shocked the classisists who "knew" that light travels in straight lines. Just what was this Einstein talking about? Was he saying that nothing in the heavens is where we observe it to be? And if the things up in the sky are not where we, with our own two eyes, perceive them to be, then what are we really seeing? Are we seeing such phenomena as ghost stars? Are we seeing bent light? If we are seeing bent light, then space may be curved after all. If space is curved, might we not be seeing the front and back of the same stars, simultaneously, without knowing it?

Above all, can't we trust what we see? The answer to the last question is a definite no. No, we cannot trust what our limited perceptions tell us is true. This is one of the adjustments we must make in our thinking if we expect to be able to comprehend even a tiny bit of the workings of the ever-present, invisible forces in our universe.

Take for example, an experience that is common to people who have seen railroad tracks. The illusion that the tracks are their normal width apart at the position of the observer, but obviously coming together a few hundred yards down the line, is a misleading one. Our eyes, we are prone to say, are playing tricks on us. Indeed they are, since they are focused to give us the sense of perspective. That is precisely the reason we cannot accept only visual proof of anything. If we cannot trust our eyes in a simple test of acuity some few hundred yards away, how much less can we depend on their accuracy looking some ninety-three million miles away at the rim of the sun, or looking at distances deeper in space which we measure in light years?

Soon after taking up his professor's post at the ETH, Einstein attended the Congress of German Scientists and Physicians in Vienna held in the fall of 1913. Here he was accepted as an equal. Most of the scientists attending were well along in years and had made their contributions in their fields years before. Einstein's greatest work still lay ahead of him. The paper he read spoke of a new gravitation; but, he did not elaborate since all the pieces did not yet fit. Curiosity was aroused, however. And Einstein watchers felt he was about to top his great achievement of 1905.

While in Vienna, Einstein finally met with his philosophical mentor, Ernst Mach. Mach was old now and had been retired from the University of Vienna to which he had moved from Prague. Now almost deaf, Einstein found Mach still possessed of a sense of humor and with his wisdom intact.

The growing Einstein mystique finally influenced the people at the University of Berlin, notably Planck and Nernst, to try to woo their former countryman back to German soil. Although conditions at the ETH were far better than he could normally expect at most universities, Einstein still was obliged to lecture to ever-increasing audiences. Not having as much time to himself as he would have preferred, he couldn't help seeing the lectures as an infringement on his time. Time was crucial for the concentration he must give to the developing gravitational theory, so that any offer made from Berlin would have to include freedom to explore with little or no demands on his time. Planck and Nernst put their heads together to try to come up with a package that Einstein could not resist. They succeeded.

15

REBEL IN BERLIN

Scientific developments and military events in Germany were soon to alter the direction the lives of Albert Einstein and his family would take. Kaiser Wilhelm II was also a part of these historic events. Wilhelm, a ruler in constant military competition with other rulers on the European peninsula, had been correctly advised that the strength of the military and their ability to perform at the highest level of efficiency would be no better than a strong scientific community could make them. With the real possibility of perhaps having to fight on two fronts, should a war break out, a heavy commitment was made to scientific research and no expense was spared to speed the construction of the Kaiser Wilhelm Institute. Located on Unter den Linden, in Berlin, and near the Prussian State Library, the Institute was to house all the sciences and be staffed with the ablest personnel that could be gathered from the entire empire. Construction was begun in 1911, and the first department to be completed was the chemical institute with Fritz Haber as *Direktor*. But, by the fall of 1913 the physics building still remained on the drawing boards. The position of *Direktor* of physics was to be held open for Einstein as one part of a three-pronged offer.

It was rumored that the Kaiser had demoted Bismarck in March of 1890 because the latter was getting old and had long before fulfilled his historical purpose, German unification. And it was also whispered that Wilhelm saw himself as a sort of Bismarck. In the east, the Russians had been practically eliminated as a military threat because of the humiliating defeat inflicted on the Russian forces by the Japanese in 1905. Germany felt secure. The Kaiser, strutting in his uniforms and flaunting his nation's obvious power had every reason for confidence. Not content, however, with his lordship over central Europe and the control over a vast land area by means of the 1897 alliance with the Austro-Hungarian Empire, he now cast an envious eye at the Atlantic Ocean. The delusion Wilhelm suffered himself to endure was the result of a childhood experience. When he was a little boy he was allowed to visit Plymouth and Portsmouth with "kind aunts and friendly admirals." He admired the proud

English ships in those harbors. Then there awoke in him the desire to build ships of his own.

The Kaiser now envisioned himself, "Admiral of the Atlantic" and built a navy to almost rival that of his English cousins. Increased German naval strength posed a threat to British dominance of the seas. The British could endure the Germans having their own way in middle Europe, but would not tolerate the Kaiser's entry into the Atlantic, Britain's front yard. Despite repeated German disclaimers and assurances of peaceful intentions, even the dullest Englishman could see that the sleek new and efficient German battleships could in no way be used against France or Russia.

Through negotiations the English learned that Wilhelm would be willing to "rein in his fleet" in return for a freer hand in Europe. When it was revealed that the freer hand meant that the Germans intended to march to the Channel coast, Britain hastily withdrew from negotiations and entered an "entente cordiale" with France and Russia.

By 1912, the lines were more clearly drawn than ever before. The French military elite, craving revenge for the disgrace of 1870, bristled with confidence once assured of support from Russia and England. War was inevitable. All that was needed to touch off the powderkeg was an incident, and that incident was not long in coming.

The early part of the twentieth century found most of Europe's population still tolerating King-Emperor dictatorships, though France and Britain at least had had the good sense to adopt the electoral process. The flash of a sword, the wave of a plumed hat, the waxed walrus mustaches, and the charge of cavalry were all part of the carry over from the days of "romance" and "gallantry." While in their death throes, these last vestiges of the princely states, still kept patriotic fervor alive and were appropriately trotted out for the public's consumption.

Czar Nicholas II of Russia retained complete control over his millions of peasants and a few revolutionaries. The "little father" could maneuver his parliament in and out of power or order his troops to fire on a group of hungry workers whenever he desired. Old Franz Josef was better suited to leading a circus band than trying to contain the bag of wildcats within his borders. Wilhelm II had been given an Empire, complete with colonies, on a silver platter. Into his trust was placed a nation, newly formed, bristling with ability, proud of performance, casting its confident but arrogant eye around to the east, west, north, and south for a suitable historical destiny. Bismarck had built fortress Germany and an efficient army second to none and had protected his flanks. But to no avail. Despite the flowering of German literature and music, the military mind still dominated. Given the leadership in science, in medicine, in technological efficiency, the nation was headed upward and forward, envied for its productivity by most of the world. The Industrial Revolution matured to its fullest in German factories.

In the summer of 1913 the sides were chosen; a weak Russia, a vengeful France, and a slumbering Britain comprised the Triple Entente, ranged against the Triple Alliance of Germany, Austro-Hungary, and Italy. Wilhelm kept screaming something about *Lebensraum*.

In the fall of 1913, as Professor Einstein was beginning his second full term at his alma mater, Planck and Nernst were putting the final touches on an irresistible package with which to lure him north to Berlin. Since the building to house the Kaiser Wilhelm Institute for Theoretical Physics existed only on paper, at this time, the duties of its *Direktor* were minimal. Even when the department would become operational, administrative duties, it was planned on Einstein's behalf, would be performed by subordinates. Einstein's strength lay in his theories, not in the ability for day-to-day administration of an institute. The heart of the deal lay in the other two provisions of the offer, a full professorship at the University of Berlin and admittance to the prestigious Prussian Academy of Science. (The exclusiveness of the Prussian Academy, which limited its members to some seventy active and two hundred associates, speaks for itself.)

When Planck and Nernst came down to Zurich and presented this deal to Einstein, he was so flabbergasted by its generosity that he begged for time to clear his mind and give the proposition careful consideration. The offer was tremendous. He could never have imagined a situation as ideal as the one his two Berlin friends had put together for his sake. To hold the title of professor and not be required to lecture; how can I refuse? To be elected to the Prussian Academy and to be handsomely paid as well—this was not something to consider lightly. And even if the directorship of the Institute required almost no work, except for occasional consultations, it showed the lengths to which the Berlin people were willing to go to assure he would accept. He was truly overwhelmed: "These Berlin people are speculating with me as if I were a prize hen, but I don't know whether I can still lay eggs."

That was not the point, whether he could still astound the world with exciting scientific discoveries. Berlin wanted Einstein for what he had already uncovered. His prestige as a great scientist and philosopher would insure the continuance of Berlin as the center of European culture for generations to come. Nernst was convinced that Einstein could not possibly turn down so attractive an offer, for, at that time, if only twelve people in the world understood Einstein's relativity, surely eight lived in Berlin. And that's where Einstein should be. But this was reckoning without due consideration of Einstein, the humanitarian and pacifist.

As a youth, not yet sixteen, he had fled once from the authoritarianism of Germany, from the egocentric illusions of destiny mixed with mythical feelings of superiority and blind obedience to nationalism. Now, some eighteen years later, he had come full circle and found himself face to face with the same challenge of conscience. If he did accept and go to Berlin, wouldn't he be compromising his pacifist principles? And surely his wife, whose distaste for the German military mentality matched her husband's, could dissuade him from accepting. Mileva Einstein did make her views known in a very few heated words of rejection. A difficult situation—and Einstein knew that he alone would make the decision. If he had decided on a purely emotional level to the exclusion of other considerations, he would have rejected the offer. Had he remained in Switzerland, his scientific future would have been assured, but, he might not have completed his greatest work, which was yet to come. Only he knew that despite help from Grossmann, he had reached an impasse in his attempt to develop relativity along gravitational lines.

Einstein's yes was based on rather pragmatic considerations, on his role as a scientist rather than as a husband and father. His obligations to his students, his colleagues, and the ETH as well as his personal feelings for his wife and sons would have to be subordinated to his life as a scientist. Great ideas were at stake, which needed safeguarding from the conflicting cares of life.

Where he did draw the line was in the matter of German citizenship. Einstein insisted that he be able to retain his Swiss citizenship when he was faced with German citizenship as a prerequisite for appointment to the Prussian Academy. But Planck would not be put off by a technicality; Einstein was German by birth, and technically he could still be considered German. Planck dug a little deeper and found that an exception to the rule had been made once before, in the case of a French scientist, Professor Haguenin, who had been allowed to maintain his French citizenship as well as membership in the Academy. Since the precedent had already been established, there remained no further obstacle to Einstein's appointment. Retaining his Swiss citizenship gave Einstein the feeling that he belonged to the whole world and not to one set of nationalistic emotions. It made the swallowing of the bitter pill of returning to Germany easier. At least, he reasoned, he was not a German citizen again.

Einstein Archives

Edward, Mileva and Hans Albert Einstein, circa 1913.

16

EUROPE LOSES SANITY

Personal feelings aside, Mileva knew that her husband was close to something big, something in the field of gravity that had never before been conceived. She did her best to suppress her complete distaste for Berlin's people, streets, and weather as they moved into their flat in the Dahlem section, with the construction site of the physics building only a short walk away. Nothing could have pleased her at this point other than a return to the pristine air, blue skies, and snow-capped mountains of Switzerland.

The academy professors, most of whom were twice Einstein's thirty-four years, were finally treated to a glimpse of the young rebel with the sloppy clothes and long hair. As he approached the podium, he resembled a violinist more than a physicist. Nevertheless, he was well accepted after he spoke these words of appreciation: "I have to thank you most heartily for conferring the greatest benefit on me that anybody can confer on a man like myself. By electing me to your academy you have freed me from the distractions and cares of a professional life and so made it possible for me to devote myself entirely to scientific duties. I beg that you will continue to believe in my gratitude and my industry even when my efforts seem to you to yield but a poor result."[91]

The astronomer, Erwin Finlay-Freundlich, as well as other well-wishers, stopped by to welcome the Einsteins to Berlin. The two scientists were working feverishly on plans for the forthcoming astronomical expedition. It was already April of 1914 and the solar eclipse would occur late in August. The expedition to the Russian Crimea was scheduled to leave at the end of July. There wasn't much time.

While the professor was beginning to feel comfortable in his new surroundings, Hans Albert wasn't adjusting too well to his new school; he complained that he had to commit everything to memory. Mileva, in the background, continued grumbling about Berlin. It's ironic that while the Berlin appointment was the high academic point in Einstein's career, his wife couldn't wait to get away from Berlin, even if only for the summer months. Well, June didn't come around too soon for Einstein. With his family away he settled down to his

Credit: AIP (American Institute of Physics). Niels Bohr Library.

Fritz Haber and Albert Einstein in Berlin, 1914.

work, unencumbered by domestic interruptions, to finally formulate the gravitational theory. His previous attempts, in 1907 and 1911, and a succeeding work with Grossmann were, at the most, preliminary. Now, without lecturing duties, "performances on a trapeze" he called them, or family squabbles, he could really concentrate.

Einstein yearned for the peace of a monastery, but people and events kept intruding. Hardly had he dispatched his family to Switzerland, hardly had he settled in for a quiet summer of work, when the continent exploded in a frenzy of war.

June 28, 1914 was the day Archduke Franz Ferdinand, heir to the Hapsburg throne and commander-in-chief of his Imperial Majesty's army, was to personally direct the maneuvers of the Austro-Hungarian army in and around the southern provincial capital of Sarajevo in the province of Bosnia. The hostility that prevailed between the Serbs living within the boundaries of Austro-Hungary and their Hapsburg masters had its origins at the end of the last century when Turkey relinquished control of the two provinces of Bosnia and Herzegovina. Austria won out over Serbia and grabbed control of the two provinces in a bloodless move. The annexation angered not only the Serbs in Serbia, but also the Serb nationalists who remained virtually captive within the borders of the two "stolen" provinces.

Perhaps the Austrians felt the Serbs should be treated to a show of strength, to let them know who really controlled things. If that was the thinking behind holding the maneuvers close by the Serbian border, the strategy backfired. King Peter of Serbia was infuriated at what he considered a provocative gesture. There was already hard feeling enough in that area. Franz Ferdinand's assumption of command was yet a further insult. The choice of Sarajevo was also regrettable; it had long been known as a hotbed of Serbian nationalism. To expect to put on a show of military strength without some type of reaction from a volatile populace must have been considered as the height of naivete on the part of the Austrians.

So far as Ferdinand was concerned, he was merely taking advantage of an opportunity to test his leadership qualities; he would soon be Emperor. His uncle, Franz Josef, who had held the dual monarchy together for almost sixty years, was now in his eighties, and would undoubtedly soon die. It was a strange situation that the old Emperor was faced with regarding the status of his nephew. Though the heir to the throne, Ferdinand was out of favor with his uncle and the court at Vienna as well, because of his marriage to a Czeck girl, Sophie Chotek, the "scullery maid." For the Archduke and his wife, the trip south was a welcome breath of fresh air away from the humiliations they were subjected to in intrigue-ridden Vienna, and an opportunity for Sophie to assume her rightful place, beside her husband. The two were still very much in love and looking forward to a few days together free from court criticism and their three children.

Of the seven conspirators who made up the assassination group, only the aim of Gabriel Princip proved accurate. Ferdinand and

Sophie, riding in an open carriage along a parade route were shot at close range; and within half an hour both were dead. This act of murder did not reflect the sentiment of the majority of the Serbs. The deed was not meant to topple the empire, nor was it intended as a vengeful retaliation of some kind. It was simply a ploy to retrieve the lost provinces for Serbia. The outcome of the catastrophe it provoked —known in history books as World War I, or the Grear War—had actually the opposite effect; Europe was further Balkanized and Serbia disappeared from the map of Europe.

Never before in the history of any continent, or of any civilization, has such a singular incident caused so total and complete an engagement of so many powerful neighbor-states in such a frenetic and fratricidal fight to the death. The assassination of two relatively unimportant personages did not warrant the wanton slaughter that followed. Some, on both sides, predicted that war was inevitable; the desire was there. If it hadn't been for this incident, another would have happened along or been manufactured.

Ferdinand's death could easily have been glossed over by Franz Josef with no more punishment meted out to the Serbs than a diplomatic slap on the wrist. Ferdinand's relative importance to the continuance of the Hapsburg dynasty can be gauged by the fact that there was no automatic declaration of war; the Emperor did not even attend his own nephew's funeral, and a new commander-in-chief was appointed without delay. But the old man did not exert complete mastery over his ministers, who saw in this incident the "cause célèbre" for which they had been waiting, an opportunity to deal with Serbian obstinacy once and for all. The ministers and generals, represented by Berchtold and Hotzendorf, respectively, convinced Franz Josef that the "land of thieves and assassins was a viper to be crushed" or the dual monarchy could not survive. "We must have satisfaction." By satisfaction they meant another piece of Serbia.

To this end, Berchtold, as foreign minister, handed up a list of excruciatingly harsh demands (which he knew could never be met) to the Serbian king, whom he held responsible for Ferdinand's death. As if the demands were not severe enough, the Austrians made it more difficult for King Peter to deal in good faith by attaching a forty-eight hour ultimatum. This was diplomatic madness at its maddest. King Peter immediately notified his Russian backers that it would be impossible to fulfill all the Austrian demands and still maintain Serbian sovereignty. They also knew that anything less than complete compliance would not satisfy Austria; Austria was bent on war. Stalling for time, Peter notified Austria that it would grant almost all demands. Berchtold, feeding misinformation to the German Kaiser, was in turn assured of German support for a "cheap little war." Berchtold manipulated the sending of information so well and so much to his own purpose, that by the time the Kaiser learned the degree of Serbian compliance and was happy to see that the reason for war no longer existed, Berchtold had already sent the following telegram to Peter, on July 28th:

The Royal Serbian Government not having answered in a satisfactory manner the note of July 23, 1914, presented by the Austro-Hungarian Minister at Belgrade, The Imperial and Royal Government are thus pledged to see to the safe-guarding of their rights and interests, and with this object, to have recourse to force of arms, Austro-Hungary consequently considers herself henceforth in a state of war with Serbia.

> Count Berchtold, Austro-Hungarian
> Minister of Foreign Affairs

With German armed might in their corner the Austrians moved their troops menacingly near the Serbian border. Peter had no alternative but to call for mobilization, when to do so was considered tantamount to war. Then, like falling dominoes, forces on both sides were set in motion, and it became too late for the Kaiser to realize that his proud Germany was fettered to the adventuresome Austro-Hungarian corpse; it became too late also to halt the forces on the move to destroy nine million military and twenty-seven million civilian lives.

France's motive in keeping the action alive was to get back the lost provinces of Alsace and Lorraine, which Germany had wrested from her in 1870. It was also advantageous for France to encourage an unprepared Russia to act tough. When Russia grumbled at Germany's adventure, Germany grumbled back. And then not even an exchange of almost amicable letters between "cousin Nicky" and "cousin Willy" could prevent the march towards destruction.

In the meantime, Britain had ordered her fleet to war stations. Prior to this series of events, it wasn't only the menace of having German troops stationed on the Belgian coast that pushed the English into the conflict; it was also the dreaded thought of German naval vessels poised in Belgian ports free to roam the Atlantic Ocean and North Sea. Sir Edward Grey, the British foreign minister, hoping to avoid hostilities, for which his military forces lacked adequate preparation, confronted his German counterpart with a plea for meaningful negotiations. The Kaiser, by this time assured that his ally would deal swiftly and forcefully with the Serbians, took off on his long-planned North Sea cruise. From his distant retreat he notified Grey of his approval of a "localized war." While Wilhelm remained aboard his yacht the ministers and generals were consulting their maps; Austria had called for mobilization following the declaration of war with Serbia.

Alarmed that the "local" situation might get out of hand, the Kaiser cut short his cruise and returned to port on July 27th, furious that his ministers were not able to contain the mushrooming incident and just in time to be informed of the Austrian declaration of war on July 28th. It was already too late. No more the "local war" which the Kaiser gave sanction to, the ensuing conflict was soon to spread to and engulf almost all of Europe. On August 1, with Grey's last minute promise to keep France neutral, which would give Germany a free hand in the east, Wilhelm summoned his generals and attempted to call off the massing of German soldiers on the western front. But again, it was too late; Russian mobilization had begun on July 30th, followed by German mobilization on the 31st. His flabbergasted generals protested that it would be impossible to stop the movement of eleven thousand railroad cars that were moving four million men to the east and west. The process, already in motion, could not be stopped without placing the country at the mercy of her enemies; complete chaos would result and Germany would be left defenseless. Faced with a situation beyond even his control, Wilhelm found it convenient then to join the new crusade and proclaim that "God has called us to civilize the world." Now, nothing barred the way to needless slaughter; the continent was in the hands of the generals. In retrospect, S.L.A. Marshall sums up: "The unthinkable happened because in each of the great states, leaders did certain things that influenced the crisis, or failed to do things that might have eased it. All shared in some degree the responsibility for the general failure.[92]

When the Germans wonder why they are so hated, they might ponder the question as to why such a peaceful nation as Belgium, which had never before been involved in a war, had built her fortifications in the east and not in the north and south. And when the Germans, without provocation, attacked Belgium on August 4, 1914, the move was the first stroke of the heralded "Schlieffen" plan, the purpose of which was to capture Paris in forty days; three days to knock off little Belgium and then wheel south to Paris. In the east, the Russians vowed to be in Berlin by Christmas. The festive air which greeted the call to arms also encouraged the Austro-Hungarians to promise to "crush" Serbia. None of these prideful boasts and none of the well-laid plans were to be fulfilled.

In the east, because the Russians mobilized more quickly than expected, the first few battles went their way. But soon, the lumbering Russians fell victim to the Germans under Ludendorff and von Hindenburg at Tannenberg. The German offensive in the west fell behind schedule because of the stubborn resistance put up by the Belgians. The Schlieffen plan wasn't working, and the two weeks that the brave Belgians held off the highly superior German military machine gave the French added time to deploy troops north to the border; this, despite the Belgians lack of experience and though they were overwhelmingly outgunned and outmanned. Not only were the French given the needed time to fully assess the German move and deploy accordingly, but the English also were then able to land a one hundred thousand man expeditionary force on the northwest coast of France. The two weeks were indeed crucial to the survival of France. The German plan had called for a quick, one stroke, knockout drive; but the delays on the eastern front and the unexpected resistance by the Belgian forces had thrown the time-table off schedule.

The cruelty with which the Germans dispatched tiny Belgium brought back to Berlin an overwhelming storm of worldwide indignation, which could not go unanswered. Instead of the respect and admiration which they expected from the world, the systematic and efficient killing perpetrated by the Germans aroused only world revulsion. How, the rest of the world wanted to know, could the German people, whose music was loved and whose science was admired, be capable of such unlawfulness and atrocities? In an obviously hasty attempt to rebut the horror stories escaping from the war zone the German government sought support from the intellectual community. By having writers, artists, academicians and scientists sign the "Manifesto To The Civilized World," which claimed the legitimate right of Germany to protect her borders and her culture, the government sought to dampen the protest. The six major points of the manifesto are:

1. It is not true that Germany was guilty of this war.
2. It is not true that we criminally violated Belgian neutrality.
3. It is not true that the life and property of a single Belgian subject were interfered with by our soldiers except under the direst necessity.
4. It is not true that our troops behaved brutally in regard to Louvain.

5. It is not true that we disregard the precepts of international law in our methods of warfare, in which there is no unbridled cruelty.

6. It is not true that fighting our so-called militarism is not fighting against our civilization, as our enemies hypocritically allege.[93]

The Germans further elaborated on point number two:

It can be proved that France and England had resolved to violate it (neutrality), and it can be proved that Belgium agreed to this. It would have been suicide not to have anticipated them.

On point number three, the Germans explained:

Again and again, despite all warnings, did the population lie in ambush and fire on them, (German soldiers) mutilating wounded men, and murdering doctors even while actually engaged in their noble ministrations. There could be no baser misrepresentation than to say nothing about the crime of these assassins and then call the Germans criminals because of their having administrated a just punishment to them. . . .

We cannot deprive enemies of the poisoned weapons of falsehood. All we can do is to cry aloud to the whole world that they are bearing false witness against us. To you who know us, who, together with us, have hitherto been the guardians of man's highest possessions—to you we cry aloud, 'Believe us; believe that to the last we will fight as a civilized nation, to whom the legacy of a Goethe, a Beethoven, and a Kant is no less sacred than hearth and home,'. . . . This we vouchsafe to you on the faith of our name and our honour.[94]

The emotional appeal had its effect, but only on Germans. Max Planck signed the manifesto, and so did Walther Nernst and Fritz Haber, as well as Wilhelm Foerster, Philip Lenard, Wilhelm Rontgen, Wilhelm Wien, Richard Willstater, and Paul Ehrlich, the chemist; Max Reinhardt, from the theatre signed it. And from the field of music, Engelbert Humperdinck and Siegfried Wagner signed. The signers, it must be understood, were under tremendous pressure to do so; not to sign would have been treason. In all, some 93 intellectuals signed.

As a Swiss citizen, the national of a neutral country, Einstein had no patriotic responsibility to Germany or to the war; he enjoyed the freedom to travel and had none of the duties incumbent upon a national of a country at war. When the other scientists rushed to donate their talents to the war effort, Einstein was not asked to, and he didn't.

Science itself knows no geographical boundaries, has no country, but scientists do. Science then became localized, narrow and chauvinistic, because of the war. With few exceptions, scientists patriotically put their talents at the disposal of their governments. One such exception, on the Allied side, was Arthur Eddington, the British astronomer and a Quaker, who would accept no work related to the war. In Germany, Einstein was almost alone in refusing to sign the manifesto. With the protection of his Swiss citizenship he could have remained silent and gone on about his work oblivious to the treachery and killing. He little realized that with his denunciation of the war he was initiating a communication with the outside world, which was never to end during his lifetime. His love affair with humanity would no longer be conducted solely from the university lectern, or in the privacy of a quiet retreat, where one needn't be brave to be bold.

Georg Nicolai, a professor of physiology at the University of Berlin, who was equally horror-struck by the destruction unleashed by his fellow-Germans, was joined by Einstein in drawing up an intellectual challenge to their war-bent colleagues, a "Manifesto To Europeans." In this manifesto, the authors made no attempt to place the blame for the outbreak of hostilities, nor did they take sides; instead they made the point that "the war raging at present will scarcely end in victory," "Would Europe," the manifesto asks, "suffer the same tragic fate as ancient Greece . . . . gradually to be exhausted by fratricidal war and perish?" The writers felt it was time "for all Europe to be united", that instead of just good Frenchmen and good Germans, what Europe needed now was good Europeans. "It is needful that Europeans should unite, and if there are enough persons to whom Europe is no mere geographical term, but something which they have profoundly at heart, then we mean to attempt to found such a union of Europeans."[95]

However humanistic, however well-intentioned, however appealing its call for peace and a united Europe, the manifesto found "no takers" among the men of German Kultur or among the German men of science. Some who were quietly sympathetic were prevented from signing by the predominant prowar sentiment prevailing in Germany. For their unpopular, antiwar statement Nicolai and Einstein were regarded with suspicion by their fellow professors; and the usually filled chairs next to Einstein's, during the weekly colloquium, suddenly stood empty. Later, in the twenties, when the ultranationalists rose to power in Germany, they never let him forget his antimilitarist stand.

The war continued to escalate with hardly a whimper of protest from the German people or the Austrians, or for that matter, from the English or French peoples. The war craze roused the populace of all the participating countries to a frenzy of hate and nationalism; no country lacked for volunteers to man the guns, or for cheering crowds to encourage them onward. The deeper towards Paris the German armies penetrated, the greedier became their appetite for more and more land. In Berlin every headline proclaimed victory, and with every victory came a resurgence of confidence in the military.

Correspondence had always kept Einstein in touch with colleagues around the world. At this particular time when he was quite alone, he wrote to his friends in Leiden, Henrik Lorentz and Paul Ehrenfest. Ehrenfest hadn't been able to find suitable employment in his native Russia or in Prague, where he first met Einstein. So, the ebullient little Ehrenfest headed for Holland and found an assistantship with Lorentz. Shocked, but not truly surprised by the ferocity of his onetime countrymen, Einstein wrote to Ehrenfest in August of the insanity prevailing in Europe. He also voiced concern over the fate of Freundlich, who had departed for the Russian Crimea sometime during the latter part of July to photograph the solar eclipse. (Freundlich and his crew were caught within the Russian borders when the war broke out, but by year's end they were back in Berlin without photographs, having been part of an exchange for some Russian officers.)

Einstein, while devoting a great deal of time to his studies, also became active with a clandestine antiwar group that espoused the end of the war as its main purpose, the New Fatherland League (*Bund Neues Vaterland*). The league's secondary goal was to fight chauvinism and help create a united Europe. It was through his work for the *Bund* that Einstein began corresponding with Romain Rolland, the French writer and pacifist, who had chosen exile in Switzerland in preference to serving his native France in war. Einstein initiated the correspondence with a letter written on March 22, 1915, in which he spoke of the folly of war: "Will future centuries really be justified in glorifying our Europe in which three centuries of intense cultural work have only brought about the transition from religious mania to nationalist mania? . . . . Even the scientists of various countries behave as though eight months ago they had had their brains amputated."[96] Rolland answered to the effect that it was because of their own shortcomings and lack of foresight that the calamity had unfolded: "We cannot flatter ourselves that this will be the last folly of mankind; and we must at least see to it that the intellectual elite will never again take part."[97]

No pacifist's words could persuade as well as bullets, nor could words of reason be heard above the din of victory by a completely submissive people whose government was bent on conquest. The French system of defense on the Rhine all but closed off activity on that front. As the Germans swung southward to the north and northeast of Paris, their communications and lines of supply also grew longer, making it difficult to keep up with their advancing troops. The French Command decided to make their stand along the banks of the River Marne. After maneuvering the rampaging Germans into an untenable position, and aided with reinforcements brought up from Paris by some twelve hundred taxis, the French were able, almost single-handedly, to hand the Germans their first defeat. This was early in September. After the Marne the contest of slaughter settled down to futile but deadly trench warfare. And while most of Europe was feverishly engaged in exterminating the flower of its youth, Professor Einstein retreated to his bachelor's quarters, cooking his own meals (when he thought of it) hoping to complete his theory.

The dreariness of war-time Berlin, the disgust he felt at the roars of approval from the crowds as "victory" after "victory" was announced to the public, together with the impasse he had reached in his work, all weighed heavily on his shoulders, and he decided to visit his family in Zurich. Mileva had stubbornly refused to return to Berlin, war or no war. In the autumn of 1915, travel for German citizens was severely restricted. But as a Swiss national, Einstein was free to travel "home". The visit was reduced to a veritable shouting match. Mileva had every right to ask her husband how he could possibly have any desire to remain in a country that had exhibited such brutality, where food was rationed and where he lived without his family? His response was how could his work progress in the face of constant arguments. Obviously, neither party showed any clear willingness to resume the marriage. The visit wasn't altogether a failure, however. The bright spot for Einstein occurred when he and son Hans embarked on an overland trip on foot into the northern part of the country. They avoided the high peaks; they preferred tramping the low hills in the open spaces.

On their return, they found Mileva no less insistent that she and the boys remain in Switzerland. She would not return to Berlin. Hans

Albert and Edward could not have understood the nature of the conflict that kept their parents apart. It's doubtful if anyone, friend or biographer, knew the real reason or reasons. The boys, however, were anxiously eager for the family to reunite and travel back to Berlin together. But the father shook his head and told them that they were to remain with their mother, that it was agreed that they were to be educated in Swiss schools. The matter was settled, but to no one's satisfaction. The possibility of a divorce had not been broached.

It was after visiting with his family that Einstein extended his trip to meet Rolland in the town of Vevey. Einstein told Rolland about the conditions in wartime Germany, alluding to the miracles the scientists were working to provide synthetically materials unavailable because of the British blockade and natural shortages. He also talked of German "greed" for land, their blinding belief in force, and of a decent but weak Kaiser manipulated by his officers. Rolland noted in his diary that Einstein "hopes for an Allied victory which would destroy the power of Prussia."[98]

17

GRAVITATIONAL THEORY

Back in Berlin, and with a fresh start, Einstein finally was able to complete work on his general theory of relativity (the gravitational theory). The publishing of this theory in the *Annalen der Physik* in the latter part of 1915 was eagerly awaited by physicists everywhere, despite the war, including his prowar colleagues. It was no secret that he was the sole physicist daring an attempt to formulate a new theory of gravitation. Often alone and unaided "Einstein devoted ten years of his life to this problem (that of gravitation) when no one else was interested in it . . . To ponder on a problem for ten years without any encouragement from the outside requires strength of character. This strength of character, perhaps more than his great intuition and imagination, led to Einstein's scientific achievements."[99]

There were three questions involving gravity to which Einstein attempted to provide answers; whether light bends in a strong gravitational field, whether his equations could account for the "perturbations" of Mercury, and does a clock tick slower in a stronger gravitational field than in a weaker one.

Of all the phenomena uncovered by scientists to date, gravity, without doubt, is the most mysterious and most pervasive. Other phenomena, such as gamma rays or other invisible rays given off by the sun, can be shielded against, but not gravity. One can sound-proof against sound and pull down a window shade to block light; but nothing affects gravity. Lead plates can deflect radiation but not gravity. Gravity is present everywhere in our everyday lives, affecting every bit of matter.

Newton's contributions, which were many in the fields of optics and motion, was popularly known for his theory of gravity. What Newton did was to equate that force (gravity) which caused the apple to fall from the tree with the force that, he hypothesized, moved the moon around the earth and the earth and other planets around the sun. Newton's universal law of gravitation, which seemingly accounted for all these infallible motions stated that: "Every two particles of matter in the universe attract each other." It was a neat little package that satisfied the doubters and radicals of the day. It seemed so perfectly sound in fact that it was not called into question for two centuries. So ingrained and accepted was Newton's concept of gravity that for two hundred years scientists believed that "Newton will have commentators but no successor."

Newton's statement implies that the sun exerts a gravitational force throughout the planetary system that keeps the planets in their respective orbits. It may sound perfectly logical to us; and most people, today, still retain that impresson. But it didn't sound logical to Einstein in the first decade of this century. Why not? Well, taking its implications a step further, Newton's law suggests that the sun's gravitational pull affects planets hundreds of millions of miles away, instantaneously. This, in scientific parlance, is called "action at a distance." In order for that (assumed) vast power of the sun to affect planets and other matter hundreds of millions of miles away, instantaneously, that force would have to travel at an enormous speed, a speed that would far exceed that of light. If we are to accept Einstein's premise that the speed of light is the fastest known of all phenomena, then we must discard Newton's "action at a distance" and continue to search for a different explanation as to why planets are held in their orbits around the sun. If, as Newton claimed, gravity is propagated instantaneously throughout the universe, it's speed would amount to seven million times that of light. Einstein doubted that the gravitational pull of the sun is so great as to keep a planet in orbit some three billion miles away, for the simple reason that gravity's pull as compared with that of magnetism and electromagnetism comes out the weaker of the three the farther away it travels from its source. Measurements taken in later years show gravity's speed to be the same as that of light, no faster.

Einstein concluded that large bodies of matter do not attract each other over vast distances; that the moon's path around the earth is simply where it should be, in a warp in space around the earth; not that the sun attracts the earth into a centrifugal course around the sun, but that the earth has found its own elliptical path around the sun, in a certain space groove, a dent in space created by the presence of the sun. The space groove, the shortest distance between two points in space, is called a geodesic. Gravitation then is not a force acting on matter, as Newton stated, but rather a curved field in the space-time continuum created by the presence of a mass (the earth or the sun).

By way of illustration, picture a medicine ball placed in the middle of a trampolene. Its weight will create a depression (a dent). Then, place a tennis ball on the outer edge. As the tennis ball moves towards the medicine ball, we cannot assume that the tennis ball was "attracted" by the gravitational pull of the medicine ball, but see instead that the tennis ball was attracted by the dent or depression caused by the presence of the medicine ball. The tennis ball was not pulled by the medicine ball at all.

We all know from Galileo's experiments that two objects of differing weights will fall at the same speed in a "vacuum." This is because, in a vacuum, the upward push of inertia equalizes the downward pull of gravity. In that part of his gravitational theory which he called the "principle of equivalence," Einstein stated that there is no way to distinguish between an "inertial force" and a "gravitational force"; that they are one and the same thing. Einstein used this example: Picture a man asleep in a room-sized elevator somewhere out in space, far removed from any gravitational pull, in a state of weightlessness. Now, a huge sky-hook is attached to the top of the elevator and soon the man and his elevator are being pulled through space at a continually increasing speed, in what is known as an "accelerated system." Then the man is awakened, and since there are no windows, he doesn't know where he is, on earth or in space, and does not know his elevator is moving. The first thing he experiences is the same effect he would encounter if his elevator were stationary on earth—a gravitational effect. He can stand erect, with his feet planted firmly on the floor, without free-floating; objects such as keys or flashlights would drop to the floor, just as if he were on the surface of the earth. This moving body, this accelerated system created a gravitational system where none existed before. In this case, an inertial system is masquerading as a gravitational system. In other words, the man in the space elevator experienced the effects of gravity and imagined he was in a gravitational field on earth, when in reality he was perhaps billions of miles away from the nearest pull of gravity. (Figure 3.)

For the second part of the equivalence example, we place another sleeping man in another elevator room. This second elevator is freefalling, under the pull of gravity, in the highest building imaginable, on some part of the earth. Now, since the man is falling under the influence of the earth's gravitational pull at the same rate as the elevator, he will not feel the pull of gravity and his feet will not be firmly planted on the floor when he wakes up. He will be freefloating. His keys will not fall to the floor, but instead will float around the elevator, since they too are falling at the same rate of speed as the man himself and the elevator. The man might say from his experience that he is somewhere out in space where weightlessness exists, but not gravity. In this case, a gravitational system is masquerading as an inertial system. (Figure 4.)

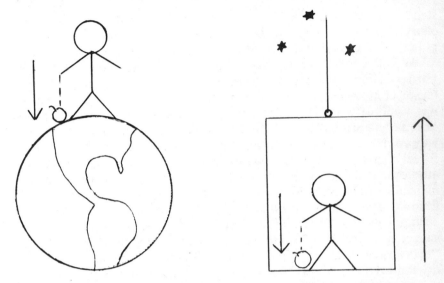

Figure 3. A uniform accelerated system, somewhere in space, creates a gravitational system where none existed before.

Figure 4. A gravitational system masquerading as an inertial system.

Implicit in Newton's law of gravitation was the premise that gravitation would not effect the direction of a ray of light. Before Einstein, determining the distance of stars depended on the accepted hypothesis that light is propagated through space in perfectly straight lines. If Einstein's theory replaces the straight lines with curved lines, all observations of the heavens to date would have to be recalculated. New calculations would show that the stars are much farther away than previously supposed, and that the universe is much larger and much older than previously thought.

Again the conservatives clapped their hands to their heads in a state of panic and disbelief; the implications of the new Einstein theory were shattering. But their anxiety was somewhat relieved when they heard that Einstein had also suggested methods to test his latest thought theory. First, Einstein suggested, with Newton's gravitational equations scientists were unable to account for the perturbations in the exaggerated elliptical orbit of Mercury around the sun. Mercury's exaggerated elliptical orbit around the sun takes on the shape of a football. But that's not the problem scientists were concerned with. What bothered the scientists was that when Mercury had completed one orbit of the sun it did not return to the same position relative to the sun. (Figure 5.) Instead it "advanced." Well, for that matter, so did the other planets. But not such a great deviation in the orbit of Venus, the Earth, Jupiter, Mars, or the other planets could be observed. The advance motion of Mercury clearly violated Newton's law and the mathematical discrepancy remained. Until Einstein. Einstein's mathematical equations predicted what the motion of Mercury must be. Einstein's equations could account for that irregularity.

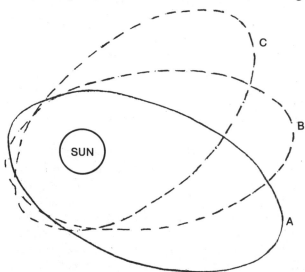

Figure 5. The advance motion of Mercury.

Second, test for the deflection of light passing close to the rim of the sun. (This is the test described in chapter one.) Third comes the most difficult part of the theory to test and not the easiest to put into words. Because of the difference in gravitational fields, Einstein said, the same clock would tick slower on the sun than on earth; but, the difference would be ever so slight, hardly measureable at all. Therefore, we must look for a body in the heavens with a much stronger gravitational field, and we find it in the "white dwarf" star known as the "companion of Sirius." The white dwarf's density is so great that one cubic inch of its matter would weigh a ton here on earth. The white dwarf's gravitation is so strong that, in effect, its gravitation slows down its own radiation to the degree that the radiation can be measured here on earth. These effects are measured by means of the color spectrum. Over a period of time, spectroscopic observations have shown that the light (radiation) from the white dwarf is indeed reduced as Einstein predicted. This reduction is known as the "Einstein effect" and constitutes an additional verification of the general relativity theory. This test, sometimes called, the gravitational "red shift" was successfully proved by W.S. Adams in 1924 in California.

But even before 1924, Max Planck, in 1919, heralded Einstein's achievement: "It surpasses everything previously suggested in speculative natural philosophy and even in the philosophical theories of knowledge. Non-Euclidian geometry is child's play in comparison."

Implicit in Einstein's gravitational theory was the premise that if a radar signal was transmitted from earth past the rim of the sun and eventually bounced off either Mercury or Mars, whenever either of these planets happened to be in the earth-sun line, then it will be found that the radar signal will be slowed down. The delay, it was theorized, would be due to the effect of the sun's gravitational pull on the radar signal. (Figure 6.) When the same signal is beamed at the same target far from the vicinity of the sun, then the delay is not observed.

In tests conducted by Irwin I. Shapiro et al at the Massachusetts Institute of Technology, J. Brenkle et al at the Jet Propulsion Laboratory in Pasadena, and W.F. Cuddihy et al at the Langley Research Center, NASA, Hampton, Virginia, a preliminary result suggests agreement with Einstein's predictions to within 0.5%.

There have been several tests of the radar signal propagation method, in 1968, 1972, and 1975 and 1976, all based on Shapiro's 1964 premise that the propagation time of electromagnetic signals travelling between points (in space) will be increased (delayed) by the

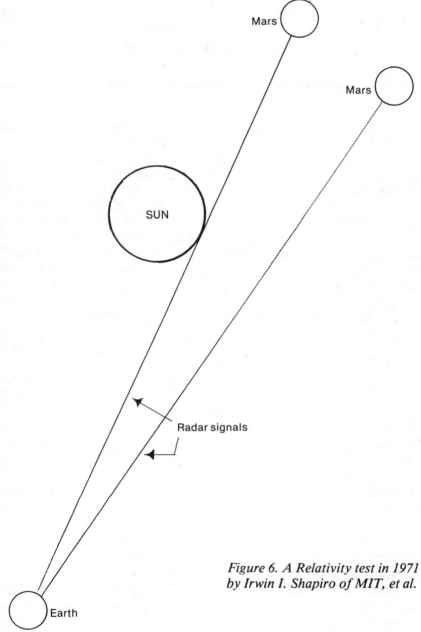

Mars

Mars

SUN

Radar signals

*Figure 6. A Relativity test in 1971
by Irwin I. Shapiro of MIT, et al.*

Earth

presence of a massive object near the signal path. The proof of this premise is one more modern day confirmation of Einstein's gravitational theory.

18

WORLD WAR I ENDS

Save for the excitement at the completion of his general theory, the world of Albert Einstein was filled with gloom. The newspaper headlines of October 12, 1916 reported that the Austrian prime minister, Count Karl von Sturgkh, had been assassinated; and by no less a figure than Einstein's former fellow-student, Friedrich Adler. Adler's action was precipitated by the refusal of the Austrian parliament to reconvene to debate the advisability of continuing the bloodshed. Adler was jailed and duly sentenced to death. But his father's influence and the question raised by the defense as to the state of his sanity had the effect of reducing his punishment to life imprisonment. (After the war, he was given a pardon and released from prison.) Meanwhile, on the western front at the Battle of the Somme, more than a million men were either killed or wounded, with no meaningful advance on either side.

Unable to contain the disgust he felt for the ongoing war, Einstein once again sought refuge in a neutral country, Holland, and the warm friendship of Lorentz and Ehrenfest. After dinner at the home of Lorentz, once Einstein was provided with a good cigar, discussion on the bending of light rays could begin. Lorentz, ever patient and incisive, handled the subject with such familiarity and depth of understanding that Einstein no longer suffered the loneliness of the single wanderer. Ehrenfest conveys the feeling of this meeting to us: "Lorentz sat smiling at an Einstein completely lost in meditation, exactly the way a father looks at a particularly beloved son—full of secure confidence that the youngster will crack the nut he has given him, but eager to see how. It took quite a while, but suddenly Einstein's head shot up joyfully; he had it. Still a bit of give and take, interrupting one another, a partial disagreement, very quick clarification and a complete mutual understanding, and then both men with beaming eyes skimming over the shining riches of the new theory."[100] Ehrenfest had also noted that Einstein had lost weight and complained about stomach pains.

On the war front, Germany was restrained by American warnings of retaliation should any of her ships be torpedoed. On the German homefront, however, the clamor for renewed and unrestricted submarine warfare was deafening. To Rolland, Einstein wrote, "I know people in Germany whose private lives are guided by utter altruism, yet who awaited the declaration on unrestricted submarine warfare with the utmost impatience."[101] To Ehrenfest, in June 1917, he wrote, "The ancient Jehovah is still abroad. Alas, he slays the innocent along with the guilty."[102]

In April, 1915, the *Lusitania,* a British passenger ship, which had sailed from New York on a trip to Liverpool, carrying some 1,198 persons, 128 of whom were Americans, went to the bottom after being hit by two German torpedoes. Strangely, this intentional murder of unarmed civilians, many of whom were women and children, did not immediately draw the United States into the war on the side of the Allies. The United States, under President Woodrow Wilson, maintained a neutral status as long as it could, to the tune of "peace at any price." The Lusitania incident served only to sway the fence-sitters away from sympathy for the Germans and over to the Allied cause. But soon after the Germans resumed unrestricted submarine warfare in January, 1917, with the sinking of two American ships, the City of Memphis and the Illinois on March 16, Wilson reacted with his now famous "The world must be made safe for democracy" speech, as he asked Congress to declare war on Germany. He got his mandate in an overwhelming vote on April 2, but there were few American troops prepared to cross the Atlantic to do battle alongside the weary French and British. Meanwhile, the Russians were close to capitulation. The large-scale riots in Petrograd in February, had forced the abdication of the Czar. The new Kerensky regime "conned" the Russian soldiers into one last attack against the Austrians, but this, too, failed. By then the Russian soldiers had had it. Having fought bravely, they simply dropped their rifles or "broom-handles" and either surrendered or went home or joined the revolution.

When Lenin and the Soviet Bolsheviks took power in October of that year, the Russians had neither the will nor the ability to continue fighting the Germans; Lenin, therefore sought peace for his new regime and found it, but at a tremendous price. The Germans, tasting victory, were not to be denied the loot and other spoils of war as they quickly raced as far into the Ukraine as their boxcars could carry them. A peace treaty was finally signed in the spring of 1918 at Brest-Litovsk, giving Germany about a third of Russia, lock, stock and barrel—and all that she could steal. Here, the Germans were given the opportunity to learn a hard lesson, an opportunity which unfortunately was wasted on them, and one which they were bound to repeat—that it was infinitely more difficult to hold on to Russian soil than it was to take it. When Russian guerillas began ambushing large numbers of German soldiers deep inside the annexed territory, then too late the Germans realized that they had come too far; much too far to be extricated before they lost most of their million-man army. With lines overextended, the Germans paid too heavy a price for their greed and for their brief occupation, in men and materiel, at a time when all possible help was needed on the western front now that the American buildup was beginning to be felt.

By November 1917, there were more than one hundred thousand Americans on French soil. At first the Americans were not used as a cohesive fighting force. They trained with experienced troops and went into their first battles as part of British and in aid of French units as they were needed. Neither the Allies nor the Germans made a proper evaluation of the gum-chewing, wise-cracking "Yank." But to the war-weary French, who had borne the brunt of the heavy losses totalling over one million dead and who were low on morale, the reckless Americans were welcome companions. And with the Germans gathering their remaining forces for an all-out campaign to capture Paris, the Allies needed every available man.

While Einstein continued to write scientific papers, even after the general theory (he completed thirty important papers between the years 1915 and 1918), his stomach trouble became worse, and his doctor ordered him to bed. Providentially, Albert's uncle, Rudolph Einstein lived close by with his daughter, Elsa, and Elsa's daughters, Ilse and Margot. They insisted that the professor's health would best be served by family care and a good dose of homemade soup. Elsa, a warm, unpretentious and outgoing "hausfrau" immediately took charge of her cousin's welfare, insisting that he remain with her family, and proceeded to nurse him back to good health. "Sorry to interrupt your work, Herr Genius, but first get something good and solid into your stomach for a change; then you can go back to your numbers." Elsa bossed him into a better state of health in a few months, and since his privacy was respected, he simply stayed on; he had found a home. The neighbors talked; but as with most comments about himself, Einstein ignored them.

The well-planned German offensive in the spring of 1918 met with great initial success; but, not having the momentum to continue to Paris, it floundered and failed. Meanwhile, American manpower increased to over a million. The last desperate attack mounted by the Germans, in May, was directed at Château-Thierry and Belleau Wood. The Americans turned them back. In August, General Pershing commanding mainly French and American forces gathered for what turned out to be the final offensive of the war. By this time, exhausted and hungry Germans were surrendering by the thousands. After the hard-fought Meuse-Argonne battle the Kaiser was ready to abdicate; German soldiers had mutinied, morale in what was left of the German army was at its lowest, and there were riots in the streets of Berlin.

In October, the Germans threw in the sponge and asked for a "peace of justice." After the barbaric acts committed by the Germans during the four years of war, the Allies were hardly in a mood to respond favorably to an appeal for leniency. To gain a better bargaining position and to humiliate the Germans further, the Allies put off signing the Armistice agreement until November 11, 1918. It was rumored that some exacting underling thought it significant that the date that went down in the history books as the cessation of hostilities read the eleventh hour of the eleventh day of the eleventh month.

19

SECOND MARRIAGE

The forty-day war that hung on for four tragic years found a defeated Germany still blockaded by Allied, mostly British, shipping. Other than to flaunt their victory and otherwise starve the Germans and Austrians, it had no useful purpose. For the Germans to make good on the extremely heavy reparations written into the Versailles treaty, Germany's beleaguered industry would have had to operate above peak capacity. This was, of course, impossible. The condition of Germany's industries precluded even a partial compliance with the terms of the treaty, which in essence, delivered most of the Ruhr's coal to France and Belgium. The victors snorting revenge, couldn't see at the moment of supremacy the impossible corner into which they forced the Germans. They became fully aware of the desperation of the Germans only some twenty years later when German rearmament once again threatened Europe with another fratricidal conflagration.

Already suffering from unemployment and starvation, further domestic disasters were visited upon the German people because of the lack of fuel and a gargantuan inflation. Germany couldn't hope to get her industries back in shape without raw materials, which were unavailable because of the blockade and without coal, the supply of which the Allies were draining off. Meanwhile France, the most injured party in the war, claiming the largest share of reparations, threatened to station her troops on German soil should Germany falter in her payments.

In Germany, there were those who argued that they had been "sold out"; that the just peace that Woodrow Wilson had promised was nowhere to be seen in the pages of the treaty. They protested that they had not been defeated on the battlefield and hoped to continue the war. These sentiments were expressed by the perennial militarists, ultranationalists, antiunionists, diehard ex-soldiers, and right-wing malcontents. The agitating groups were staunchly backed by the German General Staff, who saw in these groups the backbone of their next army and fresh cannon fodder for the next war.

After Einstein had fully recovered in Elsa's home, he resumed his post at the university. Sooner or later he would have to decide whether to continue living with his cousin and her family, which was tantamount to asking Mileva for a divorce, or to go back to his flat, bachelorhood, and an outside chance of reconciliation. The decision to remain where he was, with Elsa, was made because of her deference to his needs and her ability to handle his everyday affairs. She provided an effective shield against the social climbers who vied for the company of Einstein as a "centerpiece" for their dinners and parties. It was an agony for the father, now approaching forty, to realize that the family had broken up, that his children would suffer. But his work, which was his life, had to come first. And if furthering his work meant the breakup of his family, then so be it. The divorce was made final and Elsa and Albert were married in 1919. Now Einstein had two families to support.

Mileva resented the second marriage. After all, it was she who had labored through the difficult years in Switzerland, and now it was Elsa who would ride the crest of her Albert's success. This was not, however, the main topic of conversation when Einstein came to visit his first family. Hans Albert was now fifteen years old and would soon be choosing a career. He obviously had a mind of his own and told his father that engineering would be his field. His father did not approve of the choice. But, showing his inherited stubborn streak, Hans Albert stuck to his decision and later went on to attend his father's alma mater, the ETH. Edward, at the age of eight, showed remarkable proficiency at the piano, playing pieces difficult for most pupils his age. His technical ability was good, but his father detected that the playing was more mechanical then warm; he tried too hard, straining more for approval then for the love of the music. Einstein could begin to see the effects of being tied to a calling that forced upon him the unintentional neglect of loved ones. Mileva took events calmly, knowing that in his own way he still loved her. They somehow got along better after the divorce.

Elsa, who was five years older than her cousin, remembered more vividly than he the years of growing up in her home town of Hechingen, visiting the Munich Einsteins and teaching games to her shy little cousin, Albert. She still retained, as did her husband, the musical intonations, the soft-spoken dialect that fell easy on the ear. Plump and jovial, Elsa never pretended to intellectuality. When asked if she understood relativity, she responded that her mathematics was confined to adding up the sum on her grocery list.

Elsa Einstein was not physically beautiful; she was short, full-figured, somewhat myopic, and not what you'd call a "fashion plate." To the intellectual snobs in Berlin the hausfrau seemed hardly deserving to be the wife of a genius. To her husband, however, she proved to be an ideal mate and companion, with the good sense to withhold from her "Albertle" the feeling that he was being managed. They had known each other from childhood, so there were no pretenses, no surprises, and no deep, dark family secrets. They were family. She was the homemaker, completely devoted to her husband and daughters, almost to a fault. Ilse and Margot did not inherit their mother's vitality nor her stamina. But, at the dinner table, when the professor had left his equations in the study, there was lively family talk and the latest jokes; they were happy together. There was never a sense of intruding, or the feeling of a step-father relationship. They thoroughly enjoyed each other's company. It hadn't been this way in his first marriage.

At the beginning of 1919, Lorentz wrote to Einstein that Arthur Eddington, in England, was readying two astronomical expeditions for a late March departure to photograph the May 29th solar eclipse. Welcome news to Einstein. Not only was he confident that his theory would be proved but he felt fortunate that technology was advanced enough to permit tests of his theory within his lifetime. This is not always the case.

What was then a new experience for the German people, a representative form of government, was instituted in 1919. The thankless job of attempting to steer the course towards democracy, without violence, fell to Karl Ebert, a socialist who became the first president of the Weimar Republic.

Einstein, who was optimistic about the prospects of the new government, felt that once the German people were given the opportunity to govern themselves, to make their own decisions, buttressed by the humanist philosophies of Goethe and Schiller instead of the irrational chauvinism of Treitschke and Nietzsche, they would put militarism aside. He saw, in the near future, a new spirit of cooperation and brotherhood.

Einstein hoped; but Ebert had his work cut out for him. He was faced with the frightening but likely prospect of a grab for power by either the right or left-wing political parties. Devastating inflation made it all but impossible to buy food. A barrel of Deutschmarks would pay for but one egg, and farmers were forced to barter needed food for scarce coal. Miracles of economy and production were required to reduce inflation and put people back to work.

Walther Rathenau, a Jewish industrialist, who had distinguished himself during the war as head of the War Materials Board by keeping supplies and food moving to wherever they were needed, was appointed by Ebert as reconstruction minister. An energetic man, with a reputation of being a mover and shaker, Rathenau had kept the people eating and the soldiers shooting. With confidence in the revitalizing power of Germany, Rathenau put the war behind and set about getting the factories back in operation. He believed his country was headed for a spiritual renewal and a new birth; that it would reject militarism and socialism.

In his enthusiasm for a new and democratic Germany, Einstein became more and more involved with the political events of the day, lending his name to pacifist pamphlets and conferring with political leaders. When Einstein and Rathenau met, in the work of the postwar reconstruction, they became fast friends, often visiting each other's homes and discussing the future of Germany in a united Europe. Einstein realized that making contacts abroad would go a long way towards paving the way for better relations and reestablishing Germany among the family of nations. He could not have known, however, that he would be among the first to be called on to build bridges to Germany's former enemies, to reach beyond national boundaries towards world cooperation.

In September 1919, Einstein wrote to Ehrenfest asking his colleague if he had heard any news of the results of Eddington's expeditions. Lorentz cabled back on September 22nd that "Eddington found star displacement at rim of sun, preliminary measurement between $\frac{9}{10}$ of a second and twice that value."[103] This was indeed confirmation of Einstein's theory. The dutiful son then wrote to his mother telling her the good news, that the English astronomers had actually measured the light deflection at the rim of the sun, and that the figures agreed with his prediction. He also expressed sorrow that he could not be with her during her illness, but explained that he had to hurry to Holland to verify the details. From Holland he wrote further that the measurements taken by the British were indeed correct.

The findings of the expeditions occasioned an otherwise infrequent joint meeting of the Royal Society and the Royal Astronomical Society in London on November 6, 1919. Almost to the day of the first anniversary of the signing of the armistice, it was announced at the joint meeting that the results completely confirmed Einstein's predictions. "The night photographs show the circle (of stars) a little smaller than the day photographs. This is exactly what was predicted by Einstein. The only possible cause that could have made the circle larger is the following: The sun must do something to the rays of light as they pass close to its surface on their way to the earth. In other

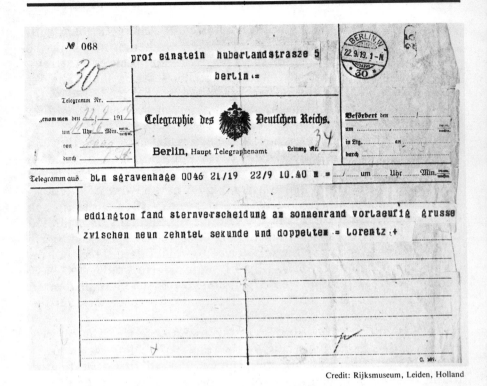

Credit: Rijksmuseum, Leiden, Holland

Lorentz telegram to Einstein, dated September 22, 1919 reads:
"Eddington found star displacement between nine-tenths of a second
and twice that value. Lorentz."

words, the sun must bend the rays of light. When the night photograph was made by the observers the sun was not there and the rays came straight through."[104]

Scientific discoveries are not the usual fare of which newspaper headlines are made; they are more often relegated to the science page, if any, or to an inside column. But the Einstein story was an exception. It was uncanny the way the newspapers spread Einstein's picture around the world. Though the theories remained incomprehensible, what people saw in the face of the Berlin professor they could understand; what they saw was compassion and kindness. They read about his reaching to the rim of the sun, unraveling some of God's tightly held secrets, bringing them down to earth, and setting them down gently before the peoples of the world. He was the provider bringing sustenance, the prophet revealing a message from on high. World wide publicity inevitably attracted worldwide attention and some of the attention proved to be self-seeking. A cigar manufacturer wanted Einstein's endorsement for the relativity cigar. Weekend inventors asked his approval of their pet project. His advice was sought on a failing marriage, on life-prolonging potions, on what course to follow in college. The freeloaders abounded. Einstein was dumbfounded as to why people were interested in a man whose theories they could never hope to understand. There were also many letters of genuine congratulations from non-designing citizens with no ulterior motives; these were answered first.

In a letter to the *Times* (London), Einstein expressed his appreciation.

> After the lamentable breach in the former international relations existing among men of science, it is with joy and gratefulness that I accept this opportunity of communication with English astronomers and physicists. It was in accordance with the high and proud tradition of English science that English scientific men should have given their time and labour, and that English institutions should have provided the material means, to test the theory that had been completed and published in the country of their enemies in the midst of war. Although investigation of the influence of the solar gravitational field on rays of light is a purely objective matter, I am none the less very glad to express my personal thanks to my English colleagues in this branch of science; for without their aid I should not have obtained proof of the most vital deduction from my theory.[105]

After the words of gratitude to his English audience, he attempted to reassure his English colleagues that Newton's star would never be eclipsed.

> No one must think that Newton's great creation can be overthrown in any real sense by this or by any other theory. His clear and wide ideas will forever retain their significance as the foundation of which our modern conceptions of physics have been built.[106]

As a postscript to the letter, and in a gibe at those who would attempt to nationalize creativity, Einstein wrote:

> By an application of the theory of relativity to the taste of the reader, today in Germany I am called a German man of science and in England I am represented as a Swiss Jew. If I come to be regarded as a "bête noire" the description will be reversed, and I shall become a Swiss for the Germans and a German for the English.[107]

In the English-speaking world, only Eddington's version of the Einstein theory, entitled, *Relativity Theory of Gravitation,* was available in print. This had first been published in pamphlet form in 1918, but the publisher dusted it off and reissued it in 1920. Sales soared into the thousands. Later, when called upon to lecture on this subject to a lay audience, Eddington "played" to overflowing crowds. His lecture, "Space, Time and Gravitation," also became a bestseller.

That same year, an American named Eugene Higgins offered a prize of $5,000 for the best essay on the Einstein theory of relativity in three thousand words. The entries were sent to the periodical, *Scientific American* and the best were sorted out by the "Einstein Editor." But all the hopefuls operated under the handicap of not being able to find adequate reference material, for the simple reason that it didn't exist. Only the pens of Einstein and Eddington had written anything about the new interpretation of gravitational phenomena. Relativity, it seems, was not clothed in familiar terms.

Leopold Infeld, then a student in Berlin, entered the competition, along with such known astronomers as Willem de Sitter of Holland and William Pickering of Harvard. Infeld wrote later of the excitement generated by the contest: "For students in a country with inflation, such a great sum ($5,000) was almost beyond imagination. I helped my friend with his entry and in my wretched room we put the finishing touches on an essay. As we counted the words, we dreamed about the rain of gold that relativity theory and the USA would bestow upon us. No, we did not win."[108]

Of the many entries the one that stood out above the others was submitted by Mr. Lyndon Bolton of London, under the pen name, "Zodiaque." "The reason why his essay was ultimately chosen over its most pressing rivals was the extraordinarily fine judgment which he used in deciding what he had to say and what he would leave unsaid."[109] Coincidentally, Bolton was employed on the staff of the British patent office.

20

SUDDEN WORLD FAME

In Germany, Einstein's sudden fame was greeted on two levels by German society; exultation that once again a German man of science had led the way to a glorious achievement and bitterness from the right-wing ultranationalists, who blinded by their anti-Semitism condemned Einstein's nonpolitical theories as "Jewish mathematics" and "Bolshevist physics." It takes a curious but lop-sided logic to describe Einstein's scientific theories as Bolshevist physics when the Kremlin denounced relativity as the product of the "bourgeois class in decomposition . . . . reactionary of nature, furnishing support for counter-revolutionary ideas." It was plainly a case of unadulterated fury blended with jealousy that a pure Aryan had not conceived of relativity first.

Jews in general were being blamed for both starting and prematurely ending the war, for Germany's defeat, for the inflation and starvation that followed, and for whatever else happened to be on the hate list on any given day, and Einstein, one of the most prominent Jews in Germany, was especially singled out. The ultranationalists hated the Jews, liberals, and democrats with equal venom; and Einstein was all three.

They lashed out at his pacifist stand taken during the war and criticized his close contact with British scientists. They became so intent at smashing the Einstein image that they formed the "Anti-Relativity Society," the purpose of which was to show that relativity was foreign to the German people. To Einstein, the very suggestion that scientific concepts and theories could somehow be confined to the citizens of one country, to one cultural strain to the exclusion of others, that intellect could be bound by borders was utterly absurd. He resented being thrust into the open marketplace of the political scene, where he was not prepared for the attendant gutter-fighting. But he learned fast. His friends advised him to ignore the insults. But the Anti-Relativity Society persisted to the extent of hiring the hall of the Berlin Philharmonic for an "Anti-Einstein" meeting. They showed a token physicist, to be sure, who disagreed with Einstein, but who also had his own equations to peddle. The remainder of the program was given over, not to a scientific disproof of relativity, but to a politicizing of it. And when the crowds looked up to see the source of the inappropriate laughter, they saw that it was Einstein himself; he managed to totally destroy the effectiveness of the propaganda. Einstein's friends did not approve of his performance, his public display; they said it was beneath his dignity. But the doughty professor wasn't quite through; he had an encore to present to his critics. In the *Berliner Tageblatt* he wrote: "The theory had the misfortune to have been worked out not by a reactionary deutsch-national German, but by a Jew with progressive ideas."[110] This statement was no solace to the paranoid Germans.

These forays into the forum of public controversy by Einstein aroused indignation among some German Jews as well. So far as some Jews in Germany were concerned, many considered themselves Germans first, Jews only secondarily, and often practiced their own brand of discrimination against their poorer, eastern brothers. This, too, Einstein was unable to understand. That these German Jews, eager for assimilation, were willing to appease the excesses of the ultranationalists was an attitude Einstein could not comprehend.

With all the flak aimed at him, Einstein decided that it was time he accepted some of the speaking engagements that were piling up. So Elsa packed a small bag, and armed with the inevitable violin, her husband took off an a lecture tour; first north to Norway, then south to Holland. He continued on to Prague. Philipp Frank picks it up from there:

> Early in 1921 Einstein returned to Prague, where I was then teaching, as his successor. I had not seen him for years . . . . When I met him at the station, he had changed very little and still looked like an itinerant violin virtuoso . . . . It was Einstein's first popular lecture that I had heard. The hall was dangerously overcrowded since everyone wanted to see the world famous man who had overthrown the laws of the universe and proved the curvature of space . . . . After the lecture the chairman . . . . gathered together a number of guests to spend the evening with Einstein. Several speeches were made. When Einstein's turn came to answer, he said: "It will perhaps be pleasanter and more understandable if instead of making a speech I play a piece on the violin." It was easier for him to express his feelings in this way.[111]

Einstein then went on to Austria where he was accorded the same enthusiastic welcome. Here the lecture hall was too small to contain an enthusiastic crowd of three thousand people who wanted to attend; it took a concert hall. Again, there was no hope of the audience understanding, they came simply because they wanted to be in the presence of a human being who "worked miracles."

On his return to Berlin Elsa informed him that his mother was ill. When he learned that the nature of her illness would leave Pauline Einstein only a short time, he had her moved to Berlin. She died a few months later.

Anti-Semitism had not disappeared while Einstein was away. The Germans could not accept the fact of their defeat, nor would they place the blame where it belonged, squarely on the shoulders of the German General Staff. To exonerate themselves the blame had to fall elsewhere. And the scapegoat for their mistakes continued to be the Jews, the minority least able to defend themselves.

Einstein paused to reflect on the condition of his fellow Jews in the midst of a hostile environment. Unable to gain admittance to universities in eastern Europe, Jewish students came to Germany searching for an education, but there, too, they found the doors closed to them. When they appealed to Einstein, he set up special classes for them. Even with help from Max Planck, discrimination continued.

Throughout Einstein's adult life, his religion had been of little consequence. He had married a Greek Orthodox girl. Their sons were not raised in a Jewish environment, nor with any sense of being Jews; and his friendships certainly were not based on the accident of race, religion, or nationality. Only when he returned to Germany did he became more conscious of being a Jew. He said that he owes this discovery more to non-Jews than to Jews. He followed closely the travail of the Polish and Russian Jews. "It was among the eastern Jews, the poorest and the most faithful to tradition, that he found the most passionate desire for knowledge, an almost superstitious cult of education, a respect for the man of letters. Among the starving students who came to him, barely able to express themselves, the study of science had replaced that of the Torah, but the passion had remained the same. The desire for knowledge for its own sake seemed to him the most striking feature of the Jewish masses and the link that bound them to himself. He wanted to find out if there were any other links among the widely differing Jewish elements."[112]

Einstein spoke of these matters to Rathenau, who exemplified the integrated, almost totally assimilated Jew. Rathenau pointed out to Einstein the salient difference between Jews and most Germans. He told Einstein, that if a Jew told him that he was going hunting for the pleasure of it, then he knew he was a liar. Einstein laughed at the comparison. But later, when he was alone he realized that it was just this quality of the Jewish people, the respect for life, concern for the human condition, that bound him intimately to them. His longing for independence and an almost fanatical love of justice were identical with the traditional principles of the Jewish people. These principles Einstein instinctively put into practice, as in the case of Leopold Infeld. Infeld had taught school in a small town in Poland, and when relativity went "public" he gave a lecture on the subject; but even the largest building in town could not accommodate the crowds. Later, when Infeld came to Berlin to study further "at the university where Planck, von Laue and Einstein lectured," he was greeted with broken promises and indifference. In desperation, after walking the cold and unwelcome streets of Berlin, he phoned Einstein. He was asked to come right over.

> Einstein greeted me with a smile, offered me a cigarette, talked to me as an equal and showed a child-like trust in everything I said. My short interview was an important event in my life. Instead of thinking about his genius, about his achievements in physics, I thought then, and later, about his great kindness, about his loud laugh, about the gentle way he talked, about the brilliance of his eyes, about the clumsiness with which he looked for a piece of paper on a desk full of papers, about the queer mixture of great warmth and great aloofness. I did not see Einstein for the next fifteen years. I had a few letters from him on scientific matters, always full of kindness. To me, as to others, he never refused help when it was needed—always writing with simplicity and grace, never with impatience . . . .[113]

Einstein knew that he could not reenter Judaism as a practicing Jew, in the orthodox sense. He felt, however, that there were areas where his name and position might help to ease the desperate plight of his fellow Jews. Anti-Semitism and the degradation of life in eastern Europe had taken its toll in the ruined dreams of the ghetto-dweller, but those who had escaped the stranglehold of persecution were not content to exchange one set of chains for another. The new arrivals yearned for liberty, education, a sense of identity, and the freedom to pursue their own destiny. Many of these "dreamers" embraced Zionism, which promised a solution, but Einstein declined. He did not wish to be associated with a cause that advocated nationalism; on the other hand, he could not turn aside the demand of his conscience that he accept the role of his "brother's keeper."

Chaim Weizmann was the leader of the world Zionist movement at this time. A forceful speaker, it wasn't difficult for him to convince his downtrodden people of the blessings and virtues of having their own homeland. In the democratic lands of the western countries, however, he ran into opposition and found it harder to raise not only the necessary endorsements but also much needed funds. The Jews of the west had flourished in the climate of freedom and did not personally feel threatened. For this reason Einstein was approached and asked to accompany Weizmann to America in April of 1921. Einstein at first refused; giving the reason that he disliked begging for money. But when Kurt Blumenfeld explained that the money raised on this trip would be used to construct the very first Hebrew University in Jerusalem, he gave in.

When news of Einstein's joining the Zionist cause was spread throughout Germany, he again became the target of criticism from diverse groups. The German ultranationalists were the first to cry out that Einstein's true sentiments were not with the welfare of the fledgling Weimar Republic, charging too that he was abandoning the Fatherland. Those German Jews who saw a threat to their assimilationist goals if Zionism gained support denounced his Zionist sympathies. Fritz Haber, too, warned Einstein not to have anything to do with that radical trouble-maker, Weizmann. Just when some Jews were intent on trying to prove to the nation what good Germans they were, why did Einstein cast doubt in the minds of the rightwing elements by embracing Zionism?

Before he sailed to aid the cause of the people to which he was inexorably tied, Einstein became a German citizen again. What he had denied to the Kaiser, his allegiance, he gave to the fragile Weimar Republic. He gave up the independence and neutrality safeguarded by his Swiss citizenship, and cast his lot with the new Germany.

21

U.S.A. AND ZIONISM

On April 2, 1921 the liner *Rotterdam* sailed into New York harbor, where the host city put on a reception second to none. With typical American exuberance the mass of reporters and photographers ran down the decks, cornering the bewildered professor and his wife. Bewildered, because in Europe, scientists, no matter how famous, were hardly fussed over and were never the subject of public display. They remained aloof. Einstein could not understand why he was singled out for publicity. When the initial excitement died down, the questioning began. No questions were asked about the war; he was not interviewed as a German national, but rather as a Jewish scientist. He was news.

For the most part, the reporters wanted an easy explanation, and in as few words as possible, of the theory of relativity. Knowing how impossible it was to respond to such a request, but at the same time not wishing to disappoint, Einstein offered them this: "Till now it was believed that time and space existed by themselves, even if there was nothing else—no sun, no earth, no stars; while now we know that time and space are not the vessel for the universe, but could not exist at all if there were no contents—namely, no sun, earth, and other celestial bodies."[114] Great, thought the reporters, today Einstein eliminated time and space. What next?

The reporters continued, is it true professor, that only twelve people in the whole world understand relativity? "Oh, it isn't so bad as all that," smiled Einstein. "Of course, a theory is a matter of mathematics, it is very difficult for the layman to grasp them."[115] As to why he received such disproportionate attention from the people, he could only shrug his shoulders and suggest "psychopathological investigation."

After the interviews, came huge crowds. Weizmann was as astonished as Einstein:

> We intended, of course, to proceed straight to our hotel, settle down and begin planning our work. We had reckoned—literally —without our host, which was, or seemed to be, the whole of New York Jewry. Long before the afternoon ended, delegations

144

Credit: Zionist Archives and Library, New York.

Aboard S.S. Rotterdam in New York Harbor, April 2, 1921. Left to right: Menachem Ussishkin, Chaim Weizmann, Mrs. Weizmann, Einstein, Elsa Einstein, Ben Zion Mossensohn.

began to assemble on the quay and even on the docks. Pious Jews in their thousands came on foot all the way from Brooklyn and the Bronx to welcome us. Then the cars arrived, all of them beflagged. Every car had its horn and every horn was put into action. By the time we reached the gangway the area about the quays was a pandemonium of people, cars and mounted police. The car which we had thought would transport us quickly and quietly to our hotel fell in at the end of an enormous procession which wound its way through the entire Jewish section of New York. We reached the Commodore (Hotel) at about eleven-thirty, tired, hungry, thirsty and completely dazed. The spacious hall of the hotel was packed with another enthusiastic throng; we had to listen to several speeches of welcome, and I remember making some sort of reply. It was long after midnight when we found our rooms.[116]

Credit: Library of Congress

Elsa and Albert Einstein, aboard ship in New York Harbor, April 2, 1921.

But the rush was just beginning; the next morning they began a hectic, six-week, hop, skip, and jump tour of the East and Midwest. In between lunches and dinners with businessmen, doctors, and Zionists, Einstein managed to squeeze in a few side trips to universities. At Princeton, he received an honorary degree and spoke there in a series of four lectures on "The Meaning of Relativity." Einstein liked the feel of the university town which he found "free from all outside disturbances, an island of scholarly seclusion amid the bustle of American life."[116] In May he visited the Yerkes Observatory in Williams Bay, Wisconsin and also met with President Harding at the White House. At a demonstration of the transoceanic wireless at the Radio Corporation of America he talked with Charles Proteus Steinmetz and David Sarnoff.

Weizmann and Einstein worked well together. The Zionist leader accepted with grace the accolades directed at Einstein, but kept the Sunday punch for himself. He did the "hard sell":

When a pioneer cames to Palestine, he finds a deserted land, neglected for generations. The hills have lost their trees, the good soil has been washed into the valleys and carried to the sea.

We must restore the soil of Palestine. We must have money to sink in Palestine, to reconstruct what has been destroyed . . . . When you drain the marshes, you get no returns, but you accumulate wealth for generations to come. If you reduce the percentage of malaria from forty to ten, that is national wealth . . . . The chalutzim (pioneers) are willing to miss meals twice a week. But cows must be fed, and you cannot feed a cow with speeches . . . . Give us your help. I am trying to build up a country which has lain waste for two thousand years.[118]

Invariably this appeal drew thunderous applause. Einstein, in turn, kept his remarks short and to the point: "I agree with Dr. Weizmann. He is our leader. Follow him."

The crowds of American Jews whom they addressed, who stood to gain nothing personally for their backing of Zionism, flocked to the support of the itinerant "fund-raisers." Before this trip, support for Zionism came mostly from the poor and orthodox Jews, those who had suffered the most. But now, despite the sameness of the speeches, the monotony of the dinners, and the interminable train trips, the cause of Zionism flourished. The greatest response came

Credit: Brown Brothers, Sterling, Penna.

Einstein in New York City, near City Hall.

May 6 1921

Credit: AIP

Visitors, staff and Einstein in 1921 photograph at Yerkes Observatory of the University of Chicago at Williams Bay, Wisconsin.

from Jewish-American doctors. The doctors' generosity made up the larger part of the two million dollars raised in the six weeks the Einstein-Weizmann team trod the American scene.

Before departing on the return trip to Europe, Einstein took some time out to attend to a personal matter, a visit to his boyhood mentor, Max Talmey, now Dr. Talmey, a practicing physician in New York City. Like most people, Talmey was unaware of relativity until November of 1919; even then he did not connect his bookish friend from Munich with the discoverer of relativity; the name "Einstein" was not uncommon in South Germany. Upon learning the true identity of the inventor, he immersed himself in every book on the subject the librarians at the New York Public Library were able to supply. When Columbia University was considering bestowing the Barnard Medal of Science upon Einstein (the medal was given to him in 1920) it was to Talmey that Professor George Pegram was instructed to turn for biographical material on Einstein.

Einstein's last meeting with Talmey, in Bern, in 1902 had been clouded by despair and disillusion. Now, with deep respect he greeted

Talmey: "But Doktor, you distinguish yourself indeed, through eternal youth."[119]

The intervening years gave them a great deal to talk about, and characteristically, the great scientist played piggyback with Talmey's younger daughter, and listened attentively as the older daughter played her latest piano piece. They were destined not to meet again until Einstein re-visited the United States, some nine years later.

From New York the Einsteins headed back across the ocean for their first visit to London.

22

BRITAIN AND FRANCE

The ancient hall of Kings College was filled with apprehension and optimism. Apprehension, because a Berlin professor would soon mount the dais and proceed to speak in the hated German tongue, in a city where only a few short years ago dachsunds were slaughtered for their German affiliation and British tears still fell for the dead in Flanders Field. Optimism for those who recalled that the professor had made a courageous antiwar stand during the war. Optimism also for those who had had enough of war and hatred and who looked forward to reestablishing an exchange of culture and commerce. Like Jan Christian Smuts, the South African leader, they looked forward once again to welcoming a German recipient of a Rhodes scholarship.

With a sprinkling of Scotland Yard men strategically placed around the floor, Lord Haldane, host for the evening, introduced their guest. Einstein was greeted with predictable silence. Unperturbed however, he proceeded to present an extemporaneous one-hour talk that was carried off without interruption. And at the conclusion he was greeted with a three-minute-long standing ovation. One reporter enthusiastically exclaimed that this was the turning point . . . . "that sanity, understanding and harmony are being restored by men of creative genius."

At least in the scientific field the goodwill engendered by Einstein's visit to some degree reduced the suspicion and tension the English scientists harbored towards their German counterparts and vice versa. As an unofficial ambassador he was praised more in England for his conciliatory visit, and for his effort to help relax the barriers, than he was in the country of his birth. The effect of Einstein's successful cultural visits to the United States and Britain, in his own mind, was a reinforcement of the hope that the hospitality he was accorded in both former enemy countries would be but a first step in a larger international effort at reconciliation and would result in more frequent exchanges across frontiers between intellectuals and political leaders.

In England he met, among other notables such as George Bernard Shaw and Lord Rothschild, Arthur Eddington and Bertrand Russell. The latter two he made a particular point of seeking out, for unlike the scientists of both countries who lent their talents to the war effort, they had refused war work. Eddington came to his pacifist beliefs by way of his Quaker religion. Russell, a philosopher and mathematician, was fired from his position at Cambridge University for his pacifist stand during the war. Einstein also seized this opportunity to express his thanks to the American and British Society of Friends for their generosity and humaneness, for their shipments of food to the starving children of Germany.

Once back in Berlin, Einstein found many more invitations to travel and lecture, far more than could ever be fulfilled in one lifetime. These he put aside, temporarily. He needed a respite from travel and time to think, to develop his theories further. What seemed to Einstein a logical step forward from the special and general theories was the "unified field theory." This theory, upon its formulation, would record in one set of equations the workings of both the electromagnetic world of the atom and the gravitational world of space; one set of equations for the workings of the entire universe. For Einstein, it was unthinkable that these two separate worlds would operate under different mathematical principles. "God wouldn't do things that way." He devoted the remainder of his scientific life to the pursuit of this elusive set of equations. Though he issued several papers on the subject through the ensuing years, Einstein never did accomplish the unification he desired, nor could he devise a satisfactory test for the theory as he had for the gravitational theory.

Through the summer and fall of 1921, with the exception of a short visit to Leiden, Einstein curtailed his social life, reduced the number of speaking engagements, and set himself a Spartan routine in order to lay out his first attempt, and a qualified one it was, to formulate the unified field. He did, however, take time out from his studies for a brief trip to nearby Potsdam for the dedication of the Einstein "Turm", an astrophysical observatory tower used to study universal phenomena. In Sweden, meanwhile, his name was suggested for the 1921 Nobel Prize for physics.

That same year, Einstein's good friend, Walther Rathenau, was appointed foreign minister of Germany, by the newly-elected Chancellor of the Weimar Republic, Wirth. Rathenau's policy was to restore normal relations with all nations, and if this meant paying the reparations, then pay the reparations he would. This policy, unfortunately, didn't sit well with the militarists who would neither admit to losing the war (the resumption of which they eagerly awaited), nor agree to the reestablishment of relations with the Allies or payment of any kind of reparations. Under Rathenau's direction the peace treaty of Rapallo was concluded with the Russians; under it both countries dropped their territorial and financial claims on each other. But in the West, relations with France improved not at all. The bitterness and hatred on both sides continued to fester.

Politics once more bred strange bedfellows. Einstein, in his anger towards France found himself in an uncommon alignment with the sentiments of the right-wing nationalists; the mediating factor was the insistence by the French government on extracting every last possible monetary and material reparation from Germany. He had seen for himself the suffering which the war, the blockade, inflation, and starvation had inflicted on German children. Einstein, thereupon turned down an invitation from the Collège de France to lecture in Paris despite the fact that it was his friend, Langevin, who had initiated the invitation. After discussing his dilemma with Rathenau, however, he found he was able to reverse his decision. "How else", Rathenau asked, "can we get Europe rolling again if we do not stretch out our hands in friendly cooperation instead of looking back with suspicion and mistrust"? The dream of a united Europe was rekindled and Einstein wrote to Langevin: "Rathenau has told me that it is my duty to **accept, and** so **I accept.**"[120]

Walther Rathenau

Several French intellectuals, who secretly looked forward to the visit of a renowned internationalist such as Einstein, yet not wishing to appear pro-German to the public, attempted to persuade Langevin to rescind the invitation. Langevin, a staunch relativist and Einstein devotee, persisted not only in this matter, but also in every other effort at reestablishing ties with Germany. Objections to the Einstein visit were not confined to a few fearful French intellectuals and varied right-wing elements, their German counterparts shrieked "traitor" at anyone attempting to reopen contact with the French. Needless to say, Einstein stood fast.

Not able to gauge the degree to which the French nationalists might go to prevent Einstein from entering Paris (there were rumors of a demonstration to be held at the Gare du Nord), Langevin hurried, along with astronomer Charles Nordmann, to the Belgian border village of Jumont, on March 28, 1922, to personally escort Einstein to Paris. Upon a safe arrival, the secretive party left the train station by a side entrance, thereby avoiding reporters and cameramen—and the possibility of an ugly confrontation. As it happened, the group of students massed at the train station were not the "patriots" (they failed to turn up), but rather a group of Einstein supporters led by Langevin's son.

Credit: Einstein Archives

Einstein solar observatory designed by
Erich Mendelsohn, Potsdam, Germany

With complete security precautions in effect and admittance by invitation only, Einstein spoke to his French colleagues on March 31. He addressed them in French, be it all in a south German accent. (In England and the United States he had to use German, and rely on translators.) Whatever the atmosphere, at least one newspaper sounded hopeful of a return to sanity: "Einstein in Paris? It marks the beginning of a recovery from international madness. It is the victory of the Archangel over the demon of the abyss."

On the way back to Berlin, Maurice Solovine, a friend from the early Bern days, who had been translating relativity into French, accompanied the Einstein party north to view the untouched devastation of the battle zone. No nationalist spirit was aroused there, only horror at the site of the remaining ghost villages. They saw shell-pocked fields, with the gaunt blackened limbs of dead trees standing stark in tortured protest, where nearby gravelike trenches still scarred the land. The rubble remained, silent, where no other earthly creature moved. Einstein stood "at the very gates of Rheims, where for four years men stood still to be slaughtered."[121] As Einstein picked his way through the rubble he muttered again and again, "War is a terrible thing . . . . and must be abolished at all costs."[122] An ashen-faced Einstein turned to his friends and exclaimed: "We ought to bring all the students of Germany to this place, all the students of the world, so that they can see how ugly war is."[123] They left the battlefield, quiet and solemn and drove to a nearby restaurant.

Nordmann describes the scene at the restaurant: "A few tables away from us two French officers of high rank in full uniform were lunching with a very distinguished looking lady. I could see that they quickly recognized Einstein, and one of them, as I found out afterward, went out to make sure by asking our chauffeur. When we got up from the table, they all rose without saying a word, all moving together, and bowed low and respectfully to the great physicist."[124] The scene could have been taken from a romantic novel; Nordmann considered it "profoundly moving."[125] Mounting the stairs of the train at Cologne, for the return trip to Berlin, a weary Einstein could manage only a wan smile for his companions. As he waved goodbye, with his great hat in his hand, he shouted above the train's whistle: "I shall tell all that I have seen to the men over there."[126]

On the long ride back, Einstein did not nap in his second-class seat. For the most part he just stared out the window without seeing the unscarred German countryside.

From Berlin he wrote to Rolland, "I was particularly glad that

Credit: Einstein Archives

Einstein lecturing on relativity at the Collège de France in Paris,
Spring 1922.

the people I met displayed a sense of responsibility and did not show
the arrogance or superiority born of victory."[127] In a subsequent letter he expressed optimism for the future relations of the two former
antagonists. "Fruitful cooperation must be based on mutual confidence, and confidence can be created only by cultivation of personal relationships. The invitation extended to me by the faculty of
the Collège de France was a first courageous step in this direction. I
hope that similar gestures will be made in both nations."[128]

Einstein exemplified his own brand of fruitful cooperation by
accepting the invitation to become the German representative on the
Committee For Intellectual Cooperation of the newly-formed League
of Nations. The strong feelings that still persisted against Germany
precluded her membership in the League. In the long run, however, a

man of Einstein's international reputation, it was felt, would help ease an eventual acceptance of the outlaw nation by the League members. The members of this particular committee were sitting not necessarily as representatives of their respective countries, but rather as citizens at large with the task of implementing methods of spreading education throughout the world. Their actions and opinions were not subject to the whims of political parties or the caprices of their national leaders; they answered only to their own individual consciences. Because of Einstein's enormous world prestige, the Committee was able to also attract to membership, Henrik Lorentz and Marie Curie. Lorentz, like Einstein, seldom turned down humanitarian pleas. And Madame Curie, having been compelled to leave her native Poland in search of an education, was sensitive to the need for an open and international approach to education. Her consent to serve on the committee was obtained at Einstein's personal request.

Einstein again served as a catalyst for better relations between the Germans and the French when a group of distinguished Frenchmen and a coalition of German pacifist organizations held a meeting at the Reichstag in Berlin to help promote greater understanding. The height of good feeling came when one of the French delegates, buoyant with enthusiasm, brought the gathering to its feet by pointing to Einstein and shouting: "Here is ample proof that men of goodwill of both countries could come together peacefully." Einstein's address before that meeting called for a new political organization, a larger world community, where language and mental barriers are transcended.

The attempts to bridge the gap, the many sincere efforts to establish a humane approach to a mutually beneficial relationship between the former enemies suffered a severe setback with the assassination of Walther Rathenau. On the morning of May 24, 1922, while riding in his open car from his suburban home, Rathenau was shot by right-wing extremists. The reason for the killing, Rathenau's continuing efforts at a rapprochment. Rathenau represented what was anathema to these Nazi murderers, contact and peaceful relations with their former enemies. The Nazis' only means of gaining and holding power lay not in a thriving, industrious, and prosperous Germany, but in a Germany, cold and hungry. They could not be effective in a Germany moving towards respectability and democracy; only where there was chaos could they gain a foothold. Like birds of prey they feed on carrion, they thrive on human misery.

Einstein's loss was twofold. He lost not only a friend and political mentor, but with Rathenau's death, progress towards international understanding was brought to a halt. The revolution of the right had begun, and rumor had it that other liberals, Einstein among them, were also ticketed for the same treatment.

The threats however did not deter Einstein from his daily routine until his friends and Elsa converged in protest at his lack of concern for his personal safety. Elsa was especially upset. Subsequently, Einstein wrote to Solovine that he had cancelled his lectures and "absented" himself from Berlin. Anti-Semitism had reached a new high with the death of Rathenau. The assassins were caught and imprisoned but never convicted despite a great outpouring of worker sentiment throughout the country in a memorial tribute to the fallen foreign minister.

Though in seclusion for several weeks, Einstein was not idle. His initial shock now turned to anger; he threatened to resign from the committee of the League. He felt he could not represent a nation where his fellow Jews were targeted for assassination. He explained in a letter to Madame Curie that it was not only because of Rathenau's murder, but because he had observed a strong feeling of Anti-Semitism among the very people he was supposed to represent. And if they were so disposed, he felt he was no longer the right one for the job. Madame Curie was quick to admonish Einstein for deserting the very goal he had previously urged her to pursue. Rather than serve as justification for leaving the League, Rathenau's death should be the very reason for remaining with the committee to further with increased dedication, international understanding through education. In his reply to Madame Curie, Einstein wrote of settling down somewhere where he would be able to work . . . . that conditions in Berlin were impossible. He did not go through with the resignation.

These were violent times, when political differences were settled by force and murder. But it was not Einstein's way to remain cooped up in fear of the assassin's bullet. He brushed aside his protective wraps and the well-meant advice of friends and family and joined the "No More War" peace rally of August 1. Through the streets of Berlin, in one of a long line of open cars, rode Einstein in a gesture of defiance hurled in answer to the assassins' threats. Elsa was petrified, and eventually she did prevail, by packing him off to Leiden for a few weeks. Unknown to her husband, though, she had him closely "tailed" by two plainclothesmen. Since the trip turned out to be uneventful, he wondered why so much fuss had been made about his safety and chided his wife for becoming unduly alarmed. But Elsa wasn't listening; she was busily packing and completing arrangements for a long boat trip to Japan.

23

JAPAN AND PALESTINE

Two events of scientific significance were noted by Einstein before he and his wife embarked on the first leg of their journey to the Orient. The first event took place on the other side of the world, in the almost inaccessible northwest coastal town of Wallal, Australia, where teams of astronomers had converged from the United States, Canada, and Australia to photograph the solar eclipse of September 21, 1922. Einstein's gravitational theory, the so-called "Einstein deflection" was again to be tested. Though the 1919 tests were sufficient to prove to the satisfaction of most the deflection of light according to Einstein's prediction, newer and much improved equipment, with lenses specially designed to produce sharp images, were gathered by W.W. Campbell and his team from California's Lick Observatory, and moved into place to photograph a different field of stars, to hopefully obtain a more precise result. The eclipse photographs taken on September 21 would have to be compared with those taken of the same star field at night from a location in Tahiti, which is almost on the same latitude. The night photographs in Tahiti would be taken without the disturbing influence of the sun, thereby making it possible to take a measurement of the difference in the position of the same stars at the two different occasions. Since the laborious process of making minute measurements would consume several months time and the results, therefore, could not be known before the next spring, Einstein put thoughts of the test behind him and concentrated on his forthcoming voyage. His self-assurance was unshakable. But what if the results had contradicted your theory? he was later asked. "Such questions," answered Einstein, "did not lie in my path. That result could not be otherwise than right . . . . I did not for one second doubt that it would agree with observation. There was no sense in getting excited about what was self-evident."[129]

The other event was the 87th meeting of German Natural Philosophers, which took place from September 17-24 in Leipzig. Einstein did not attend. Physicians, mathematicians, and philosophers with strong anti-Semitic sentiments managed to dominate the proceedings. These purveyors of hate intentionally subverted the purposes of the convention by collecting signatures protesting the theory

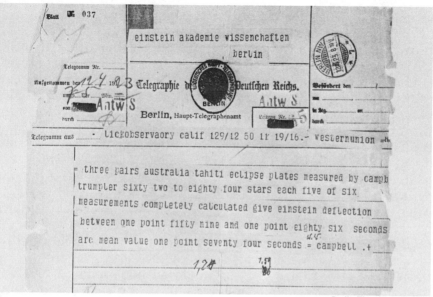

Telegram from W.W. Campbell to Einstein in Berlin, dated April 12, 1923. Gives the results of the 1922 Australian eclipse expedition.

Astronomers of Australian Eclipse Expedition in 1922, headed by W.W. Campbell, seated center. The final calculations of the Expedition found the deflection to be 1.74 compared to Einstein's prediction of 1.75.

of relativity which they described as a hypothesis without proof, full of contradictions and a logical piece of fiction. In Berlin, at the time, David Reichenstein observed: "Contemporary scientists felt themselves paling, as the great star, Einstein, appeared on the horizon. And as it is often the case, rotten motives found their expression in rotten methods. The wounded egoism of the scientific functionaries sought a way out in anti-Semitism."[130] In 1920, before certain scientists bared their anti-Semitic fangs, Einstein did attend the meeting of the German Natural Philosophers and Physicians at Bad Nauheim. After Wilhelm Weyl spoke on his elaboration of the theory of relativity, Mie spoke on gravitation, and Max von Laue on the deflection of a ray of light. Philip Lenard was irked that relativity could not tell him whether the earth is in motion or whether the entire universe is in motion around it; whether, when we are jolted by the sudden stop of a moving train, it is because the train changes motion or because we detect the movement of the earth. Lenard was so fiercely resentful that an Aryan mind had not produced relativity that, in order to cast doubt in the minds of the scientists as to the accuracy of relativity, he attempted to resurrect, of all things, the "ether." In soft tones Einstein confronted Lenard, without malice and to the point, that in respect to the motion, it was immaterial as to which of the two bodies was moving with respect to the other. As to the ether, he reminded Lenard, that it had long ago been abolished by Michelson, Morley and Lorentz. The attempts to discredit relativity and Einstein continued almost constantly until Einstein left Germany for good in 1932.

No matter how the galloping events, since the end of the war, affected her husband's career, Elsa Einstein herself, was not prepared for the harshness or the brutal realities of the postwar period. With the death of Rathenau and attempts on the lives of other officials, Elsa was thrown into an almost constant state of panic. Her first instinct was to flee the scene with her husband for she envisioned him meeting the same fate, lying somewhere in a pool of blood. Only after the Japanese steamer cleared the port of Marseilles, early in October, was Elsa able to breath a sigh of relief. Free at last, from the violence, the intrigues, the opposing political forces jockeying for positions of power; free from the Prussianness of Germany for at least six months. There would be new lands to travel, different customs to observe, fresh faces to meet and others to forget. The professor was indeed fortunate in that there were always invitations to accept when he felt the need to get away. He told his wife to drink it all in, before they have to wake up.

At a brief stopover in Ceylon, Einstein came face to face with the most deplorable conditions of human existence he had ever encountered. He was appalled at the suffering endured by his fellow human beings. Whether they worked on the docks in the searing heat or pulled rickshaw's transporting human cargo, the existence of the Ceylonese was played out at the most primitive, starvation level. There was no hope for any improvement in their social or economic conditions while they remained victims of the caste system. In his diary, Einstein recorded that he "was bitterly ashamed to share responsibility for the abominable treatment accorded fellow human beings but was unable to do anything about it. These beggars of regal stature hurl themselves en masse at every tourist until he capitulates. They know how to beg and implore in a way which tears at your heart."[131]

Upon their arrival in Shanghai, Einstein was notified by telegram that the Nobel Committee had awarded him the physics prize for the year 1921. It was sixteen years late, but a time lapse is not unusual in these matters. It was also a curious choice, a compromise by the committee, in that they awarded the prize to Einstein not for either of his relativity theories, but for his 1905 work, "The Law Of The Photoelectric Effect." The relativity theories were still considered a bit too controversial, whereas some developments stemming from the photoelectric law were already finding practical application. The Nobel Committee has sometimes been criticized for failing to recognize Einstein's greatest scientific achievement, relativity, and perhaps justly so. However, the committee's defense of its choice had to do with the word "discovery," which according to their interpretation meant something of practical use for mankind. True, relativity is mostly speculative, at least it was in 1922, but since then Einstein's equations have been used as the basis for laser beams, atomic energy, space exploration, and a theory about black holes—and as time goes by, the list continues to grow.

Late in November the Einsteins arrived in Japan to a tumultuous welcome, there to remain until February. From the start they were charmed by the friendliness and hospitality of the Japanese. Their daily excursions among the people included an ever-present interpreter, but when they were received by the Empress, they conversed in French. With a background of music represented mostly by Mozart, Bach and Beethoven, the Einsteins found the cacophonous Oriental music strange to their ears and not entirely enjoyable. But they good-naturedly suffered through it. When it came time for the inevitable lectures on relativity, Einstein spoke only in German. Though translated, and here the quality of the translation has to come into question, it was clear that the meaning of relativity escaped his audience. In addition, the patience of the Japanese must have been sorely tried, for the total time consumed by the lecture, including the translation, was over four hours, on a subject totally incomprehensible to them. He attempted to pare down subsequent lectures to a reasonable two and a half hours, only to be met with hurt feelings by those who felt slighted by a shorter lecture. Einstein felt sorry for the plight of his listeners, having to endure his lectures on inner fortitude alone.

Credit: Einstein Archives

The Einsteins at tea ceremony in Japan, 1922.

Everywhere in Japan they were received by large crowds of curiosity seekers and the inevitable interviewers. If the two months of lecturing, handshaking, strange foods, and gifts did not overtax the patience of the visitors, then there is much to say for their indulgence and forebearance in the face of a killing schedule. They were given no time to rest, except on the ship heading back to the Mediterranean. What was his impression of the Japanese? "Intellectual naiveté coupled with common sense." After taking leave of the country, he said, "I loved the people and the country so much that I could not restrain my tears when I had to depart from them."

Einstein did not go to Japan only to receive honors, conduct lectures and create goodwill, he was also a keep observer of economic and political conditions. He later warned: "Japan is now like a great kettle without a safety valve. She has not enough land to enable her population to exist and develop. The situation must somehow be remedied if we are to avoid a terrible conflict."[132]

Einstein resolved his seemingly contradictory statements regarding his critical attitude towards "nationalism" and his encouragement of the rebirth of the Jewish state, when he referred to the situation of the Jewish people as a special case. Not special in the sense that they should be given special priority before other nationalities in any specific regard, but special in the sense that the Jews are a national people without a homeland. This is quite extraordinary in the history of the peoples of the world. Every other national group in the world has its own territory under its feet. Other national and racial groups have been warred against, and perhaps decimated as well, but their remnants were not scattered, homeless and wandering, over the face of the earth. The Jews were forcibly dispersed from their native Palestine after they were conquered by the Romans in 70 A.D. And since then they have found themselves in various states of servitude, never entirely welcome, and subject always to the political winds of the times. Wherever they wandered, whatever the land, the one human condition that they shared in common was that of the defenseless minority. Einstein envisioned a Jewish "renaissance" where creative abilities could be brought into full play without hindrance when he said: "For me Zionism is not merely a question of colonization. The Jewish *nation* is a living thing, and the sentiment of Jewish nationalism must be developed both in Palestine and everywhere else."[133] Einstein saw his role in Zionism primarily as that of an educator, helping to provide a university education for the large numbers of young Jews from eastern Europe, from Germany, from anyplace where they faced bigotry, discrimination, and persecution.

It was hard for him to witness the low condition in which European Jewry was hopelessly enmeshed; deprived of the most fundamental human rights, the ownership of land, denied citizenship, and prevented from developing their potential. These deprivations often resulted in bitter, internal conflicts. Instead of divisiveness, Jews needed a "re-awakening sense of national solidarity."[134] It pained Einstein deeply to see the "assimilative" Jew in Europe taking on the airs of an Aryan and turning away from his brothers. German Jews sometimes sought to escape anti-Semitism in this way. To be German was to be strong, it meant having a permanent home, and escaping the humiliations to which Jews had been subjected; it meant strength not weakness. Einstein felt none of this. Zionism, for him, pointed the way towards self-respect: "We must have more dignity, more independence, in our ranks. Only when we have the courage to regard ourselves as a nation, only when we respect ourselves, can we win the respect of others."[125]

Welcomed to Palestine as the "most outstanding Jew in the world," Einstein was further honored when he was asked to deliver the dedication speech at the beginning of construction of the Hebrew University in Jerusalem. The Einsteins went on to plant trees in a forest later named for them. In the Palestine of 1923 they visited the agricultural settlements (*kibbutzim*) and encountered native born Jews (Sabras) as well as new immigrants, Jewish farmers. They met Jewish construction workers and Jewish day-laborers. When the land had to be cleared of ancient rocks, it was done by Jews. When the infested swamps had to be cleansed of malaria, it was done by Jews. Breaking the long-arid soil and piping in water over long distances was done by Jews. And the crops that were planted, cared for, and gathered and shipped to market—they were produced by Jews. The land they worked, the industries they established, the very homes they built was on land that was bought and paid for. These sturdy Zionists displaced no one. Particularly in the all-Jewish city of Tel Aviv, which they built on a sand dune, adjacent to Jaffa, all func-

Credit: Central Zionist Archives, Jerusalem.

Einstein planting a tree in Migdal, Palestine, 1923.

The Einsteins with Moshe Glikin, manager of Migdal farm.

tions from the paving of the streets to working the docks, were carried out by Jews. And when problems arose, they were settled by Jews.

Residing in their own homeland for the first time in almost two thousand years, Jews would not be subject to bias or prejudice; they would not be strangers in a foreign land, they were home, not a helpless minority anymore. And most important, in the Promised Land, the Jew was no longer the wanderer of the world, longing for the freedom and equality that he himself had been espousing for five thousand years. All they had to contend with were the hostile Arabs and pro-Arab English.

Einstein took pride in the accomplishments of these pioneers: "When one travels through the countryside and sees young pioneers men and women of magnificent intellectual and moral calibre, breaking stones and building roads under the blazing rays of the Palestinian sun; when one sees flourishing agricultural settlements shooting up from the long-deserted soil under the intensive efforts of the Jewish settlers; when one sees the development of water power and the beginnings of an industry adapted to the needs and possibilities of the country, and, above all, the growth of an educational system ranging from kindergarten to the university in the language of the Bible—what observer, whatever his origin or faith, can fail to be seized by the magic of such amazing achievements and of such superhuman devotion?"[136]

While Einstein marveled at the accomplishments of his fellow Jews, he also saw the necessity for establishing a *modus vivendi* with the Arabs. If the Jewish people had learned nothing else in the past two thousand years in the Diaspora, then they should know how to dispel fear and distrust, and allow no irreconcilable differences to stand in the way of peace between Jews and Arabs in Palestine. "We are convinced that we shall be able to establish a friendly and constructive co-operation with the kindred Arab race which will be a blessing to both sections of the population materially and spiritually."[137]

The Einsteins made a brief stopover in Alexandria, Egypt when Elsa was suddenly taken ill. There, the Roumanian Consul, Max Mouschly, offered the Einsteins the hospitality of his home for recuperation. From Egypt, after a lecture in Spain, they reluctantly headed back to Germany. The few months away from Berlin had been stimulating and invigorating for the Einsteins. They had seen unspeakable poverty in India and China, and in Japan, an ancient and closeted civilization uncomfortably trying to adopt the customs of the west. From Palestine's farms and cities they came away with an optimism born of seeing accomplishments never dreamed of in the ghettos of Russia and Poland.

Credit: Mireille Nahman

Alexandria, Egypt. Left to right: Roumanian Consul, Max Mouschly, Einstein, Mrs. Mouschly, Elsa, Mrs. Rosenberg.

24

A DEMOCRATIC GERMANY

Einstein returned to find opposing social and political forces arrayed against each other, the nationalists in snarling antagonism toward those who looked forward to a "greater Europe," the industrialists and the politicians, the avengers and the revengers, all pulling in different directions, all making the road back to normalcy impossible for Germany. Because of the internal strife, the honest efforts on the part of some to democratize the German Reich were becoming almost hopeless.

France, firmly in the driver's seat, stubbornly refused arbitration when a deadlock was reached over the amount of coal to be delivered to her from Germany's Ruhr. Adding muscle to her unyielding demands the French sent troops in to occupy the Ruhr region in January of 1923. Coincidentally, and for some reason which economists cannot explain, a gigantic inflation followed. The enormity of the inflation, and the consequent effects can be comprehended only when it is viewed at the level of everyday existence. Two million Deutschmarks for a pair of shoes. Few if any escaped the devouring effects of the catastrophe, which spread rapidly, engulfing all of Germany. The savings of the poor and the fortunes of the rich both went down the drain of ever-escalating prices. While the people carefully husbanded their meager supply of food and coal and huddled together for warmth, one group, the industrialists, survived the economic scourge. Seizing the opportunity, they engaged in a spree of expansionism, buying bankrupt properties for a pittance, while the rest of Germany hungered. They were looking ahead towards the next European confrontation. They knew, as did the German General Staff, that while a battle had been lost, the unfinished war would be resumed at a later date; and this time Germany would be better prepared. The unrest and the near anarchical conditions abroad in Germany unleashed a plague of extremist groups, all promising a millenium. Socialists, Communists, National Socialists, Social Democrats and a spate of religious fundamentalist groups all vied for public support. Sanity disappeared.

Einstein was quick to assess the situation, a situation that saw the League of Nations reluctant to censure one of its leading members,

France, for the occupation of the Ruhr. Both the British and Americans demurred. A friendless Germany, not allowed membership in the League had no sympathetic ear in the councils of nations or right of appeal; protests were unavailing and she had no recourse other than to submit to the invasion and suffer the consequences.

Einstein resigned his position in the League of Nations because he was convinced that the powers in control would not move against France's aggression. With the resignation of a man of Einstein's Olympian stature, the credibility of the League was bound to suffer. Hoping to ward off a damaging blow to an otherwise fragile League, Henrik Lorentz, Marie Curie, and Gilbert Murray, chairman of the committee, hastened to assure Einstein that there was sufficient sentiment in the League for his position to be able to work things out. To Murray, Einstein replied that he no longer had faith in the work of the League, since the "dominant powers" were calling all the shots. To Madame Curie he complained of the "power politics." The "United States of Europe," which Einstein had considered vital for Europe's survival, was now only a vague dream; European peace and stability were dependent on cooperation, not on revenge. This time his resignation stood.

Prompted by similar motives, Einstein lashed out again, but in a different direction; this time his anger was directed at the organizers of the Solvay Conference. The yearly conferences which had been suspended during the war were about to be resumed. In July, in answer to an inquiry from Lorentz as to whether he wished to be invited, Einstein replied that if his German colleagues were barred from attending, he did not wish to receive an invitation, and he would be forced to decline. Einstein was not insensitive to the reasons why French and Belgian scientists were reluctant to meet with their German counterparts; the feelings were still very painful. But of recent times, these "injured parties" too had not been entirely without sin.

At the invitation of the Nobel Foundation, Einstein traveled in July of 1923 to Goteborg, Sweden to officially accept his Nobel Prize. To the surprise of his illustrious audience Einstein's address was not concerned with the "law of the photoelectric effect" for which he had been awarded the prize; he spoke instead on relativity, suggesting thereby the work for which he felt the prize should have been awarded. This duty dispensed with, he hastened south to Switzerland to visit again with his first family and turn over to Mileva the cash award, amounting to some $40,000. Although some of the value was lost because of the inflation, Mileva was able to put the remainder to good use in Switzerland for the support of herself and the

Credit: From the book "A report from the Jubilee Exhibition in Göteborg, 1923."

*Einstein speaking before the Nobel Foundation and invited guests,
Göteborg, Sweden, 1923.*

education of the boys. Hans Albert was now studying engineering at
the ETH and doing well. Not a follower in his father's footsteps,
however, he chose as his field the practical end of engineering and
preferred to study sedimentary research and soil conservation. Edward was doing excellent work at school and was happy for the duration of his father's visit. However, he had not been able to adjust as
well as his older brother to their parents separation. He often brooded
about and was resentful of what he had considered his father's
neglect.

Back in Berlin, Einstein, too, found his financial situation affected by the inflation—to the degree that his salary was no longer
adequate for the support of his two families. He was forced to call
once more upon his skill as a patent examiner and served as a part-time consultant to firms in need of expert patent advice.

The unstable situation in Germany peaked on November 9, 1923
with Hitler's unsuccessful march on the Munich city hall. The
Munich police fired on the ambitious group of Nazis; several were
killed, but their leader escaped. Hitler was later tried for treason, but

In Leiden: Front row, Arthur Eddington, Henrik Lorentz. Standing,
Einstein, Paul Ehrenfest, Willem de Sitter.

spent little more than a year in a comfortably appointed jail, where
he used his time writing the hate-filled *Mein Kampf*.

After the failure of the Nazi coup, Einstein once again left for
Leiden. His departure was so sudden that Planck, fearing he would
accept a foreign post and never return to Berlin, wrote to Einstein,

pleading with him not to give up on Germany. This time, Planck was right; the fortunes of Germany took an upward swing from the low point of 1923. With the leading Nazis at least temporarily in jail and the French paring down their demands, with allied money circles beginning again to invest in German industry, with some talk of inviting Germany to League membership, and with the real possibility of getting the French out of the Ruhr, Einstein began to reevaluate his hasty resignation from the League.

Gilbert Murray had wisely kept the door open for Einstein's eventual return, and Einstein did just that. By June 1924 Einstein was reelected as an old as well as a new colleague. He took an active part in working with the committee towards creating an informed, educated and peaceful world. Where he had previously been disillusioned by the power politics which had the effect of diluting the good intent of the League, now in contrast, Einstein was encouraged by a more conciliatory attitude towards international cooperation.

The Deutschmark was mysteriously stabilizing as Einstein left Berlin to attend the July 1924 meeting of the Committee For Intellectual Cooperation. Programs initiated at this session, to help encour-

Credit: AIP

Einstein with Marie Curie: Geneva, Switzerland, 1925.

age a freer exchange of information between nations included international scientific reporting, a student and professor exchange, protection of written matter, an international meteorological office, and world-wide telegraphy. Firm in the belief that universal education would be the most effective tool in breaking down national prejudice and promoting goodwill, Einstein continually emphasized this concept in his work with the League: "An educated youth, the world over, would not resort to war to settle their differences."[138]

One of the projects introduced and particularly endorsed by Einstein was the concept of an international university. This proposed open type of university would invite speakers and professors from around the world, irrespective of their politics or philosophies. Here, history would be taught not from a narrow, nationalistic point of view, the objectivity of which must be suspect, but with a broad-mindedness that would reflect the viewpoints of as many lands as possible. With renewed faith in the ability of the League to move progressively forward, Einstein wrote confidently to Solovine that there is hope after all. But, beneath the veneer of optimism loomed the fearful question that not even the most dedicated dared to ask: what lasting progress can the League hope to make without the participation of the United States, Germany, and Russia?

Credit: League of Nations Archives.

The League of Nations Committee for Intellectual Cooperation, Geneva, Switzerland. Circa 1925.

25

UNCERTAINTY PRINCIPLE

The Einstein detractors, political and scientific, seemed never to tire in their efforts to paint him a left-winger, a supporter of Socialist causes, and when their ammunition was running low, a Communist. Einstein could only chuckle; what will they think of next? The ultra-nationalist press in Germany would not give him breathing space. One right-wing newspaper, since Einstein was always good front-page copy, reported his arrival in Moscow. Various other false reports had him in different parts of the Soviet Union throughout the fall of 1923. Fact is, Einstein never traveled to the Soviet Union, then, or at any other time, and had always rejected invitations from Soviet scientific circles. Einstein could never support a dictatorship of either the left or right, nor would he imply approval by a goodwill visit: "An autocratic system of coercion, in my opinion, soon degenerates. For force always attracts men of low morality, and I believe it to be an invariable rule that tyrants of genius are succeeded by scoundrels. For this reason I have always been passionately opposed to systems such as we see in Italy and Russia today."[139] He did, however, opt for a more even distribution of the wealth of the world, having grown up in the last days of the lavish, wasteful, absolute monarchies and witnessed the poverty and starvation at the other end.

His annual visits to Leiden, to be in the company of the stimulating Lorentz and Ehrenfest, were always welcome relief from the charged pace of Berlin. Plain food, a comfortable chair, the give and take of friendly scientific discussion, followed by long walks in the beautiful Dutch countryside, smoking his usual cigar—this was the balm that relaxed the bones and regenerated the senses. The year, 1925, however, found Einstein at a different port of call, where the scenery, surroundings and language were completely strange. This year his destination was South America, where his lectures took him to Montevideo, Uruguay and Buenos Aires, Argentina. There was no special significance attached to this trip, nor any particular domestic upheaval that necessitated his leaving Berlin. It was just another invitation to be accepted, an opportunity to visit another continent, and another function of his profession. What was most surprising to Einstein was not so much the beauty of the land, nor the hospitality of the people and the enthusiastic receptions, what he was most struck by was the receptive attitude of the German consular officials and ambassadors. In Berlin, no opportunity escaped his detractors to vilify Einstein. But in South America, a different climate of opinion prevailed; there politics were laid aside and he was accorded the hospitality reserved for a celebrity. For the resident Germans, Einstein was the only show in town and would most likely be the only one of the homegrown variety for a good long time. The diplomats turned on their smiles and good manners and enthusiastically greeted their native son. "Strange people, these Germans" Einstein wrote in his diary, "I am a foul-smelling flower to them, yet they keep tucking me into their buttonholes."

When Einstein temporarily put aside world affairs and turned once again to his first passion, physics, there too he found events and critics to be reckoned with. During the 1920's the younger scientists were mostly concerned with elaborating on the quantum theory of Planck and the relativity theory of Einstein.

As far back as 400 BC, Democritus asserted that all matter is made up of tiny particles, the basic building blocks of matter. These basic units he called *atoms*. (In Greek, atom means uncuttable; the hypothesis was that all matter can be divisible only to a certain point beyond which it can no longer be divided.) Democritus's theory became a secure and fundamental premise of science for thousands of years, despite opposing opinions from Anaxagoras and Aristotle. The atom, it was agreed, could not be further divided, nor could any power destroy the atom. In 1808, John Dalton discovered that "the atoms of one element differ from the atoms of all other elements and this difference between atoms accounts for the difference between the elements themselves." The atom remained inviolable and indestructible until the end of the nineteenth century when Röntgen discovered "X rays" spontaneously emanating from matter with evidently no outside instigation. Becquerel, using uranium, came across the same phenomenon; rays emanating from matter, spontaneously. Then, Marie and Pierre Curie succeeded in isolating a powerful source of spontaneous radiation, radium. These rays which were escaping from atoms were first described as "disintegration of the atom" by two Englishmen, J.J. Soddy and Ernest Rutherford. In turn, J.J. Thompson identified the negative charge of the atom as the electron. After considerable thought and experimentation, Rutherford added the central core, the positively charged nucleus. Picture the Rutherford atom as a miniature solar system with negatively charged electrons circling a positively charged nucleus, much as our planets circle the sun, but a great deal faster. Further investigation found that the nucleus is made up of a neutral neutron and a positively charged proton. The weight of the electron was determined to be about $\frac{1}{1840}$ the weight of the proton. The size of the atom is determined by its farthest orbiting electron; the number of electrons vary with the element, and the interior of the atom is mostly empty space. The positively charged nucleus holds the negatively charged electron in its orbit because they are unlike electrical charges that attract each other. Eddington explains: "The atom is as porous as the solar system. If we eliminated all the unfilled space in a man's body and collect his protons and electrons into one mass, the man would be reduced to a speck just visible with a magnifying glass."[140]

The brilliant Danish physicist, Niels Bohr, working in England as Rutherford's assistant and later in his own laboratory in Copenhagen, arrived at the concept of atoms whose electrons had preferred orbits. That is to say, electrons circling the nucleus, but in different planes; sort of a crisscrossing of orbits, unlike our planet-sun flat orbit. The Bohr electrons could also jump orbits, from one to another, higher or lower, gaining or losing energy. When Bohr triumphantly visited Berlin, Einstein glowingly praised his concept as "an enormous contribution to the quantum theory."

Both Louis de Broglie and Irwin Schrodinger studied the characteristics of the atom and found that the electron exhibited the same symptoms as characterized the "dual personality" of light; that the electron (a particle) acted like a wave. They all, including S.N. Bose of India, showed their work to Einstein, who helped them with publication.

Where did Einstein fit in with the new theories? Was relativity a special case of some newer discovery? Was Einstein now "old hat?" The testing of Einstein's two relativity theories still continued, but otherwise he was destined to travel a theoretical road different from that of his younger colleagues. And the cause of it all was the quantum theory.

The falling away occurred when Werner Heisenberg found it impossible to determine the exact speed and the exact location of a single electron at the same exact moment. He found that an electron has a will-o-the-wisp existence. Now you can locate it, but you cannot determine its speed. If you can determine its speed, you cannot locate it physically. Heisenberg said it was useless to worry about the flight of one lonely electron when what we are really interested in is the total effect of billions of electrons, the behavior of a whole gigantic wave of particles. His thinking was that we'd have to accept this

Credit: Central Zionist Archives, Jerusalem.

Einstein and Weizmann with members of the presidium of the German Committee for Palestine, with the director of the department for the Near East in the German Foreign Office, Mr. Schubert, 1926.

new law of probability, which states that under certain conditions billions of subatomic particles will probably behave in a certain way. In other words, if you cannot follow the path of a single particle of matter, then follow the path of billions of particles, which would be easier to trace. This theory reduced scientific exactness to an uncertainty and therefore runs counter to Einstein's philosophy of determinism. According to Einstein, when things happen there is a cause which produces the effect—and the role of the scientist is to examine and determine the cause, not to guess at it. Nevertheless, the "Uncertainty Principle" caught on. The younger investigators admitted that to know the true path of every single electron was impossible and settled for a certain margin of probability. This is what had evolved from the quantum theory which Planck had originated and to which Einstein had contributed.

His colleagues wanted to know how Einstein could turn his back on the quantum theory to which he had made great contributions, some of his own work. Einstein admitted that quantum had previously fitted a certain need, which must now be considered as having been transitory. Einstein asked in turn whether his colleagues were willing to accept the premise that the universe which functions with such precise regularity, with such beauty and harmony, operates on a probability, an uncertainty. No, Einstein said, we can be more precise than that; there are causes. At the moment, they have not been arrived at, and so those who back the probability theory of matter are accepting make-shift assumptions. But, as for Einstein, he said, "I do not believe God plays dice with the universe."

Einstein's close colleagues felt his attempt to base his unified on his gravitational theory, without the quantum theory, was sheer folly and bound to lead him down a wrong and lonely road. Perhaps Einstein clung too stubbornly to the belief that causes exist for the behavior of every particle of matter and that man will eventually make individual determinations. Perhaps not; only time and further investigation will tell.

The painstaking search for that "unified foundation on which the theoretical treatment of all phenomena is based" lured few scientists in that direction. It's just as well, for discoveries are not the results of popularity contests and are not made by the decisions of committees or a popular consensus. Most scientists did not believe beforehand

Credit: AIP

Nobel Prize Winners: Walther Nernst, Einstein, Max Planck, Robert Millikan, Max von Laue; Berlin, 1928.

that the physical reality of a unified field actually existed. Very few, therefore, were willing to devote their best research years to a pursuit that appeared to them fruitless and unprofitable. Was Einstein reaching out too far? Some said that the reason he divided his time between science, humanitarianism, and Zionism was because he no longer felt creative.

Peterchens Mondfahrt.

Silhouettes of the Einsteins: Albert, Elsa, Ilse, and Margot, made by Einstein.

26

FIFTIETH BIRTHDAY

Gustave Stresemann, who succeeded Ebert as Chancellor in 1923, was turned out of office by a no-confidence vote of his own cabinet. He then took over the post of foreign minister, a role in which he served three chancellors and which he held until his death in 1929. His major accomplishment, from a historical viewpoint, seems to have been the bringing together of the factions of the right and the forces for international conciliation long enough to improve Germany's international status and image. In 1924, Stresemann got the reparations reduced; the most immediate effect was the stabilization of German currency. He was also successful in the negotiation of the Locarno Pact of 1925, which fixed the French and German borders and paved the way for the withdrawal of Allied troops from the Rhineland. Like most Germans, he despised the provisions of the Versailles Treaty and worked hard to nullify its effects. Convinced also that only international cooperation could get Germany back on her feet again, he sought German participation in the League of Nations. But he found the most vocal opposition to this proposed move came from his own party. Once in the League, however, Germany was no longer a beggar nation. Since the Versailles Treaty limited Germany to an army of one hundred thousand men, with no tanks, and to a navy with no U-boats, and it permitted no air force, Stresemann had no choice in 1928 but to emphasize Germany's peaceful intentions by signing the Kellogg-Briand Pact, outlawing war. His efforts at reconciliation did not go unnoticed; he and Briand were the recipients of the 1926 Nobel Peace Prize. The leftists called him "capitalist" and the right wing deserted him because he was too "democratic." He was tough on Communism, but took Hitler's Munich putsch lightly. From a position somewhere in the middle, Stresemann emerged as the statesman of the twenties, successful in propping up an unpopular Weimar Republic, the very form of government to which he himself was initially opposed.

Disarmament in Europe was a joke; no nation complied with it. France, having borne the brunt of the casualties was demanding secure borders and was loathe to disarm without adequate guarantees. At the same time, the appeal of the pacifists was growing and their movement gained many members throughout the world. There was great sentiment among the various peoples that war had finally been carried too far; that centuries of rampaging and ravaging, under the tutelage of a succession of tin war-gods solved none of their problems, and only brought them despair. This, of course, was a time when no war was in progress; it is much easier to swell the ranks of the pacifist cause at such a time. Peace seemed to be catching on, though, even among the politicians.

At one Solvay Conference, late in the twenties, Einstein was introduced to the King and Queen of Belgium, Albert and Elizabeth. The royal couple took their duties to the people seriously. During the war years Elizabeth had devoted her time to work in hospitals, often assisting in operating rooms. Theirs was a concerned monarchy. King Albert was a reformer who initiated change; a king without swagger, who did not shirk from the problems imposed by German occupation. The instant rapport led to many further meetings between the scientist and the royal couple. Elizabeth, who was the daughter of a Bavarian duke was also a good violinist; invariably, following dinner at the palace, the two participated in a musicale. But Einstein behaved no differently with royalty than with anyone else. Once, when he was invited to the royal summer residence at Laaken, the chauffer was dispatched to the railroad station to pick him up. When the chauffer returned without him, with the explanation that Einstein was nowhere to be found, the monarchs became alarmed. But they needn't have been, for half an hour later down the hot dusty road, violin in hand, strode Einstein. "How could I guess that you would send a car to the station?" The chauffer had to explain that he had looked for the professor in first class and never suspected that one of her Majesty's guests would be traveling third.

As mentioned before, Einstein's trips to Leiden were the ones he enjoyed most. But not so the train ride he made there in February of 1928; Lorentz was dead. The kind colleague in science, the fellow humanitarian at the League, above all, the "Master" was gone. Einstein was asked to speak at the graveside.

It is as the representative of the German-speaking academic world and in particular the Prussian Academy of Science, but above all as a pupil and affectionate admirer that I stand at the grave of the greatest and noblest man of our times. His genius led the way from Maxwell's work to the achievements of contemporary physics, to which he contributed important building stones and methods.

Credit: Le Musee de la Dynastie, Brussels.

Einstein with King Albert of Belgium; Laaken, Belgium, July 3, 1932.

Credit: Le Musee de la Dynastie.

International group of scientists gather in Laaken, Belgium, July 3, 1932. Left to right: Bohr, Einstein, de Donder, Richardson, Queen Elizabeth, Langevin, Debye, Joffe, Cabrara.

He shaped his life like an exquisite work of art down to the smallest detail. His never failing kindness and generosity and his sense of justice, coupled with a sure and intuitive understanding of people and human affairs, made him a leader in any sphere he entered. Everyone followed him gladly, for they felt that he never set out to dominate but only to serve. His work and his example will live on as an inspiration and a blessing to many generations.[114]

It was on an educational mission to Davos, Switzerland, for the League, to lecture to young tubercular patients that Einstein was stricken with a serious heart ailment. Elsa rushed down to Switzerland, but the trip back had to be done slowly. The doctors had forbidden tobacco and even the use of a pen and paper, and it was up to Elsa to enforce these orders. Once again she had a patient to care for. But this time more was required than warm blankets and homemade soup. The patient was delighted; being laid up in bed gave him the many hours to do nothing but what he craved most, think. For most of the three-month recuperative period he was a model patient cooperating with the worried Elsa in every way. Soon, however, the day would come, and Elsa knew it, when he would be asking for his pipe.

"How many have you smoked already"? she asked timidly.
"This is my first," he invariably answered.
"But I saw you just now. . . ."
"Well, it might have been the second."
"The fourth at least," continued Elsa.
"You're not going to tell me you're better at mathematics than I am," said Einstein laughing."[142]

Hans Albert became a frequent visitor to the bedside of his recuperating father. He, too, was now living in Germany with his Swiss bride, employed as an engineer in Dortmund. A year before, his father had admonished his son not to marry. Now seeing his son happily married, he threw up his hands in a jesting disbelief: "I don't understand it. I don't think you're my son."

The salt-free diet that was instituted by his doctor reduced the inflammation of the heart and soon Einstein was up and about. Speaking appearances, conferences and traveling were still off limits, and to help in the mathematical end, the brilliant Austrian mathematician, Walter Mayer, was hired. To ease the burden of Einstein's monumental correspondence, Helen Dukas took on the task of secretary. Miss Dukas, originally from Freiburg, a no-nonsense and devoted worker, made the professor's welfare her chief concern and still, to this day, administers the affairs of the Einstein estate.

With Mayer constantly at his side, Einstein applied himself to the task of putting together a first paper on the unified field theory. In January of 1929, knowing this first report to be at the most preliminary and in no way an attempt to be the complete and final word on the subject, he sent it to the publisher. When the six pages of never-before-seen equations were released to the press, the story was given headlines by the world's major papers. They couldn't make heads or tails of it, but since it came from Einstein, it was sure to sell papers. The story drew crowds in Berlin. When Einstein noticed an unusually large group of people milling about outside his apartment building he was amazed to learn that his new theory had sparked such interest among the civilian population, and just shook his head in disbelief. Why would the public be at all interested in reading about a theory, the mechanics of which Einstein himself was uncertain about, and which to them would be totally incomprehensible? The perplexed newspaper editors pleaded with him to follow up his theory with a simplified version that the public could perhaps digest. Einstein complied, but his attempt at clarification was not successful. Not only that, but Einstein himself was not happy with the approach he had used initially and immediately began working on a new angle. It gnawed at him day and night, the idea that there should exist two structures in space, independent of one another—the gravitating space and the electromagnetic one—is intolerable. In the case of his previous theories he had suggested methods for testing, but there were none for the unified field. It was infinitely more complicated than any of his previous works and resisted his every attempt to pin it down.

Hardly had the publicity from the theory receded from the front page, then another milestone, his fiftieth birthday came up on the calendar. Having had a sufficient dose of unwanted publicity and wishing to avoid more of the same, the Einsteins made preparations to leave town for the particular day, March 14, 1929. The night before Elsa was busy preparing special foods for the next day, when she, the birthday celebrant, Ilse and her husband, Rudolph Kayser, and Margot and her fiance, Dmitri Marianoff would find sanctuary at the estate of a sympathetic friend., On their return to the apartment, they found sacks full of birthday telegrams and letters. Einstein was overwhelmed with personal gifts including several violins, sweaters, and a variety of pipes. Some of these he gave away, along with the neckties and handkerchiefs. Close friends pooled their resources and surprised him with the gift of a new sailboat. This he didn't protest, even though it was a bit fancy for him, with a cabin and a lavatory down below. His taste didn't run to the luxurious, and he almost turned it down, because Einstein was most content when a boat didn't leak and had a sail, and he could smuggle some pipe tobacco aboard. But he kept it and named it, the "Tummler."

One modest gift of a small amount of pipe tobacco which was sent by an unemployed well-wisher affected Einstein more than the many others—almost to the point of tears. The accompanying note read: "There is *relatively* little tobacco, but it comes from a very good *field*."

The story of Einstein's fiftieth birthday would not be complete if the pathetic comedy involving the Berlin Municipal Council was not included. This sorry, error-strewn saga began when the council decided that it, too, would take note of the half-century anniversary of one of its most distinguished citizens. With the desire to honor Einstein in a way calculated to bring him the greatest amount of pleasure, they decided to deed over to him a country house, a peaceful place, adjacent to a lake, where the professor could sail his boat to his heart's ease—just a quiet, private place. On being notified of the council's decision the Einsteins were overjoyed; the prospect of their ever building such a dream house had never been considered. When Elsa went out to inspect the first site chosen by the council, she found it to be occupied. The embarrassed council hurriedly returned to their maps and selected a second site. That, too, was not available. This was doubly damaging to the image of German efficiency, and again they stumbled over their maps. By now, the Einsteins were consulting with an architect and enthusiastically drawing up plans for their "dream house." The third attempt to locate a setting for the "Einstein House" also ended in misunderstanding and apologies. Not only could a suitable house not be found; the council couldn't even find a convenient and available piece of land. By this time the story had leaked to the newspapers and the council suffered further ridicule. Someone finally suggested allowing the Einsteins to look for a parcel of land for themselves, wherever they wished. And when they found it, the city would supply the purchase and building funds. So, again, poor Elsa was out looking for a site, but this time her efforts were rewarded. She found an idyllic spot in the village of Caputh, near Potsdam—a few acres sufficiently surrounded by high pines for privacy and conveniently located on a lake.

Never having owned an automobile, the Einsteins were perfectly content, despite the long train and bus ride, followed by the walk to

Credit: AIP

Max Planck and Einstein: Einstein receiving the Planck medal;
Berlin, July, 1929.

the site over a badly rutted road, that the reward at the end of the
journey would be worth the trouble it took to get there. The long ride

was not without its blessings however; it would assure privacy by discouraging most would-be visitors. But wait, yet another stumbling block was placed in the road to peace and quiet. It seems that when the council convened to vote the financial appropriation for the purchase of the land and construction of the house, all voted yes with the exception of the lone right-wing member. He said that Einstein didn't deserve it and refused to go along. No amount of persuasion could induce him to change his mind. Confronted with this absurdity, Einstein stepped in to put an end to the matter. In a curt note to the mayor, he wrote: "Life is too short for me to adapt myself to your methods. I thank you for your friendly intentions. Now, however, my birthday is already past and I decline the gift."[143]

Thus ended the business with the politicians, but not with the village of Caputh. Elsa was so taken by the mix of soft breezes, pine trees, and the wide expanse of water, and since the architect had almost completed the plans for the bungalow, she wanted to go ahead and buy the land and build the house as originally intended. She had to push her husband a bit, since building the house meant emptying their savings. Again Elsa prevailed. By early fall the home was well enough along for them to have made several visits. The happy middle-aged couple had no premonition that they would be enjoying their quiet, pastoral, "Landhaus Einstein" for no more then a few summers. Events, not of their making, and soon to unfold, were to uproot them cruelly from their peaceful village and deposit them many thousands of miles away in a foreign land.

27

RIOTS IN PALESTINE

The peace and tranquility of the summer of '29 was shattered by the news that Arab fanatics were wantonly killing Jews in Palestine. The fury of the Arab mobs found its outlet not against armed soldiers or even armed civilians, but only where the Arabs knew they would meet no resistance—a rabbinical college and a farm for orphaned children. The docile students and helpless children were unmercifully slaughtered. The blame for these deaths Einstein placed squarely on the shoulders of the British officials. He called the British to account for not restricting arms in the possession of the Arabs, and yet denying Jews the right to bear arms to protect themselves. At issue, on the surface at least, was the migration of persecuted Jews. Instead of extending a warm hand of welcome to their returning kin, the Arabs had been incited to kill the homecoming Jews.

What bothered the Arab mufti and sheiks was not so much the relatively small number of Jews who had migrated, but the thought that one day the unrestricted influx of Jews might tip the numerical scale in their favor. At that time, the late twenties, 160,000 Jews could hardly have been considered a threat to 900,000 Arabs. Numerical superiority was never the intention of Zionism. Palestine was to be the home for Jews in need of a haven, and a cultural and spiritual center for the Jews in the diaspora. It was never intended then nor today that Palestine should be the home of the entire Jewish people, or even a majority. And the Arabs have always known this. If the Arabs had instead shown the warm hospitality, of which they are capable, the Jews would never have had the need to defend themselves.

The number of Jews emigrating to Palestine was only the superficial reason for the attacks; the real fear of the Arab chieftains was the high standard of living the Jews were introducing. The Jews were cleansing the Holy Land of malaria swamps, a condition which the Arabs were perfectly willing to have continue for another two thousand years. The Jews were also conquering disease, irrigating the parched and arid soil, and turning the desert into an agricultural garden; they also created an industrial capacity in the region that was unknown in any Arab-speaking land. In addition, Jews were known to be strong unionists and would soon be demanding higher wages for Arab workers as well. It was fear that their subjects would agitate for higher living standards, fear lest they lose control of the centuries-old sheik-serf relationship that prompted the Arab overlords to organize mobs for the attacks on the Jewish settlements. It was hoped that these attacks would take such a heavy toll that further colonization would be totally discouraged. But contrary to what the Arabs expected, the Jews did not turn back.

Denouncing the policies of the British Colonial Office, in a strongly worded letter to the *Manchester Guardian,* of October 12, 1929, Einstein wrote:

> Zionism does not aspire to divest anyone in Palestine of any rights or possessions he may enjoy. On the contrary, we are convinced we shall be able to establish a friendly and constructive cooperation with the kindred Arab race which will be a blessing to both sections of the population materially and spiritually. During the whole of the work of Jewish colonization not a single Arab has been dispossessed; every acre of land acquired by the Jews has been bought at a price fixed by buyer and seller. Indeed, every visitor has testified to the enormous improvement in the economic and sanitary standard of the Arab population resulting from the Jewish colonization. Friendly personal relations between the Jewish settlements and the neighboring Arab villages have been formed throughout the country . . . I submit, therefore, that the Zionist movement is entitled, in the name of its higher objectives and on the strength of the support which has been promised to it most solemnly by the civilized world, to demand that its unprecedented reconstructive effort—carried out in a country which still largely lies fallow, and in which, by methods of intensive cultivation such as the Jews have applied, room can be found for hundreds of thousands of new settlers without detriment to the native population—shall not be defeated by a small group of agitators, even if they wear the garb of ministers of the Islamic religion . . . Jews do not wish to live in the land of their fathers under the protection of British bayonets: they come as friends of the kindred nation. What they expect of Great Britain is that it shall promote the growth of friendly relations between Jews and Arabs, that it shall not tolerate poisonous propaganda, and that it shall create such organs of security in the country as will afford adequate protection to life and peaceful labor.

The Jews will never abandon the work of reconstruction which they have undertaken. The reaction of all Jews, Zionists and non-Zionists alike, to the events of the last few weeks has shown this clearly enough. But it lies in the hands of the mandatory power materially to further or materially hamper the progress of the work . . . . I cannot believe that the greatest colonial power in the world will fail when it is faced with the task of placing its unique colonizing experience at the service of the reconstruction of the ancient home of the People of the Bible.[144]

Whether playing his violin in a Berlin synagogue, or meeting with Chaim Weizmann or the German Committee for Palestine or with the Department of the Near East of the German Foreign Office, Einstein lent his time, effort, and name for many fund-raisings that served the needs of resettlement in Palestine.

The final quarter of the year saw disaster overtake crisis and overshadow all previous problems. On October 3, Stresemann died. A few weeks later on October 24, the New York Stock Exchange collapsed, and the rippling effect devastated the economies of the entire Western world. These totally unrelated misfortunes, the second compounding the effects of the first, almost overnight rent asunder the entire structure of German democracy. The miracle of German economic recovery and growth in the twenties typified by the building of highways and factories, was made possible by the influx of funds from American financial institutions. As a consequence of the "crash," the loans were being called in; this had the effect of pulling the rug out from under the German economy. Factories closed and unemployment was widespread. Once again the stage was set for the return of the Nazis and their retinue of goons, murderers, and perverts. The rock of decency was dislodged and from under it slithered the vermin, rearing their ugly swastikas, spitting blame and easy solutions. The slavery they preached could have appeal only when unemployment was high. Blame someone else for your misfortunes and your own shortcomings, and repeat it loud and often and you will gain adherents. Democracy, they screamed, leads to disaster. And as the depression spread, the Nazis gained.

Einstein was a critic of the boom and bust cycle, which was seemingly inherent in the free enterprise system. To him the depression seemed a needless and cruel manipulation of human destinies. In a synthesis of socialist thinking, he agreed with the principle of shorter working hours to insure the greatest amount of employment, a minimum wage to increase purchasing power, and price-fixing to thwart inflation. But, the country wasn't listening. They hadn't listened to his appeals for disarmament, either.

Another misfortune, this one personal, was the psychological breakdown of his son, Edward. Edward had shown what seemed to be an inherited brilliance in science and music. And at the university his work was excellent; but masked beneath his outward, outstanding performance was the boy who felt his father had deserted his family. While he admired his father and tried to win favor by seemingly following in his footsteps, Edward harbored a deep, personal resentment brought on by the separation. Angry letters to his father, gave way to depression, which led to the breakdown. His father rushed to Switzerland, but Edward would not or could not be helped. His knowledge of psychiatry was so thorough that he could anticipate the therapist's questions, thereby negating any possibility of relieving his condition. His parents brought him to psychiatrists in Switzerland and Vienna; but all attempts to rid Edward of his malady failed. Lost in anger, but not violent, Edward remained with his mother. To see his son in this state, hating his father, and to feel powerless to help was a terrible blow to Einstein. He felt tremendous guilt for his son's misfortune and blamed no one but himself. He tried to get back to work with Mayer that summer in Caputh, but nothing worthwhile was forthcoming. Elsa could only view from the distance the grief that had come over her husband. To a friend she wrote: "This sorrow is eating up Albert. He finds it difficult to cope with, more difficult than he would care to admit. He has always aimed at being invulnerable to everything that concerned him personally. He really is so, much more than any other man I know. But this has hit him very hard."[145]

Einstein's trip to London in October, where again he lectured on relativity, helped raise funds for eastern European Jewish refugees, and also met with Eddington, did nothing to cheer him up. He posed for photographers and made conversation, but the once bright sparkling eyes now seemed remote. Back in Berlin in time for the nationwide election, Einstein supported the moderate Social Democrats. Banks were closing and soup kitchens were opening and political chaos ruled. The Nazi representation in the Reichstag jumped from 12 to 107; the Communists won 77 seats; and the Social Democrats maintained an uneasy majority. The coming winter promised "nothing but sadness." Elsa wrote to a friend, "We intend to go away for a long time."[146]

28

A JEWISH SAINT?

From 1919 on, many efforts had been made to lure Einstein away from Berlin. Through the years all of these bids proved fruitless; Einstein was devoted to his work, and his work could best be done in Berlin. After the war he had hoped that the German people would seek self-representation, that democracy would somehow take hold in Germany, but instead the destructive elements on the political scene, the arrogant, the military, and the fanatical nationalists, had taken center stage. Einstein, now in his middle years, found he was less able to withstand the almost uninterrupted series of assaults on himself originating from these groups. The annual trips to Leiden that had been weeks of joy when Lorentz held court, were now reduced to an occasional visit to Ehrenfest, who had succeeded to the post Lorentz held. Without the "Master" the thread of continuity was broken; the good old days were indeed past. The events of the past few years had piled up and taken their toll. Almost inadvertently, he found his thoughts beginning to turn in the direction of friendlier shores.

Einstein had not traveled to the United States since that barnstorming, fund-raising trip with Weizmann, in 1921. This time, if he were to accept the invitation extended by Professor Robert Millikan to visit and take part in the seminars at the California Institute of Technology, he might be able to avoid the hassle of publicity by maintaining that he was on a working holiday. No such luck. Within days of Millikan's announcement that Einstein would be in residence in Pasadena from December 1930 to March 1931, floods of mail started to pour into the *Haberlandstrasse* apartment. The letters contained the usual invitations for speaking engagements, lucrative offers for his endorsement of everything from shaving soap to pipe tobacco, and diagrams of hair-brained inventions. A barrage of this type almost always also included letters from long-lost relatives invariably in desperate need of financial assistance. All this hullabaloo Einstein sincerely wished to avoid. "Why don't they leave me alone . . . . Why can't I be treated like everyone else . . . . Why popular fancy should seize me, a scientist dealing in abstract things and happy if left alone is one of those manifestations of mass psychology that is

Credit: National Archives

*With Indian philosopher, Rabindranath Tagore, Einstein discusses
Truth and Beauty. Caputh, Germany, 1930.*

beyond me. I think it is terrible that this should be so and I suffer
more than anybody can imagine.''[147]

At the outset of his world fame Einstein did not seek publicity; he
prized his privacy. But in subsequent years, he often used the press
and the many interviews he granted to air his scientific, political and
philosophical views and his altruistic purposes, almost as much as

they used him for their commercial purposes. He learned, perhaps a bit late, that with the press you cannot pick your spots; that you cannot call off the hounds once they've caught the scent.

Although Einstein resented the intrusion into his private beliefs, he found it necessary to clear the air before embarking for the United States. Some self-styled critics of relativity resented what they regarded as man's invasion of God's domain, and characterized its originator as denying the existence of God, assailing him as "atheistic." Leaders of major religious groups felt it their duty to warn their flocks to avoid this theory of relativity whose god was an "equation." One concerned rabbi, in New York City, felt that to the public was owed a clarification of the religious belief of the propounder of relativity. He telegrammed to Einstein a short question: "Do you believe in God?" If Einstein's religious attitudes were ever in danger of misinterpretation by the public or apocryphal to the men of the cloth, his response very deftly defused their fears: "I believe in Spinoza's God who reveals himself in the harmony of all people (all that exists), not in a God who concerns himself with the destinies and actions of men."[148] The philosopher Baruch Spinoza, centuries before, had substituted an "Infinite Being" for the biblical anthropomorphic Jehovah and had been excommunicated for it. But Einstein's statement sat well with the Zionists, who were relieved that their enfant terrible had dealt well with so sensitive a subject.

Einstein's reasoning concerning the Deity did not stop with the statement above. From his studies of cosmic cause and effect he felt he had valid reasons for not throwing in his lot with a belief in an anthropomorphic Creator. He reasoned that if we give over completely to the Supreme Being the power of omniscience and omnipotence and reduce man to a mere vehicle of *His* will, then God in the Final Judgment would be judging essentially his own actions. This was not Einstein's God. Einstein's God, the originator of the equations, who constructed the universe on sound geometric principles, was not the God who slew the wicked and the innocent, the young and old alike; not a jealous God, nor the God of right and wrong, nor a personal God who rewards and punishes. Einstein's cosmic religion transcends the old prophetic concept of God who comforts the bereaved and shepherds the departed souls, but in no way denies the role of religion as an instructive tool. Science can teach only what has been learned about how nature functions, but to religion belongs the responsibility of teaching human conduct and defining the goal of human existence. "My religion consists of a humble admiration of the illimitably superior spirit who reveals himself in the slight details we are able to perceive with our frail and feeble mind. Ethics are a most important matter, but only for us, not God. That deeply emotional conviction of the Presence of a superior reasoning power, which is revealed in the incomprehensible universe, forms my idea of God."[149]

Hoping to counter the expected plague of publicity and the ever-present exploiters, Einstein announced that he would remain aboard the *Belgenland* the entire five days that the ship was to be docked in the port of New York; then safely through the Panama Canal and finally north to California. Even before he reached New York, however, the critics were out in force. The German press resented the fact that Einstein had booked passage on the Belgian ship, *Belgenland,* instead of the German *Europa,* whose destination was also New York; the newspaper failed to mention, however, that the *Belgenland* was going on to the west coast while the Europa's voyage terminated in New York. An anti-Zionist Jewish group in Germany chastised him for using his scientific fame to promote Zionism. Actually, the main emphasis on this trip was to be on science and pacifism and America's responsibility towards both. Zionism was not completely ignored, but it wasn't the main thrust of the trip.

A couple of days out on the Atlantic and the Einsteins became fully relaxed with the cares of Europe left far behind. His old jovial self again, Einstein played violin with the ship's band, signed autographs, and allowed himself to be photographed with other passengers. However, he imposed a catch. Each autograph or photograph was taxed a dollar for the benefit of the Berlin poor. The trip netted over $1,000.

Realizing that the ship had a radio-telephone, Einstein quipped that he hoped the journalists would not call him up in the middle of the night and ask him how he slept the night before. They didn't—but radio broadcast equipment was set up so that he could speak to his American audience without leaving the ship. In his address, Einstein praised the high ideals of America's political democracy and called upon the United States to take the lead in destroying the dreadful tradition of military violence.

Preventing persistent reporters from pursuing their quarry generally meets with about as much success as attempting to slow down the aging process. So Einstein relented and consented to see them. He recorded his reactions in his diary: "Just off Long Island hordes of reporters swarmed aboard . . . . Then a host of photographers rushed at me like angry wolves."[150]

Nevertheless, he faced the ordeal of a "spectacle unequaled in the history of New York" (according to reporter Louis Sherwin of the

New York Evening Post,) "with a smile; the photographers never had to ask him to smile." When cameramen followed Einstein up on the deck to pose for pictures, he stepped to the rail of the boat to get his first glimpse of the world-famed sky-line since his last visit in 1921. The photographers and reporters immediately clustered about him, completely obstructing his view, and one asked: 'Are you happy to be in America?' 'I will be happy,' he said, 'if I ever see it.'[151] When one reporter showed him a photograph that was taken on his previous trip, Einstein quipped, "My, but you fellows develop pictures fast!"[152] No he didn't have a one-sentence explanation of relativity, but perhaps the following illustration would do. If a young man is with his girl friend for half an hour, it would seem like a second. But if he sits on a stove for a second, it will seem like a half hour.

When questioned about whether he thought religion can promote the peace of the world, Einstein answered that up until then religion had not done it, and as to the future, he was not a prophet and could not predict. Asked his opinion of Hitler, Einstein dismissed him with the statement that Hitler was living on the empty stomachs of Germans. And as soon as economic conditions improve, Hitler will cease to be important.

Despite his announced intentions not to, Einstein finally yielded to the overwhelming pressure that he step ashore and visit New York. The next five days turned out to be a travel agent's dream, and a visitor's nightmare. Dapper Jimmy Walker, mayor of New York City, presented his guests with keys to the city at a crowded city hall ceremony. Nicholas Murray Butler, president of Columbia University, welcomed Einstein as "one of those gifted with . . . . almost superhuman powers . . . . The territory over which he rules is not bounded by widespread seas, by high mountains, by broad rivers or by any conventional line which separates peoples and divides languages. The territory over which his fame has gone and over which his authority extends flies no one flag and speaks no single tongue. It is the realm of ideas where men and women of every race, creed and clime may meet and claim common citizenship."[153]

From the steps of the city hall, Einstein admonished his fellow Zionists to pay great attention to *our* relations with the Arab people.

With a Rockefeller he discussed economics; with John Dewey, philosophy; with Adolph Ochs, he talked about the *New York Times;* with Felix Warburg, Zionism; and with Arturo Toscanini, Mozart.

They were then whisked off to a performance of Carmen at the "Met" followed by a Chanukah Festival at Madison Square Garden.

The highlight of the tour, and an honor singular to no other living person, was the viewing of a representation of Einstein's likeness in an arch over the west entrance of the Riverside Church in Manhattan. It was chiefly through the efforts of the church's pastor, Harry Emerson Fosdick, that the bust of Einstein stands in company with Euclid, Galileo, Newton, Faraday, and Lister. Looking up at his image, overlooking the Hudson River, Einstein impishly, if not somewhat irreverently remarked: "I might have imagined that they could make a Jewish saint out of me, but I never thought I'd become a Protestant one."[154]

In a speech on pacifism, December 14 at the Ritz Carlton Hotel, he stressed the need for reaching out to those who are not pacifists: "The aim of all pacifists must be to convince others of the immorality of war and rid the world of the shameful slavery of military service."[155] Einstein suggested two ways to accomplish this desired end; first, if only two percent of those intended for military service were to declare themselves war resisters who will not fight, then governments would be powerless—the number would be too great to be jailed. And the second, he suggested that we try to legitimatize the right to refuse military service.

After the hectic five-day go-round in New York, the weary Einsteins rested briefly in Havana. Consistent with his deep feeling for the human condition, Einstein noted in his diary: "Crisis on account of falling sugar-cane prices. Fine Spanish buildings. Academy, Geographic Society, always the same. Luxurious clubs side by side with naked poverty, mainly affecting the colored people. They live in windowless shacks."[156]

Through the Panama Canal, then north to San Diego steamed the *Belgenland* and its passengers had their first glimpse of the sunny west coast. But the price of popularity continued to be the loss of privacy: "The passengers are becoming more and more annoying. There is no end to this business of taking photographs . . . . Everyone has to have his picture taken with me . . . . the autograph business for the benefit of charity is flourishing."[157] The visiting, middle-aged European couple were fascinated by the fresh, uncluttered, and uninhibited life-style of southern California. From shopping in supermarkets to the excessive dependency on automobiles, they embraced the young, brash land and secretly welcomed the change.

New York had been a whirlwind in a few days. In Pasadena, where they were afforded that rare luxury called privacy in a "shingled gingerbread house," the pace slowed noticeably. Before settling in for the seminars at the California Institute of Technology, Einstein

Credit: Riverside Church

In company with representations of Euclid, Archimedes, Galileo, Kepler, Newton, Darwin and Pasteur, Einstein was the only living human being to be portrayed among the scientists, religious leaders and ancient world leaders on the portals of the Riverside Church, New York City.

toured Hollywood briefly. Here he met movie stars, directors, and producers, but politely declined several movie offers on the grounds that they did not have a part for a professor who played the violin.

Sound was new then, and the remarkable antiwar movie, "All Quiet On The Western Front," still a classic of its type, had just been completed. The book, by Erich Maria Remarque, had been published in Germany, but the movie had been banned there after a few showings. After a private showing in Hollywood, Einstein promised he would do what he could to get the movie released again in Germany.

Credit: Library of Congress

Albert and Elsa Einstein with reception committee at San Diego, California, December 31, 1930.

Credit: AIP

Physics department faculty and graduate students; California Institute of Technology, 1932.

Through his effort, in part, and through the efforts of the German League For Human Rights, the movie ban was lifted a year later.

In the early part of this century there was no evidence to indicate that galaxies other than our own existed. The telescopes then in use had sighted some cloudy gases in the distance, but all matter was thought to be contained in the one Milky Way galaxy. Until the advent of the 100″ telescope in 1917, the existence of other galaxies remained pure speculation. It was when Henrietta Leavitt at the Harvard Observatory began studying photographs of variable stars called "cepheids" that the field of astronomy began to appreciate the huge distances between matter. Cepheid variables, in simple language, are distance indicators to astronomers.

Harlow Shapley at Mount Wilson had removed the sun from the center of the Milky Way and placed it out on one of its spiral arms. A later measurement found our solar system riding some 30,000 light years from the galaxy's center and some 20,000 light-years from the outer edge. The most accurate figuring to date of our galaxy's dimension is 100,000 light-years across; that is, it takes light some 100,000 years to travel from one end of our galaxy to the other, at the speed

Credit: AIP

At the California Institute of Technology, Pasadena. Left to right: Walter Adams, Albert Michelson, Walter Mayer, Einstein, Robert Millikan. (Man to Einstein's left is unidentified.)

of 186,000 miles per second. Opinions were divided as to whether the distant nebulae (nebulae are large gaseous formations in outer space) were inside our galaxy or nongalactic. Then Edwin Hubble, also working at Mount Wilson, employing methods pioneered by Leavitt and Shapley, found cepheid variable stars several hundred thousand light-years away, in some nongalactic nebulae. This distance, admittedly too far off to lie within our galaxy, must then be part of a neighboring galaxy.

The discovery of one galaxy lying outside our Milky Way galaxy led to finding galaxies as numerous as stars in the Milky Way; literally millions of galaxies were "discovered." Galaxies were also found to congregate in "clusters." One of the most startling discoveries made was that galaxies were receding from one another at astounding speeds, up to one half the speed of light. And it seems that the farther away they were from each other, the faster they were receding.

The expanding universe of astronomer, Willem de Sitter, disagreed with the finite and unbounded universe of Einstein. Einstein saw evidence of this ever-expanding universe when he looked through

Credit: Brown Brothers

With Abbé George LeMaître, Pasadena, 1933.

the 100-inch telescope and consulted with de Sitter. An expanding universe encouraged Einstein more than it disturbed him and had no effect on the accuracy of his relativity theories.

A dinner honoring Einstein, held at the Athaneum on the ground of the California Institute of Technology in January of 1931 turned out to be a rare gathering of a group of Einstein "collaborators," American scientists working in the same phase of scientific thought. It was a notable occasion because of the high level of accomplishment of these men, some of whom are: Albert Michelson, Charles E. St. John, W.W. Campbell, Robert A. Millikan, Walter S. Adams, Richard C. Tolman, and Edwin Hubble. While Michelson, Millikan, and Campbell lauded the "immortal theories of relativity,' Einstein, for the most part, sought to assure Michelson of the importance of his work as a stepping stone to the "special theory." "You, my honored Dr. Michelson, began with this work when I was only a little youngster, hardly three feet high. It was you who led the physicists into new paths, and through your marvelous experimental work paved the way for the development of the theory of relativity. You uncovered an insidious defect in the ether theory of light, as it then existed, and stimulated the ideas of H.A. Lorentz and Fitzgerald, out of which the special theory of relativity developed."[158]

Before leaving the west coast for the trip east, Einstein addressed several hundred students as Cal. Tech. He cautioned them to use their scientific skills and knowledge to lighten the toils of man and not to bring out his destruction: "Concern for man himself must always constitute the chief objective of all technological effort . . . . never forget this when you are pondering over your diagrams and equations."[159]

With a "peace pipe" in the crook of his arm, a war-bonneted Einstein was dubbed the "Great Relative" on a Hopi, Arizona Indian reservation. From the rear platform of a train in Chicago, Einstein told his audience that he had despaired that governments would ever cooperate to abolish war or disarm willingly. The only way to a world of peace was to force governments to prohibit war as a means of settling disputes; and this could be accomplished only by the refusal to serve in the military. He called for supporting the "objectors" materially and morally: "When governments demand criminal actions from their citizens, we must sustain the objectors."[160]

In New York, aboard the *Deutschland,* he told the delegation from the War Resister's League essentially the same thing, and then added: "If members of pacifist organizations are not ready to make sacrifices by opposing authorities in peacetime at the risk of imprisonment or worse, they will fail. When war breaks out it is too late. Only the most steeled person can be expected to resist in time of war."[161]

Unable to fulfill his speaking commitment in New York because of "urgent negotiations with Arab friends," Weizmann cabled Einstein asking him to fill in for him. Einstein seldom, if ever, turned down such an appeal, and spoke at a fund-raising dinner at the Hotel Astor given by the American Palestine Committee.

President Hoover sent a message of goodwill to Einstein expressing his hope "that your visit to the United States has been as satisfying to you as it has been gratifying to the American people."

Einstein had looked forward to a long-awaited rest from the recent whirlwind of activity once aboard ship for their return to Germany. But the crowds seeking leadership and guidance traced him even to his ship's haven. An antiwar group asked for some words of encouragement, and the pacifist warrior complied.

The essence of his message was also contained in a previous interview with George Sylvester Viereck, Einstein had said: "I agree with the great American Benjamin Franklin, who said that there never was a good war or a bad peace . . . . I am not only a pacifist but a militant pacifist. I am willing to fight for peace. Nothing will end war unless the people themselves refuse to go to war . . . . Nothing that I can do or say will change the structure of the universe. But maybe, by raising my voice I can help the greatest of all causes—good will among men and peace on earth."[162]

29

NAZIS GAIN

Hitler traveled the length and breadth of Germany, inciting the unemployed to hatred and violence. His message was simple: he promised uniforms and bread for the blood of Jews, liberals, communists, socialists, unionists, and whoever else stood in his "messianic" way. His demonic appeal was directed mostly to the dissatisfied and the militarists, those who wanted someone else to solve their problems, even if it meant the loss of their freedoms. They didn't seem to mind the possibility of that loss, since with the exception of the few years of the Weimar Republic, Germany had never in its history existed as a free or democratic nation. Someone to lead them, someone telling them what to do, and when and how to do it, is part of the German heritage. And so, when a demagogue with the emotional appeal of a Hitler told them Germany could become great again, they dutifully donned their "brown shirts" and roamed the streets of Berlin screaming, "Death to the Jews; Germany for Germans of pure Aryan stock."

The politicians and even the intellectuals allowed these street Nazis their excesses. Hasn't unrest and unemployment always prompted this kind of reaction against minorities before? Why should it be different now? Why not let the public act out its anger? Once they get it out of their system, a pogrom or two, we can get back to the business of binding up the nation's wounds. Thus they reasoned. And so, once again the great German body was being wagged by the lowly Austrian tail. And when we trace German history back only a few years do we see that to the previous alliance with Austria falls the blame for the chaotic conditions in Germany in the early 30's. Yes, some will sight the great depression of 1929 as the prime cause of Germany's woes, but it should be kept in mind that all nations suffered the disastrous effects of the stock market crash, and only Germany sought to solve their financial problems by a calculated program of systematic death and destruction on a scale of such huge proportions.

This was the shocking state of affairs when the Einsteins returned home. If Hitler seized power and put into practice the promises he was making to the German people, then truly all freedoms would be lost. Einstein was in the forefront of those who took a firm and open stand against the advancing Nazi tide. He was among those who came to the defense of Professor Emil Gumbel of Heidelberg University. Gumbel, like Einstein, was a longtime pacifist who also supported the Weimar government. Through his pamphlets and books Gumbel unflinchingly protested the several unsolved and unpunished political murders and thus incurred the wrath of the Nazi-oriented students. His disclosures of the secret rearming of Germany, which was in violation of the Versailles Treaty, brought on such violent demonstrations by the Nazis, both at the university and at his home, that he feared for his family's safety. At a meeting in Berlin in April 1931, convened by the German League For Human Rights for the purpose of supporting Gumbel, Einstein was called on to speak.

He called, first of all, for the betterment of society, not its destruction. Then he asked for a respect for honest opinion and the tolerance that existed in German universities a century ago. Einstein said:

> In those days men strove for that larger political unity called Germany . . . . Today too, there exist people who are eager for social progress who believe in tolerance and freedom of thought and who strive for a larger political unity of what is now called Europe. The conduct of the academic youth against Professor Emil J. Gumbel, by failing to live up to the ideals of tolerance, justice and truth, offers one of the saddest aspects of our time. Professor Gumbel's only offense has been to fight against political murder and in so doing he has maintained high ethical standards. What is to become of a people who brutally harass such a contemporary and whose leaders offer no resistance to the base mob? What is so terrible is the way inexperienced youth is being misled by self-seeking movements. If it goes further in this direction, we shall arrive at a reign of red terror by way of a fascist regime of tyranny."[163]

In another direction, Einstein wrote a personal appeal to President Thomas Masaryk of Czechoslovakia, a man whose democratic principles he admired, asking for clemency in the case of a Czech war resister who had been given a long jail term. Throughout the year he kept up a constant barrage of antiwar statements charging that governments have become too dependent on the armaments industry for the employment of many workers and are reluctant to reduce their military budget for fear of the resultant unemployment.

Before he left for a four-week lecturing visit to England, Einstein was informed that Americans, too, were beginning to heed the call for war resistance. An American periodical, *The World Tomorrow,* had conducted a survey among clergymen to gauge their level of anti-war feeling. Out of almost 20,000 who replied, more than half said that churches should go on record as refusing to support another war; more than half pledged personal nonsupport. Einstein was gratified that his efforts and those of others were beginning to bear fruit. He also knew, however, that peacetime declarations of pacifism all go up in smoke once hostilities begin, and so he pressed his peace campaign further in England. Giving the Rhodes lectures and accepting an honorary degree from Oxford were part of the planned program. Once these were out of the way he met with members of the War Resisters International, a pacifist organization that had established inroads in some fifty-six countries.

With her husband on the road, Elsa had been busily preparing the house in Caputh for summer occupancy; she hoped he would relax there from his exhausting excursions. Unfortunately, this was not the time for slowing down; even the peaceful waters of Caputh would have to wait. While opportunistic politicians preached peace and prepared for the upcoming 1932 Geneva Conference on Disarmament, Einstein stepped up his peace appeals. He had reserved his strongest statement to date for the conference of the War Resisters International held at Lyons, France between August 1 and August 4, 1931. Einstein cautioned the delegates that they must do more than merely talk disarmament; that to leave the matter solely in the hands of the politicians would be folly.

> Those who think that the danger of war is past are living in a fool's paradise. We have to face today a militarism far more powerful and destructive than the militarism of the Great War . . . . I appeal especially to the intellectuals of the world. I appeal to my fellow scientists to refuse to cooperate in research for war purposes. I appeal to the preachers to seek truth and renounce national prejudices. I appeal to the men of letters to declare themselves unequivocally. I ask every newspaper which prides itself on supporting peace to encourage the peoples to refuse war service. I ask editors to challenge men of eminence and of influence . . . . This is no time for temporizing. You are either for war or against war. If you are for war you must encourage science, finance, industry, religion and labor to exert their power to make your national armaments as efficient and deadly as can be. If you are against war you must encourage them to resist it to the

uttermost . . . . Let this generation take the greatest step forward ever made in the life of man. Let it contribute to those who follow the inestimable gift of a world in which the barbarity of war has been forever renounced. We can do it if we will. It requires only that all who hate war shall have courage to say that they will not have war.

I appeal to all men and women, whether they be eminent or humble, to declare before the World Disarmament Conference at Geneva in February, that they will refuse to give any further assistance to war or the preparation for war. I ask them to tell their governments this in writing and to register their decision by informing me that they have done so.

I shall expect to have thousands of responses to my appeal. They should be addressed to me at the headquarters of the War Resisters International, 11 Abbey Rd. Enfield, Middlesex, England. To enable this great effort to be carried through effectively, I have authorized the establishment of the Einstein War Resisters International Fund. Contributions to this fund should be sent to the Treasurer of the War Resisters International, 11 Abbey Rd. Enfield, Middlesex, England.[164]

Though addressed to the War Resisters, Einstein's message was clearly directed at the delegates of the upcoming Geneva Disarmament Conference. He hoped, that from the size of the response, the delegates would become convinced that millions of people in this world were demanding more than just new rules to replace the old rules for mass destruction, that the people of the world were unequivocally demanding peace. Had Einstein's appeal elicited a great response from world citizenry, then perhaps the Geneva Conference would have had a fighting chance to truly begin disarming the world's military. But as it turned out, the response was minimal, and so was Europe's last hope for peace.

Disappointment because his appeal failed did not embitter Einstein. Instead, he became even more curious as to why the warring instinct was so strong in man; why man when given a choice, invariably chooses war to settle differences. Reason obviously plays no part in why man kills his fellow man at regular intervals; neither does religion, for all religions condemn killing. Einstein could only conclude that people somehow have become convinced that their fate should be no better than that of sheep, to be helplessly led to the slaughter. There is one glaring difference, though; sheep do not know they are about to be slaughtered. Strange, he thought, that whole populations stand ready to lay down their lives, decade after decade and century after century for a man-made, artificial boundary. The psychology of it all was beyond him. Perhaps some one more knowledgeable in the workings of the mind could provide a clue, someone like Sigmund Freud. He made a mental note to inquire.

Einstein spent the remainder of the summer at Caputh in company with Mayer working on the second and newer approach to the unified field; a paper that was based on the work he did at Pasadena. In October, a flood of incomprehensible language laced with a maze of absolutely impossible equations was ready for publication. The layman easily becomes convinced that science is best left to the scientists when he is faced with language such as the following: "Kaluza's theory rests on the assumption that the physical space-time continuum is five dimensional (instead of, as formerly, four dimensional) in which the empiric four-dimensionality of the physical continuum can be accounted for by the hypothesis that the physical variables are independent of the coordinates X5."[165]

In the winter of 1931 Hans Albert had accepted the post of first engineer in the hydraulic laboratory of the ETH. Of the opinion that his father could thrive in Switzerland as well, and without the abuse he was suffering from Germany's right wing, Hans Albert tried to convince his father that he, too, should consider leaving Germany. But hampered by obligations and curtailed by responsibilities the "old man" chose to remain where he was, for the time being at least. He felt his leaving now, in a time of great stress, would be a desertion of his friends in science and pacifism. Hans pointed out to his father that in another country his work could proceed without interruption; English science would be delighted if he decided to settle in Oxford. Cal. Tech., too, by inviting him back for a second seminar in December, made it known with little adacemic restraint that they would be happy to create a suitable situation for him should he choose to work there permanently. But, middle age made him less susceptible to change; besides, he loved his "little house."

The more astute political viewers acknowledged that if the Nazis did not come to power in the 1932 elections, von Hindenburg would reestablish the military monarchy. In either case, it would be a step back towards autocracy and bode ill for freedom in Germany; the Republic would become a relic of the past. It was obvious, even to a stubborn will like Einstein's that the present unpleasant situation in Germany could lead only to an intolerable state of affairs regardless of who came to power. Was he really too old to be uprooted?

Perhaps not. He decided that he might do well to rethink his son's suggestion.

Hans Albert Einstein, his son Bernhard, and Einstein; 1932.

30

GERMANY IN TURMOIL

The Einstein's second trip to Pasadena began early in December of 1931, aboard a small ship that did not list New York City as a port of call; the very reason they booked passage on it. Einstein was not up to the hectic rounds of dinners and speeches that would have been demanded of him; of serving as a drawing card. Aboard ship, as well, he scrupulously kept apart from other passengers, allowing no photographs, autographs, or interviews. This time he abided by it; he had a lot to think about.

He thought about the unmailed letter, addressed to Max Planck, which he had left on his desk in Berlin. In the letter he had requested Planck to take the necessary steps to revoke his German citizenship, a measure prompted by "the events of recent days." The fact that he wished to retain membership in the Prussian Academy of Sciences indicated that his protest was meant only to partially sever his associations with Germany: "So far, I have always rejected offers from abroad, however tempting, which would have forced me to leave the scene of my work. I hope I shall be able to maintain this attitude also in the future."[166] He couldn't quite bring himself to make the clean and final break, but he was edging towards it, pushed in that direction by Germany's vulnerability to the caress of Fascism. Fascism was anathema to Jews and freedom.

That past September, an emerging Japan bent on expansion, had invaded a China decimated by internal strife and grabbed Manchuria "for its own good." The rest of the world registered only a mild condemnation, and not one Western nation offered to come to the aid of the "sleeping giant." How could any of them seriously object to Japan's intrusion, when most of the West had already carved their own colonies on the shores of the Chinese mainland. The League of Nations was of no help, either. Lacking any real restraining power, the League dutifully formed a committee of inquiry, which subsequently was coquettishly convinced by the polite Japanese that Manchuria needed Japanese protection from a greedy Russia. It was a classic example of a land-poor nation, lopping off a piece of her neighbor's territory without the slightest protest or counteraction from the rest of the world. Was this naked aggression conducive to the cause of disarmament or peace? Einstein thought not and pointed an accusing finger at the monetary interests. He reasoned that if the governments of the United States, France, England, and Germany demanded that Japan cease her military adventure, under the threat of a complete economic boycott, no Japanese government could long survive and would be forced to desist from aggression. Einstein demanded to know: "then why is this not brought about? Why must each person and each nation keep trembling for their existence? Because each seeks his own miserable, momentary advantage and will not subordinate himself to the welfare and prosperity of the whole."[167]

No, Einstein had to admit to himself, the nations of the world will not act in concert for the maintainence of peace; there is not yet a powerful enough world body, or group of nations, with the desire or power to guarantee each country safe national borders. Then, he was asked, how can well-meaning nations disarm, when to do so would leave them open to aggression? To this Einstein responded: "One cannot simply and categorically demand disarmament without acquainting the threatened countries with the arrangements through which they would become safe from aggression."[168] These type of international arrangements, in reality, did not exist and further supposed a cooperative international body with a strength and willingness to impose peace. At that time, the nations of the world showed no inclination to act together to avert or discourage aggression; far from it. This left the pacifists almost nowhere to turn, except to the Geneva Disarmament Conference.

Though Einstein had his own misgivings about the eventual outcome of the conference, he had no choice but to support its efforts in an increasingly isolationist America. He reminded his American audiences that by pushing her claims America helped hasten the decline of Europe and must therefore share the blame for Europe's problems: "Let us be outspoken and straightforward, the disarmament conference presents the final opportunity to you, no less than to us, to preserve the best that humanity has produced. It is toward America, the strongest and relatively speaking, healthiest among nations, that the eyes and hopes of all mankind are directed."[169]

Einstein had greater faith in public opinion than in elected or appointed representatives. He called upon the people of the world, from the villages and cities, to let their voices be heard by the delegates, and to impress upon them their belief in the futility of war. Otherwise, if left to their own devices, the delegates would turn out only compromises and newly agreed upon rules for waging future wars. He reminded the public that war is not a game with rules (he remembered the shattered village of Rheims) that are scrupulously adhered to. In time of war all rules go by the board. Nothing previously agreed to any longer applies; agreements on arms limitations are nothing but scraps of paper, which burn exceedingly well in a fire. Only the unconditional elimination of war could save mankind from disaster. There could be no half-measures.

For all his prodding, pleading, urging, and cajoling, Einstein's calls for peace and disarmament, while politely received, were accepted as nothing more than a kind of social entertainment. The prevailing attitude in America was that if Europeans wanted war, that was their business, as long as they kept it over there. Americans wanted no part of it. The isolationists reached back almost two centuries to a statement made by George Washington, in which he warned his fellow Americans not to become involved in the troublesome affairs of Europe. Einstein realized that an uninvolved and isolationist America would spell doom to a divided and quarrelsome Europe. On the other hand, an America assuming an active role in world politics could spell the difference between a war-torn and a stable and cooperative Europe.

It was an unscheduled meeting with a visiting educator, in Pasadena, that was to determine the direction of the last third of Einstein's life. Abraham Flexner, the educator, had arrived in California to seek the advice of Robert Millikan with a view towards establishing an advanced educational institution. Nothing like it existed in America: "a haven where scholars and scientists may regard the world and its phenomena as their laboratory without being carried off in the maelstrom of the immediate; it should be simple, comfortable, quiet without being monastic or remote; it should be afraid of no issue; yet it should be under no pressure from any side which might tend to force its scholars to be prejudiced either for or against any particular solution of the problems under study; and it should provide the facilities, the tranquility, and the time requisite to fundamental inquiry into the unknown. Its scholars should enjoy complete intellectual liberty, and be absolutely free from administrative responsibilities or concerns."[170] The idea was conceived by Flexner and he managed to obtain funding, several million dollars worth, from Louis Bamberger and Bamberger's sister, Mrs. Felix Fuld.

Millikan found the idea interesting and suggested that Flexner talk it over with Einstein, who incidentally just happened to be visiting. A phone call and soon Flexner found himself explaining the needs and purposes of such an institution to Einstein. The discussion lasted through lunch and into the afternoon with the two men in perfect agreement. Einstein gave his thoughts on the necessity for financial and intellectual independence in education. The conversation centered solely on the physical setup and ultimate purpose of the institute; no reference to staffing was made. Before parting, a further meeting was arranged for the coming spring when both would be in England.

That May, when Einstein lectured at Oxford and Cambridge, he met with Flexner as arranged, and they again discussed the proposed Institute For Advanced Study. Without prearrangement, Flexner seized the moment and suggested that should the professor decide that his future research could be done just as well in Princeton, he could be assured that the door would be open and on his own terms. Einstein puffed on his pipe and recalled the Princeton of peaceful meadows and streets shaded with oaks and elms, where a pipe and learning go well together. He made no decision then and there; the suddenness of the extemporaneous offer took Einstein completely by surprise. But the thought of leaving Berlin had occupied his mind ever since Hans Albert had suggested it; and this Princeton offer might just be the ideal answer. So that they might discuss the matter further he invited Flexner to visit him in Caputh that summer.

The April elections, which gave von Hindenburg a six million plurality over Hitler, were welcomed by most Germans, even if it did mean the end of the Weimar Republic and the reinstituting of rule by the military. The result was seen as the lesser of two evils, and it was hoped that the defeat would forever banish that Austrian, Hitler, from German politics.

Whatever the outcome, Einstein was thinking seriously of the future. Europe was rampant with fascism and communism and those espousing neither, if they chose to remain, would be left with little by way of freedom of expression. As Flexner saw the situation, the state of affairs in Germany would do more to move Einstein West than any promises or offers he could make.

31

GENEVA DISARMAMENT CONFERENCE, 1932

Never before, in the history of man, had so many nations gathered together for the purpose of trying to achieve world disarmament. Some sixty-six nations had sent delegates to the Geneva Conference to work towards an agreement that would require nations to settle their disagreements by international arbitration, without resorting to war. Such an agreement was the hope of the delegates and the millions of well-wishers in February 1932. And it could have become a reality had the nations been willing to abide by the decisions of an international arbitration committee.

Disputes between nations are generally settled in one of two ways, peaceful agreement or the use of force. If we are sincere in our desire to have a peaceful world, we must renounce the use of force in settling our tribal differences and find a method to arrive at a peaceful agreement. If nations find it impossible to come to an agreement by themselves, an arbitrating committee must help settle the matter. The only trouble with international committees is that their decisions would reduce the sovereignty of the member nations; and this loss of sovereignty the nations of the world were not prepared to accept.

After several weeks of no progress, the hope for real disarmament faded away and the conference delegates busied themselves with the task of trying to reduce the destructiveness of war; that is, they were engaged in the regulation of, rather than the elimination of, war. What followed amounted to nothing more than wrangling and arguing. They disagreed as to the acceptable dimensions of an airplane's wing span; the size, speed and number of battleships; the types of allowable artillery shells; how big or small a tank should be; and how many of each of the above would constitute a number large enough to be a deterrent, yet small enough not to be considered a threat. On and on it went in meaningless haggling, foundering helplessly.

Asked his opinion of the proceedings in Geneva, Einstein retorted: "You cannot regulate war, you can only abolish it." Urged by his pacifist friends, Einstein came to Geneva in the company of Lord Ponsonby, chairman of the War Resisters International, and by way of an unofficial invitation from Arthur Henderson, President of the Disarmament Conference. It's uncertain what was expected of

Einstein at the conference, but it was certain that his appearance gave the delegates a much needed lift. And his easily recognizable figure making his way through the halls of the Peace Palace gave the cameramen a new face to photograph.

It was obvious from his initial statement to the press that Einstein had not come to praise the work of the delegates, though he did concede that those gathered at Geneva were men of intelligence: "but of great human qualities I have seen as yet nothing . . . . We are not satisfied that, as a result of what officials are doing at Geneva, we shall get disarmament in our lifetime or in our children's."[171] It's difficult to imagine what Einstein hoped to accomplish by taking pot shots at the members of the conference who themselves were honestly convinced that their work would ultimately benefit mankind. Not so, thought Einstein. As long as the delegates were "appointed" representatives of their respective governments and not directly elected by the people, the delegates could not truly represent the will of the people, nor would the conference reflect the people's desire for disarmament and peace. However, it must be remembered that, at the time, few of the peoples of the world, the ones who would have to do the fighting and dying, enjoyed the privileges of enfranchisement; at best, Einstein's plan was visionary and ahead of its time. While Einstein can be criticized for criticizing, he felt his presence could do no more harm than what already had been done to the dream of a disarmed world by the delegates. His alternative would have been to sit idly by while the future peace of the world was fragmented away. No, it was not a comedy of peace as author Conrad Bercovici had derisively suggested. For Einstein it was not a comedy at all, but a tragedy; "the greatest tragedy of modern times."

The peace or antiwar or disarmament movement, like all worldwide movements, was made up of individuals and groups of various political and moral shadings, running the gamut from radical, through moderate, to conservative. One group, called the Anti-War Congress, which typified the activist groups of the day, became *so* involved in its secondary thrust, that its original purpose was completely overshadowed. The chief target of the Anti-War Congress supposedly was Japanese militarism in China; an issue that could arouse sympathy in the people of the Western world, if not in their governments. Henri Barbusse, chief mover of the congress, asked Einstein to join in the protest. He had gathered as sponsors some of the most illustrious names in the world, including Mme. Sun Yat Sen, Theodore Dreiser, Upton Sinclair, John dos Passos, Heinrich Mann, Maxim Gorki, George Bernard Shaw, Romain Rolland, H.G. Wells, and

Paul Langevin. Einstein was impressed and agreed to participate. Barbusse then sent Einstein the text of an announcement to be released to the public above the personal signatures of the sponsors. The statement correctly chastised the Japanese, but also accused the imperialist powers. It went on, in typical left-wing jargon to extol the virtues of the Soviet economy: "Cooperative of workers . . . . abolition of exploitation . . . . dedication to the great task of socialist and human construction . . . ." If Einstein admired Lenin for leading the Russian people out of a Czarist slave-state, for the same reason, he disavowed admiration for those who imposed another slave-state in its place; he refused to put his signature to the statement. Barbusse answered that Einstein should not listen to anti-Soviet propaganda; that, if he sincerely wanted to know the true conditions, he should travel to Russia himself. Einstein shot back that if Barbusse should suddenly find himself in Russia, it would be in a Russian jail or Siberia, if indeed they allowed him to survive at all. He would sign almost any declaration, Einstein said, supporting peace, but not one that praises Bolshevism and glorifies the Soviet Union. Realizing that the World Anti-War Congress was dominated by Communists, Einstein completely withdrew his support and did not attend the August conference in Amsterdam.

At the urging of the Committee For Intellectual Cooperation, Einstein wrote to Sigmund Freud and asked the age-old question *"Varum Krieg?"* (Why War?). "Is there any way of delivering man from the menace of war?" In his four-thousand word answer, Freud replied that violence was basic to man's instinct to survive; the same is true in the animal world. In society, self-preservation and acquisition are both accomplished by violence or its implied threat. Ownership of "things" was and still is decided by violence. The very laws that govern man and the land are all supported by the threat of violence. Communities of like interests, deny the use of aggression to the individual, but give over to those powers they hire to enforce the laws the power of violence: "Our logic is at fault if we ignore the fact that right is founded on brute force and even today needs violence to enforce it."[173]

Between differing communities there is unequal power, hence conflicts between geographically separated groups; between tribes, cities, states, and countries, most conflicts were resolved by war, few by mutually respected agreements. Past wars have produced larger geographical entities, while the destructive results have remained comparatively small. Future wars could possibly unify the world, but the price may be a great destructiveness.

Einstein: Why are we pacifists?
Freud: Pacifists we are, since our organic nature wills us thus to be.[174]

Freud suggests that we have been domesticated, like household pets, by our culture and civilization. And with this change we have come, unlike our ancestors, to rely less on instinct than on reason, which has the effect of mitigating aggressive behavior and rejecting war.

Einstein: How do we prevent war?
Freud: There is but one sure way of ending war and that is the establishment, by common consent of a central control, which shall have the last word in every conflict of interest.

To arrive at a verbal solution is one thing; to make it work is something else. Freud sees no way to implement the prevention of war: "it would seem that any effort to replace brute force by the might of an ideal is, under present conditions, doomed to fail."[175]

Conclusion: only the development of high cultural standards will diminish man's destructive behavior.

It was a cold, drizzly afternoon in June when Abraham Flexner, clad in an appropriate topcoat, arrived at Caputh. He found Einstein wearing summer flannels out on the veranda. "Aren't you chilly?" Flexner asked, surveying his costume. "No" he rejoined, "I dress according to the season, not according to the weather. It is summer."[176]

They talked all afternoon, about the Institute For Advanced Study, then through supper, and concluded past ten in the evening. Einstein was enthusiastic: *"Ich bin Flamme und Feuer dafur."*[177] And still he wouldn't make it final and say yes. But Flexner was completely convinced that Einstein was coming to Princeton.

Another visitor to Caputh that discouraging summer of '32 when nothing seemed to go "right" except the government, was Antonina Vallentin; she brought a message of despair to Elsa. She had recently been in the company of the commander of Germany's ghost army, General Hans von Seeckt. He confided to her that there was great danger ahead for any of her friends who were Jewish. Pointedly, he told her, "Warn Einstein, particularly. His life is not safe here anymore."[178] It hardly seemed the setting for disturbing news; the scenic lake, the quiet, dirt road leading to the lethargic village, the branches of the trees swaying in the slight breeze. Elsa mentioned Flexner's offer:" 'Does that mean he has accepted?' . . . . 'No,' Elsa answered, 'he cannot resign himself to a final departure'." Vallentin relates: "I went so far as to say that to leave him in Germany was to perpetrate murder. This word stung her to the quick."[179]

The sense of danger finally penetrated to Einstein himself; he could no longer walk alone in the woods or along the lakefront; his secretary would have to accompany him. The next morning he sent a note to Flexner in Berlin accepting the Princeton position. But still he would not make the break a complete one. His ties to Berlin and Caputh were so strong that the impending catastrophe and the warnings of friends were not sufficiently persuasive to drive him away completely. When the Nazis temporarily eased their terror, because of a rise in employment, he would needle his friends saying that perhaps their pessimism was misplaced.

The arrangements with Flexner included a five-month visit to Princeton for a period of five years; these would be the fall and early winter months. The new position would necessitate taking a leave of absence from the Kaiser Wilhelm Institute and the University of Berlin as well. He was committed to one more winter of study at Pasadena and would continue his springtime lectures at Christ Church, Oxford. The soonest then that he would appear at Princeton would be the fall of 1933. He could have obtained a similar situation at Pasadena, but at Princeton he was able to secure an appointment for Mayer as well.

In August, Hans Albert came for a visit, bringing along his wife and infant son, Bernhard. Through several sailing afternoons Hans was unable to convince his father to take a position in Switzerland. It was the last time he and Hans were to see each other for several years. Mileva and Edward he never saw again.

Einstein went sailing every day, against a backdrop of a brilliant orange-red autumn, soaking up as much of the pastoral setting as possible, in his baggy pants and old sweater; and with the glow of a summer tan, "he radiated health and well-being." When they were leaving to return to Berlin, Einstein turned to his wife and said: "Before you leave our villa this time, take a good look at it.' 'Why' she asked. 'You will never see it again,' Einstein replied quietly."[180]

32

HITLER BECOMES CHANCELLOR

The years of Einstein's tireless and constant efforts in the cause of peace and disarmament did not go unnoticed by, or win the approval of, the right wing and isolationist groups in America. Millikan, too, did not escape criticism for his friendship with and sponsorship of Einstein. And when, inadvertently, on some antiwar petition Einstein's name happened to appear along with that of a socialist or communist, by association, he too was assumed to be a "red." This guilt by association maneuver was used by the "Women's Patriotic Corporation" in their misguided effort to protect America's innocents from the impure thoughts of a pacifist. These women protested to the State Department, denouncing Einstein as a communist, demanding that he not be allowed to enter the United States. Because he was amused by the display of blind fervor so typical of the uninformed, Einstein put everything else aside, temporarily, to write his reactions:

> Give heed to the sage, patriotic, dear ladies, and remember that the capital of mighty Rome was at one time saved by the cackling of her faithful geese. Never before has any attempt of mine at an approach to the beautiful sex met with such an energetic rebuff; even should perchance such have been the case, then certainly not by so many all at once.

> But aren't they perfectly right, these watchful citizenesses? Why should one admit to one's presence one who would devour hard-boiled capitalists with the same appetite and relish as once upon a time the ogre Minotaurus in Crete devoured luscious Greek maidens—a person who in addition is so vulgar as to oppose every war, except the inevitable one with his own wife?[181]

It's axiomatic, in the world of communications, that by the time a lie gets spread halfway around the world, the truth is just getting its pants on. By the same token, the farce started by these women continued through official channels, with the State Department relaying the alarm to its consular office in Berlin. In previous departures, the matter of entry visas was handled by the shipping lines; this time the

219

Einsteins were requested to appear before the American cousul. It was an unprecedented request, but they complied. When the young subordinate questioned Einstein about his pacifism and the organizations to which he subscribed, Einstein played along respectfully. But as the questions ranged into the absurd, Einstein became annoyed.

What is the purpose of your visit to the United States? What are your politics? Who are your friends? Einstein recoiled in disbelief. He inquired, somewhat angrily, if the young man was entirely serious; that many scientific, civic and religious institutions in the United States have invited him to visit with them. And if he continued to play silly games with such stupid questions, then he (Einstein) would simply not go. And he and Elsa stormed out the door.

Of course, the newspapers printed the story, properly upbraiding the inquisitor and condemning the narrow policies of the State Department, to the latter's embarrassment. But soon there was a telephone call from an apologetic consul general assuring the Einsteins their entry visas. Before the misunderstanding was settled, Einstein in a lighter moment had said to his wife: "Ach, Elsa, here I have two honorary keys to the city of New York, and it looks as if they would not give me a chance to use even one of them."[182]

While others personally attacked Einstein, Assemblyman Frank M. Travaleine, Jr. of New Jersey introduced a resolution stating in part, "the addition of the said Professor Albert Einstein to the faculty of a New Jersey institution of learning brings with it honor to the state of New Jersey and its people." Travaleine also invited Einstein to address the Legislature.

In early December, the Einsteins once again embarked on a trans-Atlantic voyage, and again the ship made straight for the Panama Canal, then north to Pasadena. As on the previous trip, they kept apart occupying themselves with reading. Elsa was particularly worried about having left Margot in a recuperative nursing home. Though her daughter had almost recovered from a recent illness, Elsa, as always, was torn by conflicting loyalties. The completely devoted mother, she felt she could be of greater help to her daughter than the latter's husband. Margot did recover without her.

The high point of the 1932–33 session at Pasadena was the presence of Abbé George LeMaître, a Belgian priest from the University of Louvain. LeMaître had a unique theory as to the reason why the galaxies were receding from each other and the force that gave them the initial push that sent them speeding through space, "in the beginning." The theory had first been published in an obscure jour-

nal in 1927 and eventually came to the attention of Arthur Eddington. It was LeMaître's premise that the universe, as we view it today,
began somewhat violently after a "primeval atom" of gigantic proportions, for whatever reason, blew itself apart. This "big bang"
would have had to occur some ten to twenty billion years ago, and
the still receding galaxies are sufficient evidence that the effects of the
initial explosion are still in play. Today's investigations show no
evidence that the galaxies are slowing up, therefore, any thought that
the galaxies may slow down and eventually reverse direction and be
drawn back to some central point in space should not be the concern
of any creature living in our planetary family, for our sun would
already have burned itself out long before the possibility of any such
occurrence.

Einstein thought that LeMaître's explanation was the most beautiful and satisfactory explanation of the moment of creation to which
he had ever listened. LeMaître, in an uncommon balancing act, saw
no conflict between religion and science once he realized that the
whale could not have scientifically swallowed Jonah and once he accepted the scientific fact that the creation of the universe, as we know
it, encompassed some bilions of years, not just six days. LeMaître
suggests that the old controversy between religion and science
vanishes when you realize that the Bible teaches the way to salvation
and does not purport to be a textbook of science.

At that moment, the unstable political situation in Germany was
looked at with guarded optimism. Just prior to the Einsteins boarding ship (on the way to America) the elections had reduced the
number of seats occupied by the Nazis in the Reichstag; their threat
seemed to be on the wane. In December, von Hindenburg appointed
Schleicher as chancellor and told Gregor Strasser, a Nazi leader who
opposed Hitler's demand for total power, "I give you my word of
honor as a Prussian General that I shall never permit this 'Bohemian
Corporal' to become Chancellor."[182]

Meanwhile, at Cal. Tech., Einstein warned his student audiences
that freedom was being curtailed throughout the world; justice was
deteriorating, and military service was being made compulsory in
more and more countries. In softer tones this year, Einstein hoped
that America could be coaxed from her "understandable isolation."
He also warned that "the continued policy of aloofness would not
only injure all mankind, but harm the United States as well."[184]

Von Hindenburg's appointment of Hitler as chancellor on January 30, 1933 did not come as a complete surprise to Einstein. He had

predicted as much the previous summer at Caputh when asked whether a military regime might not curb the Nazis: "I am convinced that a military regime will not prevent the imminent National Socialist revolution."[185]

Now that the Nazi revolution had succeeded, what were the Einsteins to do? Through February decisions were made, plans changed, and routes altered. Mainly, Einstein kept asking himself how to deal with this new and real menace, Hitler, who had vowed death to the Jews, unions, liberals, socialists, communists, and pacifists? Or should his threats not be taken seriously, and be considered only the inflammatory oratory of a malcontent? Would Hitler, like Schleicher, hold power for only a few months; should we sit tight and wait him out? Others might, but not Einstein; he knew what to expect, brutality and slavery. The first step Einstein took to demonstrate his disapproval of the Nazi takeover was to cancel a lecture he was scheduled to deliver to the Prussian Academy of Science, at the end of March. Meanwhile Professor Gumbel hurriedly left Germany.

Hitler's first goal as dictator was to slam the iron bars shut over the nation, to gain complete mastery over the people. With new elections due on March 5 and the economic picture improving, it was not a sure-shot certainty that the Nazis would win a majority in the Reichstag or that Hitler himself would continue in power. There was a good chance that the German voters might decide on a more moderate candidate. Hitler could not tolerate the existence of a freedom of choice in elections; it grated against his political grain; and so he plotted to get rid of his opposition, to destroy them. Thereupon, he and his two closest conspirators, Goering and Goebbels, hatched a plot that was destined to propel the ex-corporal into indisputable control over Germany—the setting of the Reichstag fire. They engineered the Reichstag fire primarily to give Hitler an issue with which to galvanize the German people behind him. Secondly, they could put the blame on the communists. If the plot paid off, and the people "bought it," he could get rid of the communists with the consent of the people. After the successful completion of that mission, the dictatorship would be well on its way to controlling every phase of life in Germany. Unbelievably, the scheme worked. On February 27, 1933, while the Einsteins were still in Pasadena, the fire was set. Hitler, as chancellor, stormed about the country, campaigning every waking minute of the next six days against the perpetrators of the fire, the communists. He also blamed socialists, Catholics, and Jews. By the time the demagoguery was over the half-terrorized German people had given Hitler a mandate of supreme authority. With that mandate began the cruelest reign of terror and the coldest, most wanton mass murders that have ever befallen mankind.

March 10, on the eve of his departure from the West coast, Einstein told the press, "I am not going home."[186] He would not live in Germany while Hitler ruled. When news of his statement reached around the world, offers came pouring in from universities in France, Spain, Holland, Belgium, Palestine, and Switzerland, as well as the United States. It was also common knowledge that Oxford had long been trying to effect his residence there. Although he would not go back to Germany, Einstein put off making his decision as to where he would finally settle until after he had returned to Europe.

At a luncheon on March 14 in Chicago, in honor of his fifty-fourth birthday, the usually smiling professor had no smile for the cameras, no little jokes. His thoughts were with the reports from Germany describing the concentration camps and the summary dismissal of Jews from teaching and other professional jobs. And this was just the beginning of Hitler's reign of terror. The only bright spot in Chicago was Einstein's meeting with Clarence Darrow, whose defense in the Scopes trial he had admired.

In New York he was met aboard the train by the German consul, Paul Schwarz, who warned Einstein not to return to Germany under any circumstances; Hitler's dirty work had begun. And if Einstein did go back, the Nazis would drag him through the streets by his hair. Elsa, shaking with fear, was inconsolable; her daughters were still in Berlin. Not anticipating the speed and fury with which the Nazis were herding innocent people off to concentration camps to be "nazified," the Einsteins had made no contingency plans. With all their family and friends still in Germany, along with all their worldly possessions, they literally had with them little more than the clothing on their backs. Elsa held tightly to the return tickets to Belgium and some cash.

To further the work of the Hebrew University of Jerusalem and the Jewish Telegraphic Agency, Einstein spoke on the evening of March 16 at a dinner at the Commodore Hotel. Praising the efforts of Felix Warburg and Chaim Weizmann in support of the university, he added his now familiar theme: "Many talented Jews are lost to culture because the way is barred to them. It will be one of the foremost aims of the University of Jerusalem to alleviate such misery. May it contribute to the attainment by the Jewish people of a spiritual and moral height which will be worthy of its past."[189]

At the same dinner sat the German consul general, Dr. Otto Klep. It is worthy of note that in the face of the Nazi takeover Dr. Klep "spoke warmly of Dr. Einstein's contributions to science and extolled his services to humanity."[188]

Thousands of miles to the East in Berlin, a meeting of a totally different sort took place on the same date. At the request of the Reich Federation of Jewish ex-servicemen, veterans from other ex-servicemen's groups were invited to a nonpolitical discussion on "national consciousness." Many members of patriotic organizations such as the Stahlhelm, the Kyffhaeuser Union, and the National Socialists were in attendance. From the beginning the Nazi storm-troopers attempted to disrupt the meeting with continuous catcalls, but were eventually silenced by members of the other groups, who came to listen to their former comrades-in-arms. The gist of the message of the Jewish veterans was in the form of a proclamation of loyalty to Germany. They pointed out that of the 550,000 Jews in Germany, who comprised a bare one percent of the population, 96,000 had served in the Great War, and 12,000 had given their lives. Dr. Freund, chairman of the Jewish veterans, assured his audience that German Jews also were firm in their commitment to a new "national consciousness." He went on to complain of the "bitter injustice" of singling out the entire Jewish population for condemnation because of the faults of the few. Freund reminded them that Jewish casualties in the war were evidence that Jews stood ready in their duty to Germany no less than Gentiles. The arguments of the other groups centered around Jewish aloofness and their tendency to liberalism.

When all was said and everything was done, it was realized, perhaps too late, that meetings of this sort solved nothing. The Nazis were now in the driver's seat. Their steamroller was on the move, and goodwill gestures and assurances of loyalty fell on deaf ears. Hitler's program called for the elimination of the Jews from the third Reich, and the Nazis proceeded towards that goal by first depriving Jews of their citizenship. "Only racial comrades can become citizens and only those of our race who are of German blood, regardless of religion . . no Jew, therefore, can become a member of the Nazi racial community."[189] From then on Jews were deprived of all civil rights before the police and in the courts; Jewish judges were removed from the bench and Jewish lawyers were prevented from practicing their profession. Marching through the streets, the Nazis would sing of murdering Jews. The police were ordered by Goering not to interfere with the violence perpetrated by the Nazi goon squads; they were also encouraged to quell any last remnant of democracy. They obediently complied.

Hitler and the Nazis ruled Germany with the method of the heel and the fist. To effect complete mastery, Hitler ordered the offices of all labor unions destroyed and their leaders shipped off to concentration camps. If they put up a fight or resisted in any way, they were shot on the spot. All political parties vanished; all political activity ceased. The people were told to believe in only one slogan: "The Fuehrer is always right." And they swallowed this hogwash. They were told by Hitler that Germans were not capable of ruling themselves. They therefore had no need to choose candidates; the Nazis would do that for them. And they cheered louder. The German people needed only an iron heel on their necks to remind them of their long heritage of servility.

Albert Grzesinski, police commissioner of Berlin at that time, relates the thoroughness of the Nazi dictatorial regime:

> As early as February 4, 1933, a new decree 'for the protection of the German people' had been enacted which virtually put an end to all meetings, printing of anti-Nazi literature, financial contributions to the democratic cause and all other activities considered harmful to Nazi interests . . . . On the day of the Reichstag fire, a new law 'for the protection of the people and the state against communist acts of violence' was made public. It had obviously been prepared beforehand, just as were the warrants for about 1,500 pacifists, communists and communist sympathizers who were immediately arrested by the police after the start of the well-prepared fire. This law deprived every citizen of his few remaining civil rights and left him at the mercy of the new masters and their heavily armed sluggers now elevated to the rank of authority. Person and home were no longer inviolate. Privacy of mail, telephone, and telegram had ceased to exist. Freedom of speech, press and assembly was a thing of the past. In addition, the government reserved for itself the right to dismiss public officials of the Weimar era without being bound by the constitution."[190]

The various German labor and industrial unions had had an enviable record of accomplishment for the preceding forty years. With a 1930 membership of eight million, they could point with pride to a great record of improvement in wages, working conditions, and social and labor legislation. In fact, they were such models of efficiency and honesty that their methods were studied and copied throughout the Western world, and their bank accounts were looked on with envy by the Nazis. Grzesinski reports that on May 11:

> The Consumers' Societies with $208,000,000 assets and savings of the members fell victim to the rapacity of the Nazis . . . . The Consumers Societies were an important branch of the German labor movement. With a membership of 3,700,000 in 1930 they played a tremendous role in the economic life of the German people. They operated 13,218 co-operative stores throughout Germany and did a total business of $578,000,000 annually. Needless to say, the Nazis were anxious to obtain control of these model business organizations and their resources.[191]

On May 2 the Nazis threw the two presidents of the German Federation of Labor, Theodor Leipart and Peter Grossmann, into jail under the pretext of protecting the unions from Marxist rabble. In the hands of the Nazi party hacks, the once proud unions degenerated into passivity and corruption. In Oberhausen, six high ranking unionists were beaten to death and those who threatened to strike were immediately shipped off and never heard from again. "In many cases, heavily armed police and Nazi detachments forced the workers to return to work."[192]

When German officials quietly asked Einstein to return to Germany, he flatly refused. Other attempts to turn a smiling and innocent face toward the outside world were made by the Germans to reduce criticism of Nazi cruelties. A former German foreign minister, Richard von Kuehlmann, when questioned concerning the demonstrations against Jews in Germany, said he believed these outbreaks were sporadic and confined to the provinces and that Hitler would suppress all such movements. Meanwhile, the Nazis raided the home of Professor Martin Buber, near Frankfort. Finding nothing with which to incriminate Buber, they stole papers belonging to Gustav Landauer, which Buber was editing. From Eastern Germany, 1,500 Jews fled over the border to Poland.

Addressing fellow pacifists, Einstein called for the "moral intervention of the intelligent portion of mankind against the excesses of Hitlerism" . . . and warned that "it would be a great mistake to engage in anti-German agitation as such."[193] A few days later, the Einstein cottage at Caputh was surrounded by a squad of "valiant" Nazis, intent on uncovering a "cache of arms" and "revolutionary material." The brave assault on the unoccupied home yielded only a rusted bread knife. The "Tummler" was also confiscated.

Back on the shores of Europe, Einstein reiterated his decision not to return to Germany: "As long as I have any choice, I will only stay in a country where political liberty, tolerance, and equality of all citizens before the law prevail . . . These conditions do not obtain in Germany at the present time. Those who have done most for the cause of international understanding are being persecuted there . . . Nations usually survive these distempers. I hope that healthy conditions will soon supervene in Germany . . ."[194]

The official organ of the Nazi press, the *Volkische Beobachter* answered: "Good news from Einstein—he's not coming back . . . . Relativity is in little demand by us now . . . . So the outlook for Einstein here is very bad."

While Hitler was shoving the "Empowering Act" down the throats of the now rubber-stamp Reichstag, which gave him complete and absolute power, the Einsteins were casting around for a temporary refuge in Belgium. To further complicate matters, it was rumored that the Nazis had placed a price of some $6,800 on Einstein's head. He said he didn't know if it was worth that much.

33

WORLD'S #1 REFUGEE

Mindful of the terror being perpetrated just beyond their border, Queen Elizabeth and King Albert of Belgium, provided a sanctuary for the homeless Einsteins in the coastal resort town of Le Coq sur Mer. Presumably safe from intruders, the near-deserted village offered suitable isolation and safety since the summer season was some three months off. As an added safety precaution the hosts also provided full-time bodyguards. Miss Dukas and Professor Mayer soon arrived, while Elsa frantically tried to contact her daughters. Margot subsequently arrived with her husband, but Ilse followed alone. Her husband, Rudolph Kayser, editor of a German publication, had decided to remain with his aging father, who with many others stubbornly refused to leave his "homeland." Nervously, Ilse returned to Berlin to be with her husband and salvage what she could from Caputh and the Haberlandstrasse apartment. Vallentin notes that "Jewish journalists were being liquidated rapidly."[195]

It was an incalculable tragedy, inadvertently inflicted upon themselves that the obstinacy with which some German Jews clung to their German loyalties, and to their possessions, often led to their own destruction. Ignoring the warnings of Weizmann and Einstein, and others, they often remonstrated against both, blaming them instead of the Nazis for their sufferings.

Atypical of the experience of most Jews, but a common enough tragedy among assimilationists was the "liquidation" of Fritz Haber. Today, Berlin has an appropriate memorial, the Fritz Haber Institut of the Max Planck Gessellshaft, dedicated to the great German scientist. But in 1933, the mood was different; they were not naming important buildings after Jews, or even former Jews. Haber was "kicked out" of his directorship of the Kaiser Wilhelm Institute for Chemistry; to Hitler, he was still a Jew despite his conversion to Christianity. A forlorn Haber tried to make some sense of it: "For more than forty years I have selected my collaborators on the basis of their intelligence and their character and not on the basis of their grandmothers."[196]

All his life Haber had been an unquestioning and loyal German nationalist, who had served his country well, especially during the Great War. But even before Hitler assumed the chancellorship, Haber had modified his former anti-Zionist views to the point where he invited Weizmann to visit him at the Institute. Weizmann was suspicious; wasn't it Haber who tried to persuade Einstein not to go along on the 1921 visit to America? But Weizmann relented. Haber led Weizmann through the laboratories under his domain: "It was a magnificent collection of laboratories, superbly equipped and many-sided in its program, and Haber was enthroned as dictator."[197] A keen observer and a chemist himself, Weizmann could well marvel at the high esteem in which Haber was held in Berlin. As he was guided through building after building, project after project, Haber would suggest: "You might try to introduce that in Palestine."[198] And it began to occur to Weizmann that Palestine could greatly benefit from Haber's services if he could be convinced to emigrate. Haber was, "A Nobel Prize winner, and responsible for one of the biggest technical successes of the age, namely, the conversion of the nitrogen of the air into ammonia and citric acid. These two chemicals are essential ingredients in the making not only of explosives, but also of artificial fertilizer, which thus became accessible in large quantities at a low price."[199] But nothing came of that meeting.

In 1933, Haber escaped to England, where at Cambridge he was offered a laboratory of his own. Feelings were still running high over the German use of poison gas, however, and Haber was forced to leave for Switzerland; he arrived an ill and broken man, "stripped of everything—position, fortune and honors."[200] Weizmann and Haber met again in Zermatt in the summer of 1933, when Haber appeared to be recuperating from his state of melancholy. He sounded more optimistic to Weizmann, but once in a while he would look back to his former elite position with nostalgia: "Dr. Weizmann, I was one of the mightiest men in Germany. I was more than a great army commander, more that a captain of industry. I was the founder of industries; my work was essential for the economic and military expansion of Germany. All doors were open to me."[201]

Weizmann, at the time, had been dropped from the presidency of the World Zionist Congress but was kept busy in his own laboratory. Always in the foreground of activity that would promote the general welfare of Palestine, he had accepted the chairmanship of the Central Bureau for the Settlement of German Jews and was responsible for the emigration of several thousand German Jews to Palestine. Often in a climate that was difficult for them, under harsher conditions than they were used to, amongst Jews from other lands whose habits and language were strange, the German Jews stayed in Palestine to work hard and survive and incidentally to bring a strain of culture and orderliness that the new land lacked and needed.

Grasping the moment, Weizmann volunteered an "invitation to come out to Palestine and work with us . . . . the climate will be good for you. You will find a modern laboratory, able assistants. You will work in peace and honor. It will be a return home for you—your journey's end."[202] Haber beamed. Weizmann had offered him a new life and he accepted enthusiastically. Tragically though, in the midst of his travel preparations, Haber died in Basle. As a footnote, it must be noted here that, in Haber's behalf, Max Planck attempted to intervene with Hitler himself, citing the great scientific and cultural contributions Haber had made to the benefit of Germany. Typically, Hitler flew into a rage, pounding his fist on the desk and screaming that there can be no exceptions. Planck was forced to retreat.

Many Jews, as well as others in Germany, were convinced that they could ride out the Hitler storm, that the violence was not directed against them, but against the more recent arrivals, the eastern Jews; and did nothing. They continued to deceive themselves with the belief that once Hitler drove "them" out or otherwise got rid of "them," the persecutions would end. A form of paralysis, it was not confined to the Jews. A case in point is the example of Pastor Martin Niemoller, who during the first World War had been a highly skilled U-boat commander. With the advent of peace, Niemöller turned in his periscope for a pulpit. In 1937, because he could no longer remain silent about the brutal injustices in Germany he was thrown into a concentration camp. After the war, when he was asked why Germans, more particularly himself, had not acted against Hitler sooner, Niemöller answered that the first Nazi attacks were made against the communists, and since he was not a communist, he remained silent. Then he declined to act when the Nazis came after the Jews, since he was not a Jew. And so on when the Nazi horror was directed against Catholics, unionists, pacifists, and liberals—since he was none of the foregoing, he still did nothing. Finally, when Hitler came after the Protestants, and Niemöller looked around for help, there was no one left.

At the hideaway at Le Coq-sur-Mer, correspondence flowed in and out in a continuous stream; the cottage became a message center between Germany and the rest of the world for fellow refugees also caught up in the uncertainty of the day. Einstein saw his role clearly; to inveigh against Hitler's government, to try to bring it down, if possible, and to bring home to the "innocents abroad" that the rumors of torture and death in Nazi concentration camps were true, despite official denials. One could not wish Hitler away or hide from the consequences of his cruelty; one could only fight Hitler's terror with every weapon at hand.

To strongly emphasize his censure of the Nazi regime to the world at large, Einstein publicly tore up his German citizenship. Then he engaged the Prussian Academy of Science in a running battle of words and publicly resigned from that once prestigious organization. To the point, his resignation was meant to condemn the academy's acquiescence when their colleagues were "booted out" of their professions for no apparent reason other than the accident of birth. A second motive for his taking the initiative in resigning was to save Planck and his other long-time colleagues and friends the painful task of asking him to resign. The academy responded that they "had no reason to regret Einstein's withdrawal" because "of his atrocity mongering in France and America."[203] Einstein countered by denying that he took part in any "atrocity mongering" and suggested the academy take the trouble to get the correct text before making untrue statements: "The German press has reproduced a deliberately distorted version of my words, as indeed was only to be expected with the press muzzled as it is today."[204]

The secretary of the Academy responded, but no longer charged Einstein with atrocity mongering. Instead he asked for a "good word":

We had confidently expected that one who had belonged to our Academy for so long would have ranged himself, irrespective of his own political sympathies, on the side of the defenders of our nation against the flood of lies which has been let loose upon it. In these days of mud-slinging, some of it vile, some of it ridiculous, a good word for the German people from you in particular might have produced a great effect abroad.

Einstein was quick to reply:

You have . . . remarked that a "good word" on my part for "the German people" would have produced a great effect abroad. To this I must reply that such a testimony as you suggest would have been equivalent to a repudiation of all those notions of justice and liberty for which I have stood all my life. Such testimony would not be, as you put it, a good word for the German people; on the contrary, it would only have helped the cause of those who are seeking to undermine the ideas and principles which have won for the German people a place of honor in the civilized world. By giving such testimony in the present circumstances I should have been contributing, even if only indirectly, to the moral corruption and destruction of all existing cultural values. It was for this reason that I felt compelled to resign from the Academy, and your letter only shows me how right I was to do so.[205]

To Planck he also wrote denying any atrocity mongering, then continued: "I cannot help but remind you that, in all these years, I have only enhanced Germany's prestige and never allowed myself to be alienated by the systematic attacks on me in the rightist press, especially those of recent years when no one took the trouble to stand up for me."[206]

The professors of the academy may have been intimidated by Hitler's terror into criticizing Einstein, but saving one's own neck was the only rule of the day. But if their criticism was based on their impartial appraisal, which would have implied a deafness and a blindness and a conformity of monumental proportions, then the "book burning" on May 10, 1933 should have made abundantly clear, beyond anyone's doubt, the slavery Hitler intended for the German people. After this shameful demonstration of the contempt the Nazis felt for any freedom, no one, no professor, no clergyman, no unionist, no socialist, no Jew, no Catholic, no resident of Germany or Europe or any part of the planet, could have doubted the bloody road ahead. Books by Thomas and Heinrich Mann, Sigmund Freud, Stefan Zweig, Erich Maria Remarque, Albert Einstein, Helen Keller, and Upton Sinclair were thrown into the leaping flames by recently nazified students. Replete with a torchlight parade, and accompanied by a marching band, the bonfire in front of the Berlin Opera House was sheer regression to a caveman mentality. And this effrontery to culture and civilization was systematically repeated throughout Germany; as the flames leapt higher, freedom diminished. From that night on, science, literature, anything in print would bear the Nazi stamp. Science would no longer be an open field for speculation and free thought; it would forcibly be tailored to the military, political, and propaganda needs of Hitler. And the scientists who remained, willingly or not, passively allowed the Nazi yoke to be fastened around their subservient necks. Except for the concern he showed in the Haber case, Planck, along with Nernst and von Laue,

Einstein's closest friends for twenty years and often his defenders, continued their work, serving in silence the politics of the day.

In response to a letter from Max von Laue, Einstein wrote that he didn't agree that scientists should stay out of the political arena, pointing out that what von Laue suggested, silence, would lead, as it had in Germany, to an abdication of responsibility to those who seek to impose rule without question. To Ehrenfest he complained, as he had during the first World War, that the lack of resistance to Hitler by the intellectuals was leading to disaster. And to Langevin, Einstein reported "that a group of armed bandits in Germany has successfully silenced the responsible segments of the population."[207]

The Nazis could not attack Einstein personally and still leave his relativity theories intact; therefore, "Jewish speculative physics" would no longer be tolerated by Aryans. To try to legitimatize their denouncement of relativity, they published an article in the official Nazi newspaper, written by an old Einstein hater, Philip Lenard. Lenard's philosophy of science was infected by his obvious feeling of inferiority: "We must recognize that it is unworthy of a German to be the intellectual follower of a Jew. Natural science is of completely Aryan origin."[208] The Nazi rise to power presented Lenard with the opportunity to voice the anti-Semitic garbage he had been holding in check: "The most important example of the dangerous influence of Jewish circles on the study of nature has been provided by Herr Einstein with his mathematically botched-up theories consisting of some ancient knowledge and a few arbitrary additions. This theory gradually falls to pieces, as is the fate of all products that are estranged from nature. Even scientists who have otherwise done solid work cannot escape the reproach that they allowed the relativity theory to get a foothold in Germany, because they did not see, or did not want to see, how wrong it is, outside the field of science also, to regard this Jew as a good German."[209]

Summer was approaching and traffic to and from the sequestered cottage was increasing. Fellow refugees and former colleagues found their way there to tell Einstein that they condoned his resignation from the academy. They beseeched him for jobs, money, clothing, for a letter of recommendation, and for that intangible sense of reassurance he radiated, or came simply "to inhale a breath of faith."[210]

An offer arrived from the Collège de France to take the physics chair there. Einstein accepted. From the University of Spain came a similar offer, which he likewise accepted. England repeated its offer and included citizenship. Commitments were made to lecture in Brussels and Leiden. And Weizmann repeated his claim that Einstein belonged at the University of Jerusalem, that he need not be a wanderer among the universities of the world. Einstein's acceptance of all the offers was a gesture made for the worldwide publicity it would receive, with the hope it would reflect unfavorably on the Nazis. It was understood that he never intended fulfilling all these obligations.

The hate-mail Einstein received at this time came from two primary sources—the Nazis and his fellow Jews. The hatred of the Nazis was at least understandable. But when German Jews wrote, blaming him for the Nazis terror they were suffering, begging him to remain silent, he was dumbfounded. They didn't seem to understand that if they remained, they were doomed. They refused to believe that this could come about. A perplexed Einstein asked: "Anti-Semites often talk of the malice and cunning of the Jews, but has there ever been in history a more striking example of collective stupidity than the blindness of the German Jews?"[211]

Some American Jews, too, were of the opinion that less criticism directed against Hitler would result in less harm to German Jews. The "collective stupidity" was contagious. Rabbi Stephen S. Wise of the Free Synagogue of New York, an ally of Einstein in Zionism, also caught considerable flak for his criticism of Hitler. Turning to Einstein, Wise wrote of his frustration in trying to deal with the attitude of those American Jews who had urged him to temper some of his anti-Hitler statements. Einstein and Wise had hoped for the opposite —that protests by American Jews would help in enlisting the support of non-Jews in opposing the policies of the Nazis. Fortunately, the effect of the appeasers was minimal. And Einstein continued his messages from Belgium, warning the outside world that Germany was secretly rearming and that a new European war was in the making.

Two Belgian conscientious objectors, who had been jailed because of their dedication to the "inviolable principle of pacifism" looked to Einstein to intervene on their behalf. A world figure, with an unassailable history of pacifist views, Einstein was a logical choice; one who also had the ear of the Royal couple. But they soon found out, from Einstein, that the timing was wrong. With Germany rearming, Belgium faced an obvious crisis. Einstein and King Albert held a hurried conference on the urgent matter of "defense forces" and Einstein came away from the meeting condoning military service as it pertains to a nonaggressive country like Belgium. He wrote to the jailed pacifists that if they could picture Belgium occupied by the Germans of today, a condition that would be many times worse then the occupation during the first World War, they, too, would consider the situation to be intolerable. He said that if he were a Belgian he would volunteer for the armed forces.

Einstein's abrupt reversal from pacifism brought to his doorstep another storm of protests and criticism; this time from his long-allied pacifist friends. Those who had looked to him as an uncompromising pacifist, a pillar of antiwar sentiment, and an outspoken foe of the military, felt betrayed, even outraged. Old pacifist friends, bitterly disappointed, wrote to him in disbelief that he would condone the use of military force, that for a momentary expediency he would approve of that great evil, conscription, the elimination of which they had all struggled for, for so long. Lord Ponsonby wrote to Einstein with "deep disappointment." Ponsonby, too, could neither see the fire nor smell the smoke. Clearly, he did not approve of Hitler's insane methods, but he didn't believe Hitler was crazy enough to start another European war. Ponsonby said: "no matter how provocative a government may be, this fact is not, in my view, a sufficient justification for denying the reasonableness and effectiveness of refusing military service."[212]

A reversal of such magnitude, from one of the high priests of pacifism was considered an act "worse than treason." But Einstein never stopped to consider whether his opinions would meet with popular approval. So far as he was concerned, his views on pacifism had not changed; the conditions in Europe had. And he could not remain blind to the realities. With his eyes focused on the fragile Belgian border, he asked Ponsonby: "Can you possibly be unaware of the fact that Germany is feverishly rearming and that the whole population is being indoctrinated with nationalism and drilled for war? Do you believe for a moment that Germany's overlords will be any easier on the French than they have been on their own fellow citizens who are not willing tools? What protection, other then organized power, would you suggest?"[213] Obviously, Ponsonby's ox was not being gored.

Criticism nevertheless mounted; the War Resister's International asked him to make a retraction. Other pacifists spoke of the apostasy of Einstein, his "weakness of spirit," inconsistency, indecisiveness. Rolland wrote of Einstein's "about face," his hesitations and contradictions. Not fazed by the rash of rebuke, in an interview Einstein stated: "It is beyond me why the entire civilized world has failed to join in a united effort to make an end to this modern barbarism. Can it be that the world does not see that Hitler is dragging us into war?"[214]

In August, German gestapo agents crossed over into Czechoslovakia and murdered Theodor Lessing. Lessing, an outspoken liberal and anti-Nazi, had escaped from Germany but had not fled far enough. The news of Lessing's death threw Elsa into a new panic of fear for her husband's safety. She couldn't sleep nights, doubly suspicious of every sound and shadow within sight of the cottage. The guards admittedly found it increasingly difficult to spot a would-be assassin and advised Einstein that his safety could not be entirely guaranteed. Einstein then realized that soon they would have to move on.

With or without government sanction, scientific organizations in London, along with leading political figures and the Friends Committee, formed ad hoc groups to raise funds with which to aid escaping German scientists and writers. The Academic Assistance Council and the Academic Freedom Fund were two of the groups that had organized a meeting for this purpose at the ten thousand seat Royal Albert Hall. Invited to speak as one who truly was representative of the refugees' plight, Einstein was spirited across the English Channel and brought to the estate of his benefactor, Oliver Locker-Lampson. Here, under protective guard again, he was able to relax and get some three weeks of work done on the unified field. There followed a meeting with Winston Churchill and a few sittings with sculptor, Jakob Epstein. He found Churchill an eminently wise man and also aware of Hitler's intent. Einstein and Epstein became associated, through the English penchant for doggerel:

> Three wonderful people called Stein
> there's Gert and there's Ep and there's Ein
> Gert writes in blank verse
> Ep's sculpture is worse
> And nobody understands Ein.

No official of the English government wanted to be saddled with the responsibility if harm came to Einstein while on English soil. So, on the night of October 3, 1933, the alert representatives of Scotland Yard were generously sprinkled among the more than ten thousand people jammed into the Royal Albert Hall. James Jeans, Austen Chamberlain, Oliver Locker-Lampson, and Ernest Rutherford all spoke in favor of admitting refugees seeking a new home. None of the speakers referred specifically to "Jewish" refugees and neither did Einstein, though obviously a large percentage of the refugees were Jewish. The English wanted to protect themselves against any charge of "saving the Jews," to the exclusion of others.

Belgian bodyguard, Elsa and Einstein discussing safety measures at Le Coq-sur-Mer, Belgium, 1933.

Einstein this time spoke in English. He stayed clear of mentioning either Germany, Hitler, or the Nazis, for one particular reason; a strong current of opinion in England was in favor of a "hands off" Hitler policy. One wonders how many English still espoused that policy after Dunkirk or Coventry? Einstein said:

> It cannot be my task today to act as judge of a nation which for many years has considered me as her own; perhaps it is an idle task to judge in times when action counts . . . It is in times of economic distress such as we experience everywhere today, one sees very clearly the strength of the moral forces that live in a people. Let us hope that a historian delivering judgment in some future period when Europe is politically and economically united, will be able to say that in our days the liberty and honour of this Continent was saved by its Western nations, which stood fast in hard times against the temptations of hatred and oppression; and that Western Europe defended successfully the liberty of the individual which has brought us every advance of knowledge and invention—liberty without which life to a self-

respecting man is not worth living . . . . Today, the questions which concern us are: how can we save mankind and its spiritual acquisitions of which we are the heirs? How can one save Europe from a new disaster? . . . . If we want to resist the powers which threaten to suppress intellectual and individual freedom we must keep clearly before us what is at stake, and what we owe to that freedom which our ancestors have won for us after hard struggles . . . . we have this further duty, the care for what is eternal and highest among our possessions, that which gives to life its import and which we wish to hand on to our children purer and richer than we received it from our forebears.[215]

The immediate future for the Einstein group consisted of five months at Princeton, followed by one month at Oxford; beyond that

Credit: Library of Congress

Royal Albert Hall, London, 1933. Left to right: Oliver Locker-Lampson, Einstein, Ernest Rutherford, Austen Chamberlain, at meeting in aid of refugee assistance fund.

nothing. There was no house to which they could return and they had no belongings other than what could be carried. Millikan repeated his offer of a safe haven at Cal. Tech., but that would have left Mayer out. Neither could a permanent arrangement be reached with the English. In Southampton, on October 7, Einstein and Mayer boarded the *Westernland,* which had just arrived from Antwerp. They joined Elsa and Miss Dukas already aboard, and sailed for the United States. On October 17, 1933 they arrived at the entrance to New York harbor. Only one of them would see Europe again.

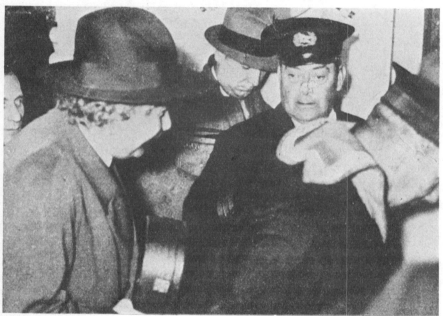

Arriving in the U. S. October 17, 1933, with violin in hand.

34

PRINCETON

The autumn foliage in the Princeton of 1933, brilliant in tones of green, red, orange, and yellow, offered a warm welcome to the new residents. And soon the uncertain refugees were comfortably settled into a rented house in the university town. The townspeople, unsure as to how to respond to the presence of a world figure in their midst, gradually became accustomed to the habits of the "professor." It soon became apparent that he liked to walk a great deal—to the near-by woods, the half-mile to the university campus every morning, and sometimes (but not too often) to the village barber shop. But they never encroached on the privacy they knew he valued. When they ran into him at the drugstore munching on an ice cream cone, at the train station, or out on Carnegie Lake, they found a simple "good morning" invariably was greeted with a smile or a wave of the hand, but they kept their distance. The professor was eternally grateful that the town did not feel it necessary to mark his arrival with a welcoming party or celebration; the other side of a cocktail glass was not the way to get to know Einstein.

Einstein found the democratic principles to which he subscribed best played out in the American system. He was pleased that the elitist manner, so typical of the European social order had been left on the shores of the Atlantic. The university people, when at home, relaxed in a way to Einstein's liking, by discarding the ceremonial garb of the professor in favor of loose-fitting, comfortable clothing.

Beyond the first impressions of his new haven, Einstein found an America, for the most part, untouched by the violence and brutality across the sea, and not at all anxious to become involved. The new-comers, with the memories of their recent European experiences still fresh in their minds and disturbing to their thoughts, perforce kept to themselves. In the comparative safety of America and beyond the danger of persecution, their thoughts continued to be with the dear family members and the many friends still in the grasp of Nazi tentacles.

When it was announced that Einstein would become permanently associated with the Institute For Advanced Study, once again their house became the focal point for those in flight and a haven for recent arrivals. These refugees, caught in a no-man's land, and not wanted by either side, could not enter the United States unless sponsored; and this is where Einstein put his reputation to work. He, and Miss Dukas, busily turned out a barrage of letters to university presidents, to financiers, to philanthropies, industrialists, and businessmen, praising the abilities of "so and so," himself, more often than not, unsure of the accuracy of the glowing terms he ascribed to the person involved. The purpose was to get these floundering refugees into the country and into jobs. The process saved many lives, for, at the time, few nations permitted even a partial opening of their doors to new immigrants. To open the gates to America, Einstein served with unflagging availability, almost to a fault. He appealed to the State Department, to the governments of France and England, for visas for people lucky enough to escape, but fearful that they might find no place to which they could go.

Irwin Schrodinger, not a Jew, left Germany and eventually settled in Dublin. Max Born left for England. One who could not cope with the Nazi threat was Paul Ehrenfest. Whether in despair over the coming catastrophe or as the result of the anguish of always having been cast in the role of follower and never the leader, the teacher instead of the discoverer, Ehrenfest took his own life. He also shot his sixteen-year-old son. Now, Leiden was part of the past, never to be experienced again. Going back was now impossible. The lines around the professor's chocolate brown eyes deepened; his gait grew slower. Absent-mindedly he puffed on a dead pipe, his eyes distant, glistening as they contemplated the eastern sky.

An unimposing, two-story frame house at 112 Mercer Street was the last home the Einsteins were to know; the wandering at last was over. With the books and furniture that Ilse had managed to salvage from Germany, Elsa began the project of furnishing their new home. The first order of business was her husband's study. She had the wall removed and replaced with a large picture window to bring him closer to the out-of-doors he loved, with a distant view of the graduate school beyond the trees.

Neighbors knew it was cold outside when they saw the professor walking by with his navy blue wool hat stretched down over his ears. Sometimes he accepted a ride back after a morning of work with Mayer. Mayer, like the younger physicists, had become convinced that Einstein's work on the unified field would not lead to the desired end. With ideas of his own that he felt worthwhile to pursue he was able to obtain his own position at Princeton.

112 Mercer Street, Princeton, New Jersey

Now that he was beginning to feel a sense of permanency, Einstein's travels dwindled to a trickle. No more the itinerant professor, complete with violin and equations, charming audiences in the far-flung capitals of the world with his relativity lectures, or proselytizing for peace; he remained in the United States, except for one brief trip to Bermuda. Yet, he didn't become a recluse either. If his feet had lost their wanderlust, his soul had not lost it ideals, and he continued to speak out and write, though not as frequently or as dramatically. To Queen Elizabeth he apologized for having to refuse her invitation to visit Europe. Now, he wrote to the Queen, his friends call him *Der Grosse Schweiger* (The Great Stone Face) because of the diminished role he played in public affairs.

Had he so desired, weekly seminars could have been arranged, as in Berlin, and once again he could have become the beacon to which overflow crowds would be drawn. But this was a new country, and a new era was beginning. He felt it to be more appropriate that he turn the reins over to the younger professors whose reputations had not yet been made and who also were closer to the current trends in physics. Beside his own work, Einstein served in the dual capacity of advisor and collaborator for the students, who for the most part were beyond graduate work and well into research. These roles suited him fine; they were far removed from teaching.

When writing to old friends or colleagues he would often refer to himself as an old "museum piece." Perhaps at times he felt old and useless, and perhaps he had lost some of life's verve, but his pursuit of the unified field never slackened. With his new assistants, Nathan Rosen and Boris Podolsky, he attempted to show that Werner Heisenberg's uncertainty principle, while not necessarily incorrect, remained incomplete; at best a transitory description of the subatomic world that would not stand up in the long run, and eventually would have to be supplanted (with the unified field theory, of course). Other abilities may have faded a little, but not his single-mindedness.

The grievous situation in Germany still overshadowed his every thought and action. Eager to discuss Europe's future and a more active role by the United States, Einstein accepted an invitation in January of 1934 to meet with President Roosevelt at the White House. Roosevelt, always the charmer, lost no time in assuring Einstein of his deep concern for the lost freedoms in Europe, and his

Einstein with a group of musical friends at the scientist's home in Princeton. Elsa Einstein is standing behind Albert.

resolve to help in every way. This was mostly lip service on Roosevelt's part, since he knew more than anyone that he had little influence in Europe and absolutely none with Hitler. He had all he could handle at the moment trying to get his anti-depression legislation through Congress. Unemployment was high; some farmers were dumping milk, and others, peaches—all to drive the prices up—while soup kitchens were feeding the hungry, and war veterans hawked apples on the street corners.

Margot meanwhile had left Belgium for Paris, where she was joined by Ilse and Rudolph. But the strain imposed on Ilse by the nerve-racking return to Berlin and the subsequent escape took a fatal toll. "There she was, trembling and fragile, her narrow face wearing an expression of painful surprise that never left it; deep shadows under her eyes, she jumped at every bang on the door."[216] She became seriously ill. By the time Margot wired her mother of Ilse's condition, it was already too late. Nevertheless, Elsa hurried back across the Atlantic alone to be with her dying daughter. Whether Ilse fell victim to an inoperable cancer or simply lost the will to live was never determined; she didn't respond to treatment by the best French doctors and soon died peacefully.

Elsa returned to Princeton with Margot, reproaching herself for her daughter's death. For his part, Einstein shared his wife's grief. Now, Elsa needed rest, a change of scene. These her husband found in a perfect retreat in a rented estate in Old Lyme, Connecticut. Though Elsa was soon again actively lavishing her dutiful attentions upon her husband and Margot, it was clear that she would never completely discard the mantle of guilt she carried for Ilse's death. Neither did she ever feel completely comfortable living a "luxurious" life in America while many friends in Germany were carted off to concentration camps, never to be seen or heard from again.

As the depression in the United States continued during the midthirties, so did the country's isolation from the troubles in Europe. Attempts by Einstein and others to convince Americans of their responsibility toward Europe proved futile; Germany, meanwhile, continued her twenty-four hour a day rearmament plans. Hopefully, to contain Hitler's expansionist aims, Einstein called for an international police force, whose united display of might would discourage any nation from aggression. But again, without the participation of the United States the smaller countries could not hope to stand up against Hitler. This proposal was an even further move away from Einstein's "uncompromising pacifist" position of only a few years

Credit: Dr. Thomas L. Bucky

With friends. Rear, Thomas L. Bucky. Left to right, Helen Dukas, Margot, Einstein, Dr. Gustav Bucky, Frieda Bucky.

before. Pacifism in the face of Hitler would indeed have been a form of voluntary suicide. One pacifist source said that he would prefer to live under Hitler rather than fight. Had this individal's philosophy prevailed over all of Europe, then many more millions in addition to the 55 million people who perished during World War II would have fallen victim to Hitler's brutality. Pray tell, what manner of butchery is this (pacifism, you call it) that would allow the slaughter of countless millions of men, women, and children, without so much as a whimper of protest? One had supposed that pacifism would be in opposition to death in war. In this case, it seemed to encourage it.

Homesickness never plagued Einstein even for a moment, though he did miss some of his old cronies. Of those friends who were also transplanted to the United States, he most often was in the company of Dr. Gustav Bucky, who lived in New York City. Dr. Bucky, who had originally migrated to the United States in 1923 with his wife, Frieda, and sons, Peter and Thomas, had returned to Berlin for a brief period, and while there became the physician for Elsa's

Gustav Bucky and Einstein

daughters. Among the world's first radiologists, Dr. Bucky applied Rontgen's recently discovered X-rays to practical medicine. On the side, he was an amateur physicist. Out of their frequent discussions,

Dr. Bucky and Professor Einstein invented an automatic timing device used in the single lens reflex cameras of today. Dr. Bucky saw the practical use; Einstein was interested only in the theoretical end and seldom was involved in the finished product. A warm, personal friendship had developed between them, and once both families found themselves within a comparatively short train ride from each other they became frequent visitors to each other's homes. The Bucky family took on the responsibility for locating out-of-the way summer places for the Einsteins and usually spent weekends in their company. Son Thomas spent every summer of his growing years sailing and hiking with Einstein, and declared that in all those years, "I never saw him lose his temper."[217]

35

GERMAN EXPANSION

Goebbel's short-wave radio propaganda was aimed not only at Germanic peoples in nearby Austria and Czechoslovakia, but also at Germans living in North and South America. The carefully screened propaganda contained only messages of sweetness and light, boasting of the virtues of Hitler's Reich compared with the despair before him. Censoring out any reference to concentration camps, Goebbel's men broadcast the music of Beethoven, described cultural events, and passed on only news that would serve the best interests of the new Germany. These interests were common knowledge to the rulers and statesmen of the world—incitement against Jews, world domination, and rebellion of immigrant Germans against their adopted countries. But, because of the preposterous nature of this propaganda, the world paid little heed.

The fruits of Goebbel's insidious propaganda campaign were first gathered in neighboring Austria. Promised uniforms and leather boots and Jews to knock about, Austrian Nazis sprang up like weeds out of the ranks of the unemployed, pledging themselves to die for Hitler. On the Austrian domestic scene, however, in February 1934, all was not going well between Chancellor Englebert Dollfuss and the Austrian Social Democratic Labor Party. Their differences on the issues of suffrage, civil rights, and badly needed labor legislation could not be resolved over the conference table; Dollfuss therefore called out the army. When the smoke cleared, they counted three hundred dead and seven hundred wounded; another casualty of the violence, not generally noticed by the Austrians, was their democratic form of government. The action proved to be a fatal mistake for Dollfuss. By alienating the Social Democrats, the party that had given him the most support, he unknowingly opened the power gap and the Nazis marched in. Guessing that the right moment had arrived, the Nazis attempted a revolution, but succeeded only in assassinating Dollfuss. Another iron fist, Kurt von Schuschnigg, the former minister of justice moved up to the office of chancellor.

Across the border in Germany, assassination fever was spreading. And Hitler pulled off a purge of his own, but this time not of Jews, labor leaders, or communists. On a quiet and hot summer weekend (the dates were June 30 and July 1, 1934) when public buildings would be closed down, when city officials would be relaxing in the country and at lake resorts, when there was no one around, Hitler and Goering ordered the assassination of the cream of the Nazi party —Hitler's best friends. Chief among the victims was Ernst Roehm, who Hitler himself had appointed chief of staff of the SA, Sturm Abteilung, otherwise known as the "brown shirts" or "storm troopers," a semi-military group numbering some two and a half million men. The "traitors" were summarily shot in simultaneous actions in Munich and Berlin. This self-serving massacre, planned and ordered by Hitler, was called the "Night of the Long Knives."

Had Hitler sincerely seen it as his messianic duty to cleanse Germany of the non-Aryan element and un-German thoughts, why one might ask was it necessary to kill so many Aryan Germans to accomplish this? Why did he put to death the very men who had supported him through all the early disappointments, the defeats and discouragements? The answer is tragically simple; Roehm's burgeoning power would soon be challenging that of his boss, Hitler. Grzesinski wrote: "This tremendous organization constituted in Roehm's hands a great power and a great threat, and it was the threat which Hitler and the army leaders promptly realized . . . Roehm had grasped more power then he could hold."[218]

Hitler realized that his main ambition, domination of the world, in the long run, would best be served by the army and not the SA. The SA could be counted on to do the domestic dirty work of secret torture, bullying, election-rigging, and midnight murders, but to conquer the world he would need the services of a well-organized, professional army; competition between the two groups would surely dilute Germany's strength. One group had to go.

Hitler knew that he could never cover up the deaths of his own "gruppenfuhrers" and "standartfuhrers." Through their misdeeds they had become too popular with the people and their absence had to be explained. So, Hitler went to the rubber-stamp Reichstag (William L. Shirer describes the Reichstag as "600 or so handpicked, sausage-necked, shave-headed, brown-clad, yes men"[219]) and proceeded to shout them into submission: "I ordered the leaders of the guilty shot. I also ordered the abscesses caused by our internal and external poisons cauterized until the living flesh was burned. I also ordered that any rebel attempting to resist arrest should be killed immediately . . . shot . . . until the flesh was burned."[220]

This madman was obsessed with death. Yet, the German people were falling all over themselves, knuckling under; the British, French and Roosevelt paid scant attention, counting on Hitler to fall of his own stupidity. Worst of all, not a word, not a peep from the SA itself. Unbelievable—the sheepishness with which the Germans accepted Hitler's every whim, no matter how outrageous, and the lack of concern by the leading nations of the world for events beyond their borders. The executions, far from ending the blood-letting, served as a mere crude curtain-raiser.

While these murders were going on, in experimental laboratories manned by Enrico Fermi in Italy, Frederic Joliot-Curie in France, the trio of Otto Hahn, Fritz Strassmann and Lise Meitner in Berlin, Niels Bohr in Copenhagen, and Ernest Rutherford in England, the indestructibility of the atom was being contested; the atom was being bombarded. Fermi found in 1934 that by shooting neutrons into a mass of uranium, a new but unidentifiable element was formed. This was puzzling. With the benefit of knowledge acquired later, we know now that Fermi had actually split the uranium atom. The term "fission" was not used to describe this process until 1938; in that year Lise Meitner and her nephew, Otto Frisch, realized the true significance of what Fermi had done.

Because of the continued persecutions and the threat of war, valuable scientists with atomic research background started to leave other European countries for England and the United States. In the United States, hope sprang eternal in the heart of Dr. Arthur Holly Compton, a Nobel Prize winner from the University of Chicago, who predicted as early as November 1931 that the atom would soon be smashed and the vast storehouse of energy from within would "yield to experiments." Ernest Rutherford thought the idea absurd: "Anyone who expects a source of power from the transformation of these atoms is talking moonshine."[221] Another Compton, Dr. Karl T., President of the Massachusetts Institute of Technology, in March of 1934, at a meeting at Columbia University, bolstered the faith of his namesake, seeing the "innermost citadel of matter . . . . yielding tremendous amounts of energy."[222]

Incongruous as it may sound, in an interview in Pittsburgh, the originator of the original equation, himself poured cold water on the whole idea. Einstein called the search for the magic formula fruitless. How could that be, the father of $E = MC^2$ refuting his own theory? Not really. Atom bombardment, in the 1930's, was in its infancy, and with the meager information available to his colleagues, Einstein could not foresee the use of atomic energy in his lifetime. He likened the improbability of success in extracting power from the atom to the unlikelihood of shooting birds in a country where there is little light and where there are very few birds. He could not have predicted that a crisis of monumental proportions, soon to be visited on the nations of the world, would greatly accelerate the search for atomic energy and lead to its eventual development.

Credit: AIP, Pittsburgh Post-Gazette

Einstein in Pittsburgh, 1934.

Self-isolation did not by any means amount to solitary confinement. Einstein liked to laugh and enjoyed the company of young people, especially those who were also musicians. He balked at first when Harlow Shapley invited him to Harvard to accept yet another honorary degree, but accepted when Shapley insisted in his second letter that Einstein bring along his violin. The frontal approach with Einstein did not always work. Once the speech-making and music were over with, and in the absence of his ever-watchful wife, he could sit back and relax with a cigar or two.

With the passage of time, the Einstein mystique should have almost vanished. Instead, his rare public appearances sent people clamoring for seats with an almost viscious determination. The announcement that the American Museum of Natural History, in New York City, would be showing a film on relativity, the so-called "Einstein film," saw a mob of near five thousand people literally tear down the doors of the museum. Even New York's "finest" were

Credit: Harlow Shapley, *Through Rugged Ways to the Stars.* New York: Charles Scribner's Sons, 1969, AIP.

With Harlow Shapley, June, 1935.

unable to contain the unruly and surely unscientific crowd as they pushed and shoved their way into the auditorium. One newspaper headline read: ''Thousands battle in museum to see Einstein film.'' The film, however, ran for several months, so that all had an opportunity to view an easy lesson on Einstein.

Another example of the Einstein influence was the suggestion from a New Jersey congressman that the U.S. immigration service waive the usual five-year waiting period and allow Einstein and his family to become citizens without delay. Appreciative of the gesture, but simply wanting to be treated the same as everyone else, Einstein declined. To legally remain in the United States, however, he would have to replace his visitor's visa with a permanent residency visa. This could be done only from outside the territorial limits of the United States. Accordingly, in May 1935 the Einsteins, with Miss Dukas, took a brief holiday in Bermuda. The business of the visas concluded, Einstein found time to do some sailing in the soft winds and aqua-blue waters off Bermuda. On returning to Princeton, the Einsteins took out their first citizenship papers.

The first phase of German expansionism began with their occupation of the Saar region on March 1, 1935. The Germans entered under the terms of a plebescite, but one that was carried out under threat and intimidation. To calm France's fears, Hitler magnanimously announced that the Saar was the last territorial bone of contention with France. The French bought it, but not William L. Shirer, the journalist, who said: "We shall see."[223] Two weeks later, Hitler showed his true intent when he tore up the military restrictions agreement of the Versailles Treaty and announced that Germany would institute universal military training. His Junker generals cried joyful tears, and the German people united behind him, Nazi or no. He had thumbed his nose at the Allied powers but proclaimed that Germany was rearming merely for the maintenance of peace. France, England, and Poland managed to fidget a bit, but in the end could only sputter a mild objection. They didn't realize then, that their combined action, at that crucial time, before Germany was fully rearmed, could have quashed Hitler and gotten rid of him forever. A keen observer of the political scene, Shirer knew what was happening: "My guess is that Hitler has got away with it."[224]

In a later speech Hitler disclaimed any intention of interfering in the internal affairs of Austria, annexing Austria, or concluding an Anschluss (unification). Then Hitler began building U-boats, so as to be on a par with Britain. Unbelievably the English approved. Assured by Hitler that he had no intentions in Austria, Mussolini invaded Ethiopia in October of 1935.

Almost a year to the day of the Saar occupation, German troops marched unopposed into the demilitarized zone, the Rhineland. Hitler's general's had urged caution but Hitler counted on the timidity of the democracies and found his assessment to have been correct. With only a minimal show of force the French army could have dispatched the Germans back to Berlin. For whatever reason, the

French didn't move to confront the Germans, and their inaction only emboldened Hitler. He was about to cut Europe's throat, and the Allies were handing him the razor.

Shirer, who was at the Reichstag when Hitler spoke there on the day his soldiers marched into the Rhineland, described the scene:

> His voice which had been low and hoarse at the beginning rose to a shrill, hysterical scream as he raged against Bolshevism . . . . Then, in a more reasoned voice, his argument that France's pact with Russia had invalidated the Locarno Treaty. In the interest of the primitive rights of its people to the security of their frontier and the safe-guarding of their defence, the German government has re-established, as from today, the *absolute* and *unrestricted sovereignty* of the Reich in the *demilitarized zone*. Now the six hundred deputies, personal appointees all of Hitler, little men with big bodies and bulging necks and cropped hair and pouched bellies and brown uniforms and heavy boots, little men of clay in his fine hands, leap to their feet like automatons,

Credit: Zionist Archives and Library, New York.

Dinner at New York Zionist Club, 1935. Left to right, Einstein, M. Maldwin Fertig, Professor Franz Oppenheimer.

their right arms outstretched in the Nazi salute, and scream "Heil's," the first two or three wildly, the next twenty-five in unison, like a college yell. Hitler raises his hand for silence. It comes slowly. Slowly the automatons sit down. Hitler now has them in his claws. He appears to sense it. He says in a deep, resonant voice: "Men of the German Reichstag!" The silence is utter. "In this historic hour, when in the Reich's western provinces German troops are at this minute marching into their future peacetime garrisons, we all unite in two sacred vows." He can go no further. It is news to this hysterical "parliamentary" mob that German soldiers are already on the move into the Rhineland. All the militarism in their German blood surges to their heads. They spring, yelling and crying, to their feet. The audience in the gallery does the same, all except a few diplomats and about fifty of us correspondents. Their hands are raised in slavish salute, their faces contorted now with hysteria, their mouths wide open, shouting, shouting, their eyes burning with fanaticism, glued on the new god, the Messiah. The Messiah plays his role superbly. His head lowered as if in all humbleness, he waits patiently for silence. Then his voice still low, but chocking with emotion, utters the two vows: "First, we swear to yield to no force whatever in the restoration of the honour of our people, preferring to succumb with honour to the severest hardships rather than to capitulate. Secondly, we pledge that now, more than ever, we shall strive for an understanding between European peoples, especially for one with our western neighbor nations . . . . We have no territorial demands to make in Europe . . . . Germany will never break the peace." It was a long time before the cheering stopped.[225]

The French protest to the League of Nations, in the matter of German occupation of the Rhineland, bore no fruit; the League's well-known impotence in these matters continued.

At the end of the summer of 1935, Elsa fell ill. The only symptom, the swelling of an eye, hid the more serious cause, inflammation of the heart. She tried to keep the seriousness of her illness from her husband and friends, but Einstein knew and tried to act as if he didn't. As her condition worsened through 1936, he spent more and more time talking to her, finding extra time to sit by her bed, reading to her. She needed absolute quiet.

36

PEACE FOR OUR TIME

It was mainly to dispel the notion that saving refugees from Hitler was directed by, with, and for Jews only that Einstein appeared with former Governor Al Smith at a dinner in New York City. They spoke over a nationwide radio network in an appeal to the American people to help supply financial aid for both the political and non-Jewish refugees from Germany.

Another cause to which Einstein gave much unpublicized impetus was the case of a German pacifist editor, Carl von Ossietzky. Thrown into a concentration camp by the Nazis, Ossietzky became the center of a secret campaign to have him awarded the Nobel Prize for Peace. With backing for this movement from Jane Addams, John Dewey, and Einstein, it was hoped to gain the release of Ossietzky, and at the same time point out to the world the utter and complete suppression of human rights instituted by the Nazis. In 1936, the Nobel Committee did award the Peace Prize to Ossietzky, but the furious Nazis passed a new dictum making it illegal to accept a Nobel Prize. Ossietzky was never released and died in the concentration camp in 1938.

In his letters and public appearances, Einstein continued to seize every opportunity to help refugees and at the same time encourage Americans to enter the mainstream of the world to help reduce the possibility of a new war in Europe: "Isolation," Einstein said, "serves neither the ideals of pacifism nor the cause of America's security."[226] It was almost a one-man campaign.

Meanwhile, Elsa's condition had not improved. In the hope that a summer at Saranac Lake might help her to recover somewhat, the Einstein household moved to that northern retreat.

Some fifteen years had passed since a despondent Leopold Infeld had received a helping hand from Einstein in Berlin. Now in 1936, residing in his native Poland, where he became the recipient of a two-year fellowship, he wrote to his former benefactor in the hope that his two years might be spent in Princeton. With Rosen due to leave soon, Einstein wired Infeld to come over and work with him. Not one for wasting time, Einstein immediately put Infeld onto the task of finding a new approach to the old unified field. Infeld, soon to become an author and professor on his own, also had the facility, to a greater degree than most, of being able to put into words the benefits other than scientific that he had received from working with Einstein. The essential Einstein, as observed by Infeld is the one who, should we strip from him all scientific achievements, the fame from his relativity theories, the Nobel Prize, and every other honor, "is the only scientist of whom I would say that, after subtracting all of this, he will remain just as great as before . . . . During the two years of my association with Einstein, while I say him almost every day—sometimes twice a day—during these many months I was more and more aware of a greatness that has nothing to do with his scientific achievements. I learned much from Einstein in the field of science. Yet, as years pass by, I am well aware that I value most the many intangible things outside the field of science that I have learned from him."[227]

While Infeld and Einstein labored daily in the sparsely populated realm of abstract thought, Elsa's condition worsened; in late December she died. Elsa's had always been a difficult role, the wife of the world's most renowned scientist, who required dedicated attention and a protective shield from an intrusive, inquisitive world. Her position demanded that she subordinate her own needs, desires, and interests, and often those of her children for the sake of her husband. Tom Bucky describes Elsa as "a very nice little lady, but a bit fuzzy.' She had just enough fuzziness evidently, to fit the bohemian habits of her husband. On one level, the scientific, Einstein remained aloof, almost disdainfully so, and unemotional about the on-going life-death cycle. When Max Born's wife asked if he was afraid of death, he answered, "I feel myself so much a part of all life that I am not in the least concerned with the beginning or the end of the concrete existence of any particular person in this unending stream."[228]

Perhaps Einstein could approach the life struggle with some degree of dispassion, having fully accepted the inevitability of the end, which finality scientists come to terms with; this is reality. But, it wasn't the detached scientist who deeply mourned the death of his wife; no one else was so close and so devoted. When he resumed work at the Institute, the loneliness, even for one who yearned for solitude, bore down heavily on him.

It was not long after Elsa's death that Einstein wrote to Hans Albert, asking him to come to the States for a visit. Taking leave of his family, temporarily, Hans Albert was somewhat shocked at how much his father had aged in the past four years. His hair was almost completely gray and his once rounded, cherubic face, was now drawn

Wearing leather jacket on sailboat; 1936. With signature.

and pale. There, on the dock, father and son greeted each other; Hans knew now for certain that his father really needed him. It was a bittersweet moment, in the shadow of New York City's skyscrapers, silent reminders of the hikes through the Alps, the summer days of sailing, the long walks, and the smelly cigars. But "he never seemed to get bored with us," Hans recalled.

After a month at Princeton and with some urging and a little financial help from his father, Hans decided to remain in the United States. Casting about for a position, he refused to trade on the fame of his name, and found a suitable position at the University of South Carolina.

Infeld's fellowship was about to run out, and he too would soon be checking into the job market. Einstein offered to pay him out of his own pocket, if he chose to remain. But Infeld would not accept Einstein's charity; instead he suggested that they collaborate on a book that would trace for the layman the fundamentals of physics from the very beginning, "The Evolution of Physics." With the power of Einstein's name, the book became a best seller. It was the receipts from the sale of the book that kept Infeld going until he was able to find a position in Toronto. Infeld felt especially indebted to Einstein: "I am well aware that if it were not for the kindness shown me by Einstein, I should probably now be among those buried in the camps of Oswiecim or Majdanek, where most of my family perished."[229]

If Einstein showed a certain stand-offishness towards the undergraduates at Princeton, it was because his routine did not bring them into close contact. Nevertheless, they didn't exempt him from their campus humor. The graduating class of 1937 dedicated the following verse to him:

"The bright boys, they all study math.
And Albie Einstein points the path.
Although he seldom takes the air,
We wish to God he'd cut his hair."

Tom Bucky, too, attempted to amuse Einstein from time to time. When Tom was successful, "his laughter—he would break out in this loud, sudden laughter, which would stop just as suddenly."[230] But Tom knew, most of the time where to draw the line. When he overstepped, he was greeted with admonishing stares from his parents. "You could go only so far with Einstein . . . . you just couldn't walk up and slap him on the shoulder and say 'Hi,'" Once when Einstein was wearing an old jacket, Tom asked, unmindfully, "where'd you get that, out of the mothballs?'' Einstein didn't laugh. When he and Tom went sailing, he would attempt to explain relativity with the greatest patience, ''but he would soon leave me far behind . . . . always trying to help, to explain.'' In 1953, at Tom's wedding, Einstein showed up, though he was not invited. ''We didn't dare.'' Einstein came to this black-tie affair wearing an old Navy pea-jacket. The groom knowingly shook his head; he recognized it as the one that bore the NRA label on the inside. It had to be twenty years old. And world leaders in the category of Nehru and Ben-Gurion got the same treatment when they came to visit—the old sweater, baggy pants, and slippers.

When Hitler ordered his Reichswehr to invade Austria on March 11, 1938, his troops met with no resistance. The local population had already been softened up by years of privation and propaganda, so that when the Germans marched in they were welcomed by well-rehearsed, flower-throwing Nazis. They unfurled their swastikas and pictures of the Fuhrer and began practising the Hitler brand of murder, torture, looting, and destruction, so quickly and efficiently learned from their ''racial comrades.'' Prior to the German takeover, Hitler had demanded that Nazis be admitted to the Austrian cabinet, and Schuschnigg gave in, in order to avoid bloodshed. Hitler's army marched and the blood flowed anyway. Suicides followed and the airports were packed with thousands seeking to escape. Three days later, Hitler entered Vienna in triumph, unopposed. Meanwhile, not a word of protest was heard from the Allies. Neville Chamberlain, the British prime minister, presented the meek, Allied response, ruling out the use of force as a means of stemming the spread of Nazism. American isolation removed them from any involvement in this affair.

Working with Otto Hahn and Fritz Strassmann at the Kaiser Wilhelm Institute, was an Austrian Jewess, the atomic physicist, Lise Meitner. Because of her nationality, she had not been liquidated when Hitler came to power in 1933. But now with the takeover of her native Austria into the fold of the German Reich, her position became untenable and she left Berlin for Sweden. Otto Frisch, her nephew, working in the Niels Bohr laboratory in Copenhagen, crossed the sea to visit her. Frisch, who was also an atomic scientist, was apprised by his aunt of the latest in the work of Hahn and Strassmann; they had actually split the atom, but did not interpret their results as such. Meitner and Frisch did.

Many of the world's leading scientists were driven from Europe by the "superrace" mania of the Nazis. Besides Einstein and Meitner, the list included Enrico Fermi, Otto Stern, Leo Szilard, Max Born, Edward Teller, Hans Bethe, Victor Weisskopf, and many others who gladly served the Allied cause. Fermi, whose wife was Jewish, was catching some flak in Italy, not so much because the Italians were anti-Semitic, but because Mussolini fell so much under Hitler's heel.

In September of 1938 Neville Chamberlain came running, hat in hand to Germany when Hitler massed two hundred thousand troops at the Czech-Austrian border. Caught unawares and devoid of any plan to thwart Hitler's designs on the Czech-Sudetenland, Chamberlain bade the Czech government turn over half their country to the Germans. Daladier of France was equally cowardly. Neither showed any inclination to come to the aid of a democracy about to be carved up. Eduard Benes, the president of Czechoslovakia, would have rallied the Czech people to fight the Germans, but without support from the French and English, it would have been a needless letting of blood. With Czech capitulation a sad reality, forced on the Czech people as much by their Allies as by the Germans, Chamberlain returned to England claiming the role of peacemaker, mouthing such mocking phrases as, "Peace for our time . . . . peace with honour." He prudently neglected to mention the price for the peace that was obtained and to whom the peace pertained—certainly not the Czechs. As for "honour," it was trampled in the mud.

Hitler's contempt for the apparent weakness of the democracies helped solidify the ranks behind him, in Germany and in the neighboring countries. The Nazis took great satisfaction in the fact that Hitler was able to make these acquisitions by the use of bluff and without going to war. A few months later, the Germans gobbled up the rest of Czechoslovakia, again without going to war.

In Copenhagen, Niels Bohr had become interested in Lise Meitner's interpretation of the Hahn-Strassmann experiment. He brought her over from Sweden and provided the facilities with which she could work out the same experiments to see if her conclusions were indeed correct. With help from Frisch, Meitner split the uranium atom and was able to measure the amount of energy released. This was a momentous discovery, and when she communicated the results to Bohr, who was then on his way to the United States, she did it by way of a one word telegram: "Success." Bohr immediately spread the word to Fermi, Einstein, and Szilard. Einstein and Fermi were at first skeptical that the necessary "chain-reaction" could be accomplished, but not so Szilard. Almost alone, Szilard saw the technical possibility of channeling the energy derived from "fission" into a bomb of huge destructive capability. Looking beyond the immediate, if the Germans developed the bomb first, in what Szilard saw as an inevitable war, this power in the hands of a Hitler would place the world under his heel and ring down the curtain on civilization.

Fermi, now at Columbia University, related the possibilities of such a vast source of destructive power to some Navy officials, who received the report with expected suspicion. With war clouds gathering, their military sights were set on the known and trusted capabilities of such old reliables as the battleship and the newly-developed aircraft carrier. The miniscule atom is a nice little guy, but its investigation and eventual use, besides being time-consuming, was not a certainty. Simply, it was too speculative.

37

LETTER TO ROOSEVELT

By the fall of 1938 the persecution of Jews in Germany had been increasingly stepped up. Their shops were boycotted and they were forced to sell their property for insignificant sums. German landlords and hotel owners were *"verboten"* to rent to Jews; no one was allowed to hire a Jew; even radios belonging to Jews were confiscated. They were systematically being deprived of their rights, their livelihood, and their citizenship. They were, under Hitler's plan, being slowly starved to death. The question here is an obvious one, why didn't the Jews leave Germany? Why didn't they just pick up and get out? Why suffer the abuse? As is often the case, there was no simple solution; it is much easier to ask the question than it is to provide the answer. The real question, and the one that gets to the heart of the matter is, if they could get out, where could they go? The English had cut off immigration to Palestine and the Americans begged off because of unemployment. Those few who were allowed to emigrate, did so, provided they had sufficient means to bribe their way out. The others who couldn't, were forced to remain, their last hope that once Hitler had vent his anger or was somehow knocked off his perch, life would be easier. Only the Netherlands opened its doors to the hapless Jews to any extent. Hungary, Poland, Yugoslavia, Italy, Switzerland, Luxembourg, France, Britain, Australia, and the South American countries took only a few.

One seventeen year-old, who came to the realization that his real home was in Palestine and not in Germany, left in 1936. Herschel Grynszpan remained for a while with relatives in Brussels and then went, illegally, over the border into France. From Paris he hoped to make his way to the Promised Land, but he never made it. On November 3, 1938, Grynszpan read a hastily written note from his sister, Berta, who reported that his family was among thousands of Jews who had been forcibly deported overnight from Germany to Poland. Their father, Sendel, later told the unhappy story:

> We were taken by train to the German border station at Neu Bentschen on the line connecting Frankfort on Oder with Posen. We arrived at about six o'clock on Saturday morning. There

were trains from all over Germany: Leipzig, Berlin, Cologne, Dusseldorf, Bieleford, Essen, Bremen. We were about 12,000 in all. That was Saturday, October 29th. When we got to the border we were searched. We were only allowed to take 10 marks; any excess was confiscated. That was German law, we were told: "You didn't have more than that when you arrived in Germany and you can't take any more with you now." We were kept under guard and not allowed to communicate with anyone. The SS told us we would have to walk about 2 kilometers to the border. Those who couldn't walk were beaten until the road was wet with their blood. Their baggage was taken away. It was the first time I realized how barbarous the Germans really are. They made us run while they shouted, "Run! Run!" I was struck down at the roadside, but my son Marcus took me by the hand and said, "Come on, Papa, run. They'll kill you if you don't."[231]

When the full import of the mass deportation and suffering of his family became clear to Grynszpan, he dropped his original plans, bought a gun, and on November 7 shot and seriously wounded the third secretary of the German Embassy in Paris, Eric vom Rath. When vom Rath subsequently died of his wounds, Hitler made it a "cause célèbre" and even attended the funeral. In retaliation for vom Rath's death, Nazis throughout Germany, Austria, and the Sudetenland spread terror and death into every Jewish community. Every known Jewish shop that had not previously been pillaged, was broken into and shattered, the goods stolen or burned. Homes were invaded, valuables were stolen, and thousands of males were sent off to concentration camps or murdered on the spot. Hundreds of synagogues were set on fire and dynamited, their sacred contents burned or mutilated, while German firemen sought only to prevent the fire from spreading to nearby German-owned property. The devastation was carried out with characteristic German precision and visciousness. There was so much glass littered on the streets from broken store windows that the outrage was called, "Krystal Nacht." That was the night of November 10, 1938.

The American consul in Leipzig, David H. Burrum, in his report to the consul general in Berlin, described the scene there:

The shattering of shop windows, looting of stores and dwellings of Jews which began in the early hours of Nov. 10, 1938, was hailed subsequently in the Nazi press as a "spontaneous wave of righteous indignation throughout Germany, as a result of the cowardly Jewish murder of Third Secretary vom Rath in the German Embassy in Paris.'' So far as a very high percentage of the German populace is concerned, a state of popular indignation that would spontaneously lead to such excesses, can be considered as nonexistent. On the contrary, in viewing the ruins and attendant measures employed, all of the local crowds observed were obviously benumbed over what had happened and aghast over the unprecedented fury of the Nazi acts that had been or were taking place with bewildering rapidity throughout the city. The whole lamentable affair was organized in such a sinister fashion, as to lend credence to the theory that the execution of it had involved studied preparation.[232]

President Roosevelt was appalled by the events in Germany, as he related his feelings in the following communication to Myron C. Taylor: "The recent wave of extreme persecution which has swept Germany and which is continuing in many of its aspects has greatly increased both the difficulty of providing refuge and settlement for the unfortunate victims and the urgency for concrete action to meet the problem . . . . we must produce concrete and substantial results and we must produce them soon."

Roosevelt's sympathy and call for action is heartwarming, and seems to promise a solution for the problems of the sufferers, until we read further in the same letter: "This government is already accepting involuntary immigrants to the fullest extent permitted by law. I do not believe it either desirable or practicable to recommend any change in the quota provisions of our immigration laws. We are prepared, nevertheless, to make any other contribution which may be in our power to make. You are authorized to make a public statement that this government can, under its existing law, accept annually 27,370 persons from Germany. This does not include certain members of the learned professions whose admission is not subject to numerical limitation."[233]

Still, in the face of the unsympathetic policies of the government of the United States, Einstein persevered. As late as mid-1941 he was still writing letters to important and influential parties to help ease the plight of the refugees. To Eleanor Roosevelt on July 26, 1941, he wrote:

Dear Mrs. Roosevelt:

I have noted with great satisfaction that you always stand for the right and humaneness even when it is hard. Therefore in my deep concern, I know of no one else to whom to turn for help.

A policy is now being pursued in the State Department which makes it all but impossible to give refuge in America to many worthy persons who are the victims of Fascist cruelty in Europe. Of course, this is not openly avowed by those responsible for it. The method which is being used, however, is to make immigration impossible by erecting a wall of bureaucratic measures alleged to be necessary to protect America against subversive, dangerous elements. I would suggest that you talk about this question to some well-informed and right-minded person such as Mr. Hamilton Fish Armstrong. If then you become convinced that a truly grave injustice is under way, I know that you will find it possible to bring the matter to the attention of your heavily burdened husband in order that it may be remedied.

Very truly yours,

Professor Albert Einstein

As the Christian world shut its eyes and its gates, any hope of large-scale immigration from Germany vanished. The holocaust occurred because the world handed Hitler a free hand with the destiny of the Jews and Europe.

Fermi, Bohr, and Einstein were not totally convinced that a chain reaction could be achieved, but Szilard was leaving nothing to chance. If there existed even the remotest possibility that the Germans would succeed in harnessing nuclear power, then ways had to be found either to hinder them in their effort, or to achieve the reaction first. It was no secret that the Germans had stopped the export of uranium from the Czechoslovakian mines they had taken over. And it was also common knowledge that the world's largest source of uranium was located in the Belgian Congo. Considering Einstein's special friendship with Queen Elizabeth, Szilard held that a letter from Einstein to the Queen would not only safeguard a supply of the precious ore for the Allies, but at the same time, deny it to the Germans.

On the morning of August 2, 1939, in Peconic, Long Island, New York, where Einstein was summering, Tom Bucky was told: "Now Tom, you stick to your house. You don't come over here. And you stay away." There were always visitors coming to see Einstein no matter where he tried to find a haven; it was therefore no surprise to

Tom that he was asked to make himself scarce. But, never before had he been told to remain in his apartment over the garage. Tom Bucky continues: "People came and stayed most of the day . . . . but I never knew about the bomb, nor did my father know about it. The only thing we did know was Einstein's great fear the Germans are building a secret weapon, something that's going to blow up the whole world, all at once . . . . He was afraid of that. But more, neither my father nor I ever knew, even though I was with him (Einstein) every single day . . . . then in the evening they said, 'Now you can show up again' That's all I knew, period, until after the bomb was dropped and up until the secret was out. Then I realized that that was when Leo Szilard, who later on I became friends with, was there with that letter business to Roosevelt."[234]

Trading on Einstein's like fear that the Germans might first discover how to unlock the power of the atom, Szilard, along with Edward Teller and Eugene Wigner, rode out to confer with him. What issued forth from that long, hot day of drafting and redrafting, was a message not for the Queen, with a copy going to the United States State Department, as was previously planned, but an approach directly to Roosevelt himself.

August 2nd, 1939

F.D. Roosevelt
President of the United States
White House
Washington, D.C.

Sir:

Some recent work by E. Fermi and L. Szilard, which has been communicated to me in manuscript, leads me to expect that the element uranium may be turned into a new and important source of energy in the immediate future. Certain aspects of the situation which has arisen seem to call for watchfulness and, if necessary, quick action on the part of the Administration. I believe therefore that it is my duty to bring to your attention the following facts and recommendations:

In the course of the last four months it has been made probable —through the work of Joliot in France as well as Fermi and Szilard in America—that it may become possible to set up a nuclear chain reaction in a large mass of uranium, by which vast amounts of power and large quantities of new radium-like elements would be generated. Now it appears almost certain that this could be achieved in the immediate future.

This new phenomenon would also lead to the construction of bombs, and it is conceivable—though much less certain—that extremely powerful bombs of a new type may thus be constructed. A single bomb of this type, carried by boat and exploded in a port, might very well destroy the whole port together with some of the surrounding territory. However, such bombs might very well prove to be too heavy for transportation by air.

The United States has only very poor ores of uranium in moderate quantities. There is some good ore in Canada and the former Czechoslovakia, while the most important source of uranium is Belgian Congo.

In view of this situation you may think it desirable to have some permanent contact maintained between the Administration and the group of physicists working on chain reactions in America. One possible way of achieving this might be for you to entrust with this task a person who has your confidence and who could perhaps serve in an inofficial capacity. His task might comprise the following:

a) to approach Government Departments, keep them informed of the further development, and put forward recommendations for Government action, giving particular attention to the problem of securing a supply of uranium ore for the United States;

b) to speed up the experimental work, which is at present being carried on within the limits of the budgets of University laboratories, by providing funds, if such funds be required, through his contacts with private persons who are willing to make contributions for this cause, and perhaps also by obtaining the co-operation of industrial laboratories which have the necessary equipment.

I understand that Germany has actually stopped the sale of uranium from the Czechoslovakian mines which she has taken over. That she should have taken such early action might perhaps be understood on the ground that the son of the German Under-Secretary of State, von Weizsacker, is attached to the Kaiser-Wilhelm-Institute in Berlin where some of the American work on uranium is now being repeated.[235]

Yours very truly,

Albert Einstein

Alexander Sachs, an economist, was the connection through whom the letter was to be shown to Roosevelt; but some two months later, and the letter still lay on Sachs's desk. The usually slow wheels of government were grinding unusually slow this year, with good reason; the world was at war. On September 1, 1939, Hitler ordered his "panzers" to invade Poland. Screaming something about his right of "counterattack" he brought the poorly equipped, outgunned Poles to the negotiating table in thirty days. France and Britain, duly shaken and now fully awake after the Czechoslovakian humiliation, had previously warned Hitler that an invasion of Poland would bring them into the war. Ignoring their ultimatum and contemptuous of their warnings, Hitler was convinced he could grab off Poland with little or no opposition from the west; and after Warsaw was reduced to rubble, the Germans occupied all of Western Poland. But the Russians weren't exactly sleeping either. They, in turn, moved west and occupied the eastern part of Poland, and shook Hitler up a bit when they also took over the northern flank countries of Latvia, Lithuania, and Estonia. Now, looming up in the east, was a far greater menace than Hitler had bargained for.

On the Western front, where the British and French troops were massed, there was no action; they called it the "phony war." In Washington, the "letter" finally landed on Roosevelt's desk. The President immediately saw its importance and acted to form the Advisory Committee on Uranium. Within the space of only some three weeks, after meeting with Fermi, Szilard, and Wigner, the committee issued a report in favor of proceeding with the investigation of atomic energy. They, too, became convinced that atomic fission could produce a source of bombs with a destructiveness vastly greater than anything known. Other meetings followed and Einstein was often consulted, but he declined the invitation to become a member of the committee. With the miserly sum of only $6,000 for the coming year appropriated for research, the work of the committee soon slackened. When Szilard came to Einstein grumbling about not enough attention and insufficient funds, Einstein wrote a second letter; this one to Sachs, to be relayed to the President. Einstein renewed his warning that the Germans had increased their research in uranium. It is also noteworthy, that for the first time, Einstein called for secrecy where atomic developments were concerned. As a result of his second letter, the committee was enlarged, but Einstein still declined to participate directly. Still, it took two more years before the "Manhattan Project" evolved.

There's no question but that Einstein was well-informed on the progress of the atomic scientists. He knew them all, and while he was called on less and less for advice as the program progressed, and while he couldn't dot every "i" and cross every "t" he knew pretty well what was happening. It was his own decision that he not occupy a seat on the policy-making committee; this deprived him of access to "top secret" status. It was just as well that he didn't serve on the advisory committee; it prevented him from joining in the determination of the bomb's eventual use.

38

WORLD WAR II

Maja Winteler, who had not seen her brother since 1932, decided to visit him in Princeton and get a glimpse of the United States as well. But once she came here, she, too, never returned to Europe; the war had intervened and the decision to remain a permanent guest in her brother's house was made for her. The townspeople enjoyed seeing them together when brother and sister stepped out-of-doors for a walk, with their wild gray hair, so similar in appearance, that from afar one couldn't tell one from the other. And when Gustav Bucky came by with his roadster and the Einsteins would ride the rumble seat—imagine two heads of hair like the Einstein's blowing in the breeze. Maja had always been a vegetarian, but after coming to America she found that she couldn't resist the uniquely native food phenomenon, the "hot dog." After devouring one, she invariably felt guilty, until her famous brother officially declared the hotdog, a vegetable.

If the British had made a strong show of their naval forces when Hitler invaded Denmark and Norway, the Germans would have retreated. But the British effort was so feeble in April of 1940 that not only did the Germans take Norway, but the almost perfect ease with which it was accomplished further reinforced Hitler's feeling that the British would not fight. Besides protecting his north, Hitler now controlled the Baltic Sea; the sea lanes to Sweden (on whom Germany depended for steel) would remain open, and extremely important for survival, Germany would be spared the blockade that had all but strangled her in the First World War.

In a lightning move in May, Hitler invaded Holland and Belgium, and after two weeks of the most barbaric bombing of civilian centers to date, swung south to invade France. Avoiding the Maginot line, and employing a combination of massed tanks and large numbers of aircraft, the Germans reduced the French army to a sorry lot of prisoners by June 14. Nowhere visible was the elan of the French fighting man who had saved Paris in 1914 and who had stopped the hated Bosch at the Marne. The French people and soldiers were betrayed by a combination of inferior and antiquated weaponry and

271

outmoded military concepts, together with right-wing sympathies in the ranks of the military. Sold out by Nazi sympathizers from within their own ranks, who comprised the "fifth column," the soldiers could do nothing but just plain quit. By having it declared an open city, Paris was spared the bombings, destruction, and death that the Germans had visited upon Warsaw and Rotterdam. Paris passed from the gaiety of the "city of lights" to the drabness of German gray.

The German *blitzkrieg* (lightning war) squeezed one hundred thousand British soldiers into the coastal town of Dunkirk, with nowhere to go but into the water of the English Channel. In the face of heavy German bombardments, most of those who made it to the beaches were picked up by the thousands of English small craft that had crossed the channel to rescue them.

After mopping up the remaining pockets of resistance in France, and garrisoning his troops throughout the once proud, but conquered land, Hitler ordered Goering's air force to begin bombing Britain, ostensibly to soften her up for the inevitable invasion. The air war over Britain began with great German superiority, but with American aid pouring in and stiffening British resistance, the tide of the air war gradually turned in favor of the Allies. Like Napoleon before him, Hitler was fearful of running the risk of a coastal landing on the shores of Britain; the nightmare of some unforeseen disaster, perhaps the fate of the Spanish Armada, haunted him.

But why risk invading England? Why consider it at all? What possible harm could the English do now, bottled up on their tight little island? Why not simply take a breather, consolidate the winnings, and exploit the recent gains? Historically speaking, Hitler had outdistanced Frederick the Great, Bismarck and the Kaiser put together. He had given to Germany "Lebensraum," the legendary dream of Germans for the past two hundred years, with the acquisition of Austria and Czechoslovakia and the military conquest of half of Poland and all of Holland, Belgium, Luxembourg, Denmark, Norway, and France. No country of substance was equal to her challenge. And allied with the lackey, Mussolini, he could control all of Europe. But peace was never Hitler's intent. His style of government, one-man decree, could not survive on a peacetime footing. Without his constant harangue to greater and greater military glory, the people would soon lose interest and Hitler would fall. He had built the German people up to a point of great expectation, a thousand-year Reich, conquest of the world, the key phrases calculated to inspire

Taking U. S. Oath of Allegiance; 1940. Left to right, Helen Dukas, Einstein, Margot Einstein.

confidence and unquestioned obedience. And hadn't he gained the right to that confidence? Just take a look at Hitler's map of Europe —his empire stretched from the Baltic to the Mediterranean, and from the Atlantic to the Russian border. The Germans were not the only people convinced that he was nothing less than divinely inspired, if not the "second coming." But, all this wasn't enough for Hitler. He ordered his armies to invade Russia on June 22, 1941. Hitler had only momentarily stubbed his toe in the "Battle of Britain," but at Stalingrad he came to disaster; the German dead there amounted to two hundred fifty thousand men. The tide had turned. The fabled, invincible German armies, the odious goose-stepping "supermen" also failed to dislodge the Russians from either Moscow or Leningrad. However, they did march well in parades.

Aiding the war effort, Einstein copied his original 1905 relativity theory paper which was to be put up for auction at a war bond rally. It brought in several million dollars. Reviewing the copy, Einstein mused that he thought he could have stated it simpler.

Finally, the Allied armies made their move, landing on the beaches of Normandy on June 6, 1944. Previous landings were made in Italy. Simultaneous with an offensive from a resuscitated Russian fighting force, the drive towards Berlin began. Given stubborn resistance, the Germans finally collapsed and begged to be captured by the Western Allies lest they fall into the hands of the less sympathetic Russians. In May 1945, Hitler and Goebbels commited suicide and Germany surrendered. Only when Allied soldiers liberated the death camps, where the extermination of countless millions of people had been carried out by means of the latest uniquely German inventions—the gas chambers, the crematorium, and slave-labor—was the world informed of the horrors perpetrated in the name of Hitler.

Over in the Pacific, on December 7, 1941, Japanese forces bombed Pearl Harbor in a sneak attack, and entered the war. Japan continued her military adventure throughout the southeast Asia area conquering Singapore, Indochina, and the Phillipines, extending her domain as far south as New Guinea, thus threatening Australia, and as far east as the Marshall Islands. Using only some 16 percent of her fighting forces, however, the United States forces began driving the Japanese back to their home islands. From the landing of the Marines on Guadalcanal in August on 1942, to subsequent naval victories, the Americans continued north to dislodge the Japanese from Tarawa, Pelelieu, Saipan, Guam, Eniwetok, Iwo Jima, and Okinawa and fulfilled General MacArthur's prophecy to "return" to the Phillipines. In the summer of 1945, they then stood ready to invade Japan herself.

The major effort to obtain a self-sustaining and controlled chain-reaction was moved from Columbia University to the University of Chicago early in 1942. Enrico Fermi, along with his colleagues, under the direction of Dr. Arthur Holly Compton, began setting up the first atomic furnace. The atomic age was ushered in in the most unlikely place, the squash court under the stands of Stagg Field in Chicago. The critical experiment was performed there on December 2, 1942. The reckoning had been correct; one uranium atom when split released the energy needed to split two atoms of uranium, which in turn released the energy needed to split four uranium atoms, and so on up the geometric-progression ladder. These actions took place within "millionths of a second," so that they appeared instantaneous. The energy released, in accordance with Einstein's equation, was enormous. Fermi and his crew had succeeded.

At Los Alamos, New Mexico, Dr. J. Robert Oppenheimer headed the team responsible for converting the sensitive nuclear apparatus into a workable bomb. The first test (only one was required) was made on July 16, 1945 when the first "atomic bomb" was fired at Alamogordo, New Mexico. This test, too, was successful. On the island of Guam, the "Little Boy" bomb was loaded aboard a converted B-29 named the Enola Gay. Since it was considered too risky to load the completed bomb on board in one piece (it might explode during take-off), it was assembled in the air. On the morning of August 6, 1945, about 9:30 A.M., in the company of two protecting B-29s, Colonel Paul W. Tibbets, Jr., brought the Enola Gay over the Hiroshima target. Major Thomas W. Ferebee released the bomb, and for the first time in history atomic power was used. Eighty thousand civilians were killed by the initial blast; there were additional casualties from burns and radiation. Three days later, the "Fat Man" was dropped on Nagasaki, with similar results. The dumbfounded Japanese quickly surrendered.

Credit: National Archives

Einstein working with Naval personnel during World War II.

Prior to its use, scientists were not unanimous in their opinions as to whether the "bomb" should be used against population centers. Some loudly opposed its use; others were in favor. Back in April, 1945, Szilard and Einstein had composed another letter to Roosevelt, begging him not to drop the bomb; since Germany had virtually been knocked out of the war, there no longer was any danger that an enemy would use atomic weapons against the Allies. Unfortunately, Roosevelt died on April 12th, and the letter remained unopened on his desk.

When Vice-President Harry S. Truman was sworn in as the new president, he was quickly informed about the destructive capacity of the new bomb and told that, if he consented to its use, the war could be brought to a quick end. New on the job, and having been kept in the dark about the entire Manhattan Project, Truman sought expert advice. He summoned a "select" committee composed of Henry L. Stimson, George L. Harrison, James F. Byrnes, Ralph A Bard, William L. Clayton, Vannevar Bush, Karl T. Compton, and James B. Conant to advise him. The committee was aided by the opinions of a panel of outstanding scientists, all of whom had had a major role in the bomb's development, Dr. Arthur H. Compton, Enrico Fermi, E.O. Lawrence, and J. Robert Oppenheimer. Also contributing to the final decision were General George C. Marshall, chief of staff of the United States Army, and General Leslie Groves, the military commander of the Manhattan Project. After all the views were expressed in detail, the committee unanimously recommended immediate use of the weapon against the Japanese homeland. Truman concurred.

Volumes have been written and spoken both by those who opposed dropping the bomb (on humanitarian grounds) and by those who favored using the bomb, seeing in its use also a means of actually saving the many lives that would have been lost in the inevitable invasion of the Japanese home islands. But, as history records, the bomb was developed too late to be used against Germany, and some who wish to attach a racial motive to the bomb's use on Japan would do well to consider that Allied fire-bombing of German civilian centers accounted for more deaths than both atomic bombs.

With the continued development of post-war atomic weapons, scientists became alarmed at the real prospects of a nuclear holocaust. They agreed that the possibility exists that millions of lives could be wiped out in a few seconds if means could not be found to prevent nuclear proliferation. Since the first bomb was dropped, Einstein had agonized that he had had his finger on the trigger. So when several scientists organized the Emergency Committee of Atomic Scientists, and asked Einstein to serve as chairman, he readily accepted. Represented with offices in Washington, New York, Chicago, and Princeton, and including such scientific luminaries as Harold Urey, Hans Bethe, T.R. Hagness, Philip Morse, Linus Pauling, Leo Szilard, Victor Weisskopf, and Edward Condon, the committee set about the task of informing the American public of the horrifying effects of a nuclear war. Einstein actively joined in the appeal for funds, regularly attended the meetings, had a hand in formulating policy, and rallied many of the splinter groups to the common cause. The committee tried to bring home to the public that they could no longer depend on sending infantry off to some distant land to fight future wars; that whole cities would be destroyed in seconds with but the push of a button, should an atomic war break out. Only a world government, Einstein believed, could forestall a nuclear war: "A world authority and an eventual world state is not only desirable in the name of brotherhood; they are necessary for survival."[236]

Suggestions on how to deal with a post-war Germany varied— whether to strip Germany down to little more than an agricultural society, for example, or divide her territory among the victors, all, however, agreed that the German potential for making war must be destroyed. Einstein, too, felt that Germany cannot be reeducated away from war; she simply must not be allowed to develop any war industries.

Einstein was not seeking revenge when he firmly rejected an invitation from the Bavarian Academy of Science to again accept membership. To Arnold Sommerfeld, an old friend, who had initiated the letter of inquiry, he wrote: "The Germans slaughtered my Jewish brethren; I will have nothing further to do with them, not even with a relatively harmless academy. I feel differently about the few people who, as far as it was possible, remained steadfast against Nazism. I am happy to learn that you were among them."[237]

Allied investigations finally revealed that the Germans had not given special priority to the development of an atomic bomb; instead, they had put their money and effort into the rockets of Werner von Braun. When informed of this, Einstein said that had he known the Germans were not working on the bomb, he would not have written that letter to Roosevelt.

39

BRANDEIS UNIVERSITY

In 1938, when Thomas Masaryk pleaded with Neville Chamberlain not to give in to Hitler's demands, declaring that the Czech people stood ready to fight for the Sudetenland, he was greeted with the icy response, "I trust Hitler." Chamberlain's appeasement cost the Czechs their freedom and their country; it cost Europe fifty million lives. A year later, with the same frigidity, Chamberlain signed the infamous "white paper" prohibiting further Jewish immigration to Palestine. This time Chamberlain appeased the Arabs and caused the death of millions of Jews who perished in Hitler's extermination camps because they had nowhere to go. At that time, making a survey of the use of the land in the Middle East, Walter Clay Loudermilk, who was sent there by the United States Department of Agriculture as a soil conservationist, observed the effect of the white paper:

> During my stay in Palestine in 1939, I witnessed a tragic by-product of the German advance into Czechoslovakia. In Palestine and Syria we were told of cargo boats, filled with refugees from Nazi-dominated Central Europe, whose captains tried desperately to disembark this living cargo on the shores of Palestine. We saw some of these old and often unseaworthy boats, whose miserable passengers were not permitted to land anywhere because of the lack of formal visas. We saw those wretched ships floating about on a steaming sea in unbearable summer heat, with refugees packed in holds under intolerably inhuman conditions. The laws governing the transportation of animals for slaughter in the United States do not permit conditions like those which some of the intelligentsia of central Europe had to undergo in these old boats on the Mediterranean. The revolting slave ships of a century ago were better; for slaves had a sale value and their ships were sped to their destination without delay. But Jewish refugees were kept floating about upon a torrid sea, just out of sight of land, with a desperate hope that the captain, though risking confiscation of his ship, would

attempt to discharge them illegally on the shores of Palestine. I was told of ships that had set out laden with refugees, and after some months turned up empty again, with no trace of their human cargo. None of them have been heard from since by their relatives.

During our stay in Beirut an old cargo boat, loaded with 655 refugees from Czechoslovakia, was unloaded at the quarantine station for a few days. The ship was so overrun with rats that the passengers had to be removed to exterminate these vermin. After obtaining permission to interview the refugees, we found that they had been floating for eleven weeks, packed into little wooden shelves built around the cargo holds. The congestion, the ghastly unsanitary conditions and sufferings that these people had undergone aroused our highest admiration for their courage and fortitude. Their food was gone, and all of them had contracted scurvy from malnutrition. We were astonished to find that these former citizens of Czechoslovakia represented a very high level of European culture. Most of them spoke several languages, and many of them were able to tell us their story in English. Of the 655 refugees, forty-two were lawyers, forty were engineers, twenty-six were physicians and surgeons, in addition to women doctors, professional writers, gifted musicians, pharmacists and nurses. Two had been staff officers of the Czech army before its dissolution by the Nazis, sixty had been army officers, and two hundred, soldiers; many others were skilled workers and craftsmen.

Without passports, without country, these useful and highly cultured refugees presented one of the most tragic spectacles of modern times. No ambassador, no consul spoke up for them to demand the rights and privileges enjoyed by the lowliest citizen of the smallest country. They were adrift without a port of entry, without a representative who could protect them. What a stigma upon our modern civilization. What has become of our conception of the infinite value of the individual?[238]

With the advent of World War II, the Jews in Palestine put aside their differences with the British and joined the fight against the common enemy. After the war, when the world's sympathy for the remnants of European Jewry spoke loudly in favor of a Palestine homeland, the British still persisted in their brutalization of a people who were simply trying to go home. Ripping them from off the

Einstein with refugee children, 1948.

beaches of Palestine, stopping ships within sight of the "Promised Land," forcing them into detention camps, beating with clubs the survivors of Hitler's death camps to force them to turn back, and generally favoring the Arab populace, the British added another inglorious page to their already tarnished history as a colonial power.

World opinion, however, was heavily favorable towards the establishment of a Jewish homeland and openly critical of the British pro-Arab policy. The British were saved additional embarrassment when the United Nations voted to partition Palestine between the Jews and Arabs; the date was November 29, 1947. May 15, 1948 was the date the British mandate ended. The following day David Ben Gurion proclaimed the existence of the State of Israel, and the gates to the homeland were at last reopened. The establishment of a Jewish state helped solve the immediate needs of the homeless survivors of the Nazi holocaust, but the day of proclamation also signaled the invasion of Israel by the five neighboring states of Egypt, Syria, Jordan, Lebanon, and Iraq. The armed struggle of Israel to repel those who wished to drive her into the sea is well documented in many personal and historic accounts; it is a struggle that unfortunately still continues today.

In his appearance before the Anglo-American Committee of Inquiry on Palestine, in 1946, Einstein testified to the effect that the bulk of the refugees should be brought to Palestine. He also stated before the committee, and to the dismay of political Zionism that, "I was never in favor of a State."[239] Nationalism to Einstein, was an infantile disease that one should expect mankind to outgrow; he believed in a mature world government. Inherent in the narrowness of nationalist goals is the corruption of human values. This was his evaluation in a general sense. But to be specific, if we search the records of various Einstein statements on the subject of Israeli statehood we find overwhelming evidence of his dedication to a "Jewish National Spirit,' to a "national renaissance." He had said, "I look upon Jewish nationality as a fact."[240] He referred to a "Jewish Commonwealth in Palestine." And again, "The Jewish nation is a living thing and the sentiment of Jewish nationalism must be developed both in Palestine and everywhere else . . ."[241] "I am convinced that every Jew who cares at all for the health and the dignity of Jewry must cooperate with all his power in the realization of Herzl's dream."[242] And Herzl's dream, of course, was the "Judenstaat."

Einstein would have preferred that this particular state not be subject to the same stresses and pulls affecting other states; that is, having to defend borders, wage wars, and having to endure the unavoidable political intrigues. He envisioned a center from which would emanate a "spiritual rejuvenation," not in a religious sense particularly, but rather in the sense of a moral and spiritual center for the Jewish people. In 1944 he went so far as to declare for a Jewish controlled Palestine. Whatever the status of the Jews in Palestine, peace could only be achieved when there was cooperation between Jews and Arabs.

It was mainly through the efforts of Rabbi Israel Goldstein of New York that the campus of Middlesex University, a floundering medical and veterinary school in Waltham, Massachusetts, became the first Jewish-sponsored secular university in the United States. C. Ruggles Smith, the son of founder John Hall Smith, made every effort to facilitate the turning over of the university, in toto, to a predominantly Jewish group from New York, headed by Goldstein. Just outside of Boston, and not far from New York, the one hundred acre campus was ideally located near Harvard, Radcliffe, MIT, Boston College, Boston University, Tufts and the many other fine educational institutions in and around the "Hub." Quick community

Testifying before the Anglo-American Inquiry Committee on
Palestine, 1946.

approval was won with warm endorsements from the presidents of
the neighboring universities as well as from Governor Maurice J.
Tobin and Archbishop Richard J. Cushing. Boston lawyer George
Alpert was brought in for the purpose of interesting local industrial
and philanthropic leaders. But to gain the maximum amount of support, financial and cultural, Goldstein had to go elsewhere:

What we needed immediately was first-class academic sponsorship. A number of eminent scholars and scientists with whom I had discussed the problem, seemed interested and glad to help, but I was ambitious to secure the endorsement of the greatest academic figure in the world, Professor Albert Einstein. I called on Professor Einstein at his home in Princeton. With deep interest he listened to the exposition of my plan for a Jewish-sponsored secular university. He agreed that it was an important objective. He had been troubled for some time past not only for the plight of Jewish scholars who found it difficult to receive appointments in the colleges and universities. He had firmly held ideas about the need of giving the faculty of an institution of higher learning significant rights in guiding educational policy. His chief concern was that the university should be first class and free from nonacademic control . . . . Professor Einstein's warm endorsement and offer of help were a source of great encouragement, gave the project prestige, and helped me in the approach both to laymen and to leaders in academic circles."[243]

Not only had Goldstein obtained Einstein's personal endorsement, but out of the discussions emerged the Albert Einstein Foundation

Credit: AIP

With R. W. Ladenburg at Princeton.

for Higher Learning, a fund-raising instrument, which if successful, "could become the mother fund to support a network of Jewish-sponsored secular universities."[244] The added prestige of Einstein's participation made it possible for Goldstein to interest a large group of distinguished sponsors from various fields, among whom were Hon. Joseph Ball, Karl Compton, Judge Anna M. Cross, Helen Gahagan Douglas, Dr. Will Durant, James A. Farley, William Green, Sidney Hillman, Dr. Alvin Johnson, Hon. H.M. Kilgore, Dr. Frank Kingdon, Fiorello LaGuardia, Wayne Morse, Dr. Hugh O'Donnell, Walter Reuther, and Owen D. Young. Goldstein would serve as president of the foundation, and Einstein as head of the Educational Advisory Committee of the University. The naming of the university was easily arrived at, Brandeis University, after Louis Dembitz Brandeis, Associate Justice of the United States Supreme Court from 1916–1939.

It was decided that if the university was to open at the earliest possible time, the first course of study would have to be a school of liberal arts, since it was the easiest to assemble in terms of faculty and cost. A medical school, which would require extensive equipment and facilities, specialized faculty, and a hospital association was considered too costly in time and money. Relieved of the burden of having to fund a medical school, previous priorities could now be attended to. The run-down condition of the existing campus required the immediate outlay of current funds to provide not only faculty but also additional classrooms, furniture, offices, dormitories, and dining rooms if the target date for the freshman class of 1947 was to be met.

Those who thought Einstein was along "just for the ride" and would serve only nominally were surprised to see that he took an active part in the committee's work. "He was deeply concerned with the choice of a faculty that should be free from the influence of the laymen, the Trustees of the university or of the Foundation . . . . Dr. Einstein felt that a body of outstanding, independent, objective men should be charged by the Board of the Foundation with the selection of an Acting Academic Head to organize the university and of an Advisory Board to advise the academic head."[245]

The idea of a denominational university in America was not a new concept. Most of the first universities founded on the continent were religiously affiliated; Harvard, Yale, Princeton, and later Fordham, Notre Dame, Holy Cross and many others were pioneered by various religious groups. Jews, who for the most part placed education second only in importance to their religion, have given inordinately large amounts for the support of institutions of higher learning, though numbering only a small minority of the population, despite the quota system which worked primarily against them. There were the expected objections from fellow Jews. Some voiced fears that a Jewish-sponsored university would develop into a ghetto school. Others turned away from supporting the school because they wished to maintain a low Jewish profile; this attitude was also present in the beginning days of Zionism. Goldstein reminded the negativists that years before there was similar resistance by some American Jews to the establishment of Jewish-sponsored hospitals. "Experience had proved, however, that Jewish hospitals, their non-sectarian character and their high standards, had rendered a service to the general community and had raised the prestige of the Jewish community."[246]

Less then a year before the freshman class of 1947 was to enter Brandeis University, a bombshell exploded in the midst of all the well-laid plans. In a letter to Goldstein, Einstein threatened to withdraw his name and support. This was an enormous shock to Goldstein and it couldn't have come at a less propitious time. The reason for Einstein's "shocker" was the approach Goldstein had made to Dr. Abram Sachar for the post of academic head. Goldstein's action was clearly going over the head of Einstein and the yet unnamed Educational Advisory Committee, and Goldstein readily admitted such in an apologetic letter to Einstein. But patching things up was not Einstein's way in this matter; there was a principle involved —whether any one individual can take upon himself the rights and duties which were clearly outlined and separated beforehand, of others charged with the enormous responsibility of choosing faculty. Einstein stubbornly refused to tolerate this incursion into the "educational program and policy of the university." If his name was to be used, then his (Einstein's) standards would be maintained. He remained, and justifiably so, uncompromising.

While the matter was conducted by private letter and the public was not informed, the controversy developed into an either-or situation; either one or the other would be forced to retire from active association with the university. It was a difficult situation and required a sense of what was best for the university. Goldstein had done all the groundwork, the speaking, the cajoling, the convincing, and the creating when famous names were not around. He had literally built a university from nothing but dust and ashes, but without Einstein's support, Middlesex would have been better left Middlesex. Goldstein pondered the question: to allow Einstein to publicly resign would perhaps be a fatal blow to the yet unborn university, more damaging than his own departure would be. He therefore resigned.

Back in 1925, when the Hebrew University was established in Jerusalem, Einstein as chairman of the Academic Council was involved in a similar entanglement centering around the office of the academic head. When Einstein strongly advocated the appointment of an academic head he came up against a formidable barrier in the person of Dr. Judah L. Magnes, who had just been elected chancellor. An academic head would, in Einstein's view, serve along and in equal capacity with the chancellor; an academic head would have to be a professional educator with substantial experience in university administration. At the time, no one was serving the academic interests of the university in that capacity, and Magnes strongly opposed naming an academic head, in what he considered to be a threat to his position. Magnes could not be lightly shoved aside. "He was chosen (chancellor) because of the requirements of the time. He was a Zionist; he was an *oleh* (immigrant); he had been, since 1913, an enthusiastic advocate of the university; he was available, had the will and the courage to devote full time to the task without remuneration; and he had the connections in the United States to enable him to successfully raise funds for the University. Additionally, there was no other candidate who commanded his qualifications."[247] But Einstein's attitude and also Weizmann's toward the stewardship of the university did not envision one-man rule; they felt the academic administration should be completely separated from the office of chancellor. Weizmann was caught in the middle. On the one hand he agreed with Einstein on the need for an independent academic head. But on the other hand, he also appreciated the invaluable leadership that Magnes had shown at a time when raising money for a university in a far-off land always proved difficult. Both sides held to their views until 1932 when an impartial investigation was made and held with Einstein as opposed to Magnes. Magnes was later elected president of the university. In the years that followed, both in Jerusalem and in Waltham, after the departure of the prestige names and prime movers, the universities survived to attain the high standards, academically, all had desired.

In the aftermath of the war the Soviet Union assumed the mantle of a major world power. During the last few months of the war she had placed under her domination most of middle Europe—Poland, Rumania, Bulgaria, Czechoslovakia, and the eastern half of Germany. Fearing that the Russians might have dreams of annexing more or all of Europe, the United States immediately began circling the territories under Russian tutelage with a string of air bases. The

Soviets, in turn were afraid that, with the atomic bomb, the United States would attempt to bring the Soviets to their knees. At that time, there were some, on both sides, who would have liked a final showdown between the two super powers, but cooler heads prevailed, especially after both sides realized that the destructiveness of these atomic weapons would be so devastating that neither side could hope to win anything in a nuclear war.

While some pressed for international control of atomic weapons, Einstein held out hope that the United Nations organization would develop into a higher supra-national authority "vested with sufficient legislative and executive powers to keep the peace,"[248] and eliminate the need for each nation to be separately secure. "The United Nations is an extremely important and useful institution *provided* the people and governments of the world realize that it is merely a transitional system toward the final goal, which is the establishment of a supra-national authority."[249] "Security," Einstein wrote in an "open letter" to the United Nations, "is indivisible. It can be reached only when necessary guarantees of law and enforcement obtain everywhere, so that military security is no longer the problem of any single state"[250] . . . . "If . . . . every citizen realizes that the only guarantees for security and peace in this atomic age is the constant development of a supra-national government, then he will do everything in his power to strengthen the United Nations . . . . the UN must act with utmost speed to create the necessary conditions for international security by laying the foundations for a real world government."[251]

In the same letter he challenged the Soviet Union to join the family of nations in a world government.; if she didn't, the rest of the world should start without her, but that its doors would remain open. Einstein realized the shortcomings and limitations of the UN, but nevertheless had high hopes for its development. "The UN now and world government eventually must serve one single goal—the guarantee of the security, tranquillity, and the welfare of mankind."[252]

Four Soviet scientists replied to Einstein's challenge—Sergei Vavilov, A.N. Frumkin, A.F. Joffe, and N.N. Semyonov. First they praised Einstein's efforts for peace and his out-spoken anti-Nazism, then continued up and down the party line calling his suggestion for Soviet participation in a world government "absurd," suggesting, in turn, that he was a tool of "capitalist monopolies" and that the "out and out imperialists . . . . were using it as a screen for unlimited expansion."[253]

Credit: AIP

At a summer place.

Former Vice-President Henry A. Wallace seeking endorsement from Einstein for forthcoming Presidential election in 1948. Left to right: Wallace, Einstein, columnist Frank Kingdon, actor-singer Paul Robeson.

Einstein's response indicated that he understood the nature of their fear and suspicion of Western motives. He went on, "We should not make the mistake of blaming capitalism for all existing social and political evils, and of assuming that the very establishment of socialism would be able to cure all the social and political ills of humanity."[254] Then rising to the attack, Einstein wrote:

> The suggestions of the American government with regard to atomic weapons represented at least an attempt towards the creation of a supernational security organization. If they were not acceptable, they could at least have served as a basis of discussion for a real solution of the problems of international security. It is, indeed, the attitude of the Soviet Government, that was partly negative and partly dilatory.

Finally, standing above the battle, Einstein appealed for an overview of the clear and present danger to all.

> Is it not true that all the controversies and differences of opinion which we have touched upon in our strange exchange of letters are insignificant pettinesses compared to the danger in which we all find ourselves? Should we not do everything in our power to eliminate the danger which threatens all nations alike? If we hold fast to the concept and practice of unlimited sovereignty of nations it only means that each country reserves the right for itself of pursuing its objectives through warlike means. Under the circumstances, every nation must be prepared for that possibility; this means it must try with all its might to be superior to anyone else. This objective will dominate more and more our entire public life and will poison our youth long before the catastrophe is itself actually upon us. We must not tolerate this, however, as long as we still retain a tiny bit of calm reasoning and human feelings.
>
> This alone is on my mind in supporting the idea of "World Government" without any regard to what other people may have in mind when working for the same objective. I advocate world government because I am convinced that there is no other possible way of eliminating the most terrible danger in which man has ever found himself. The objective of avoiding total destruction must have priority over any other objective.[255]

The two meetings between Dr. Albert Schweitzer and Einstein took place in the 1930s; one in Berlin and the other in England. Over the years, they had followed similar paths, working towards a more secure and more peaceful world. When it became known that Schweitzer would be leaving his jungle hospital and visiting Europe, Einstein wrote and asked him to be his guest in Princeton. Schweitzer responded:

> Dear Friend: So often, indeed, have I written you in thought because from afar I follow your life and your work and your attitude towards the happenings of our time . . . . But now that, through circumstances, I am obliged to forego the opportunity to meet you in Princeton, I cannot do otherwise than to tell you in writing how sorry I am about it. And now I see in an issue of Life magazine, which came into my hands, pictures of the Institute which further increases my regrets about the renunciation. The picture of Dr. Oppenheimer with you is touching. And

when I see a picture of you there always emerges the memory of the beautiful hours at Berlin which I spent with you.[256]

Einstein's letter to Schweitzer on the occasion of the latter's eightieth birthday, on January 14, 1955, was but one of the many messages of congratulations that poured into the jungle hospital at Lamberene; it was the one that touched Schweitzer most deeply. Einstein wrote in part:

> I have scarcely ever known personally a single individual in whom goodness and the need for beauty are merged to such a degree of unity as in the case of Albert Schweitzer . . . . He did not preach and did not warn and did not dream that his example would be an ideal and a comfort to innumerable people. He simply acted out of inner necessity."[257]

Schweitzer's reply concerned itself with peace and atomic weapons:

> About the question of new tests with the most modern Atomic Bomb, I cannot understand that the UN cannot make up its mind to bring the matter to a discussion. I am getting letters asking that you and I and some others should raise our voices to demand such action of the UN.[258]

Schweitzer and Einstein shared the same concern for the future of mankind to the extent that each made appeals for an end to the nuclear arms race. Schweitzer lived long enough to write to President John F. Kennedy in August, 1963 about the American-Soviet test ban treaty.

> (It) gives me hope that war with atomic weapons between east and west can be avoided . . . When I heard of the treaty, I thought of my old friend, Dr. Einstein, with whom I joined in the fight against atomic weapons. He died in Princeton in despair. And I, thanks to your foresight and courage, am able to observe that the world has taken the first step on the road leading to peace.[259]

Growing old was a difficult time for Einstein. Now at the age of 69 his mind remained alert, but his body was continuing to fail. The death of Langevin, of his first wife, Mileva, and of his sister Maja, all in a short space of time, deepened the cragginess around his deep-set eyes. His now completely white hair looked like a halo. The sailboat lay gathering dust in the boat-house. He used to joke that the boat had fallen into a state of disrepair like its owner.

40

FINAL DAYS

After successful surgery for the removal of an intestinal cyst late in 1948, Einstein recuperated in Florida. In the spring he returned to Princeton, refreshed in mind and spirit, to tackle his long-neglected equations once more. The years of work on the unified field theory could never be considered as wasted, for if his approach was premature, and not the correct one, the publication of it would perhaps serve as a warning to scientists who followed of some of the roads not to pursue.

When it became known that a new and more powerful nuclear weapon, the "fusion" or, more commonly called, the "H" or hydrogen bomb, could theoretically be built, pacifists and individual members of the concerned public wrote to Einstein asking him to use his influence to prevent its development. Einstein replied that a unilateral decision on the part of the United States not to make the H bomb would be impractical; that the "cold war" was the responsibility of both sides who evidently found it in their interest to have it continue. Then in January 1950 President Truman announced his decision to go ahead and manufacture the H bomb, stating that this policy was prompted by the desire to keep ahead of the Russians. Now the nuclear arms race was accelerated to possibly disastrous proportions. The casualties as the result of a careless push of a button, in this age of instant catastrophe, could range into the hundreds of millions.

When Einstein saw that neither side showed a willingness to reduce armaments or to keep nuclear weapons to a reasonable level but instead both had embarked on all-out programs of maximum production, especially of the H bomb, without concern for the consequences, he accepted an invitation from Eleanor Roosevelt to appear on her NBC-TV program. Speaking from his Princeton home, dressed in a sweater and open-neck shirt, Einstein told a nationwide television audience that security through armaments is a disastrous illusion. Alluding to the American-Soviet arms race, he said it "assumes hysterical character." He warned further that if the development of the H bomb was successful, then "radioactive poisoning of the atmo-

292

Credit: AIP

Einstein pointing out to a television audience the dangers involved in an H-bomb race between the United States and the Soviet Union. 1950.

sphere and, hence, annihilation of all life on earth will have been brought within the range of what is technically possible.''[261] To head off the appointment with disaster for which the two giant powers were headed, Einstein called for peaceful coexistence among nations, and the "solemn renunciation of violence.''[262] He proposed that a restricted "world government would considerably reduce the imminent danger of war.''[263] His speech appeared in all newspapers, and the New York Post carried this headline on its February 13, 1950 front page:

"Einstein Warns World

OUTLAW

H-BOMB

OR

PERISH.''[264]

Credit: New York Post

Headline from the New York Post, February 13, 1950

With the drive for nuclear armament superiority, the military became more visible on college campuses and loyalty oaths among government workers became a hotly debated issue. In the United States, "witch hunts" were conducted by the House Un-American Activities Committee, for the purpose of rooting out and punishing anyone who held unorthodox views. The witnesses who were summoned to appear before the committee and refused to testify—choosing instead to fall back on the first amendment to the Constitution which guarantees the right of free speech and on the fifth amendment which protects a citizen against having to make self-incriminating statements —came under suspicion of being either communists or fellow-travelers. If after warnings they still refused to testify, they were held in contempt by the committee and were fined or imprisoned or both. One of those who refused to be browbeaten by a committee turned to Einstein for help. William Frauenglass, a Brooklyn teacher, who was faced with the dilemma of whether or not to testify wrote to Einstein for advice. Einstein created a sensation with his published reply:

> The problem with which intellectuals of this country are confronted is very serious. Reactionary politicians have managed to instill suspicion of all intellectual efforts into the public by dangling before their eyes a danger from without. Having succeeded so far, they are now proceeding to suppress the freedom of teaching and to deprive of their positions all those who do not prove submissive, i.e., to starve them out.
>
> What ought the minority of intellectuals to do against this

Princeton. Left to right, Indira Gandhi, Einstein, Prime Minister Nehru, Madam Nehru. Circa 1950.

evil? Frankly, I can only see the revolutionary way of non-cooperation in the sense of Gandhi's. Every intellectual who is called before one of the committees ought to refuse to testify, i.e., he must be prepared for jail and economic ruin, in short, for the sacrifice of his personal welfare in the interest of the cultural welfare of his country. However, this refusal to testify must not be based on the well-known subterfuge of invoking the fifth amendment against possible self-incrimination, but on the assertion that it is shameful for a blameless citizen to submit to such an inquisition and that this kind of inquisition violates the spirit of the Constitution. If enough people are ready to take this grave step they will be successful. If not, then the intellectuals of this country deserve nothing better than the slavery which is intended for them.[265]

These "witch hunts" reached the height of absurdity with the scurrilous behavior of Senator Joseph McCarthy, the junior senator from Wisconsin. McCarthy's claim to fame, his "ace" was a theoretical list of fifty-seven card carrying communists who, he fantasized had infiltrated the State Department. If indeed this was true, a serious threat to the security of the United States existed and should have been dealt with immediately. But McCarthy refused to divulge the names to his senatorial committee, to the FBI, and even to the president. If the list truly did exist, then McCarthy was acting against the interests and security of the United States in not revealing the names so that the agents of a foreign power could be apprehended. That, in itself constituted an act of treason.

McCarthy revealed what he was when he appeared on national television as one of the antagonists at the so-called Army-McCarthy hearings. After all the bluff and bluster, McCarthy was unable to expose one single communist, in or out of government. Finally censured by his own colleagues in the senate, McCarthy left in his wake ruined reputations. Those he "accused," still under suspicion, were often deprived of the means of providing a livelihood for their families.

On November 9, 1952, death came to Einstein's longtime friend, Chaim Weizmann, who in his final years had served as the first president of Israel. In a matter of two days, Einstein received a hand-delivered note sent by the Israeli Ambassador to Washington, Abba Eban. Eban's message asked whether he would accept the Presidency of Israel if it were offered by a vote of the Knesset (Parliament). Einstein replied that he was "deeply moved by the offer from our State

Credit: AIP

Standing in study, Princeton home.

of Israel.''[266] He then proceeded to list, apologetically, the reasons he could not accept. First of all, now in his seventy-third year, his health was failing. Then, the many years of thinking in abstract terms would prevent him from dealing with people in an everyday, practical sense. There was also the question of conscience, should he disagree with the policies of the government. "I am more distressed over these circumstances (having to refuse) because my relationship to the Jewish people has become my strongest human bond, ever since I became fully aware of our precarious situation among the nations of the world."[267]

In a letter to Queen Elizabeth, Einstein complained that he had finally put his fiddle away; that it was becoming more than he could bear, having to listen to his own playing, which like himself had not escaped the ravages of time.

As late as 1952, Einstein was haunted by the image of himself as the "father of the A-bomb." A Japanese editor, acknowledging Einstein's role as a great scientist, asked why he cooperated in the production of the bomb when he knew of its great destructive power? Attempting once again to set the record straight, as he had to do countless times in order to erradicate the erroneous impression that had gathered credence through the years, Einstein explained:

> My part in producing the atomic bomb consisted in a single act: I signed a letter to President Roosevelt, pressing the need for experiments on a large scale in order to explore the possibilities for the production of an atomic bomb.

Credit: AIP

Ben Gurion visits, Princeton 1951.

I was fully aware of the terrible danger to mankind in case this attempt succeeded. But the likelihood that the Germans were working on the same problem with a chance of succeeding forced me to take this step. I could do nothing else although I have always been a convinced pacifist. To my mind, to kill in war is not a whit better than to commit ordinary murder.''[268]

In other correspondence, he reiterated that he never condoned the use of atomic bombs, but that it had not been his decision to make.

Babies, streets, astrophysical towers, and schools have been named after Einstein. Many are the honors he received and many are the contributions he made in fields other than science. Though he was not attached to Yeshiva University in an academic sense, the board of the university chose to name its new school of medicine, the Albert Einstein College of Medicine. And without much ado, they received his permission. On March 15, 1954, on the occasion of the dedication, some of the officers of the University including its president, Dr. Samuel Balkin, former New York State attorney general Nathaniel L. Goldstein, and Dean of the Albert Einstein College of Medicine, Dr. Marcus D. Kogel traveled south to Princeton. At the location of the Princeton Inn the architects model of the proposed college was viewed by Einstein for the first time. In an era when the United States was feeling the pinch from the lack of sufficient medical facilities Einstein's words were especially meaningful as he addressed the media cameras. ''I am grateful that Yeshiva University has honored me by using my name in connection with the new college of medicine. There is a shortage of physicians in this country and there are many young people able and eager to study medicine, who under the present circumstances are deprived of the opportunity to do so.''

For an honorary degree which he highly prized Einstein traveled to Lincoln University in Pennsylvania to receive. Here, Dr. Horace Mann Bond presented Einstein the degree in appreciation for his call for full equality for minorities and in particular for his support of the defendants in the Scottsboro case. On the subject of racial bias Einstein said, ''There is . . . . a somber point in the social outlook of Americans. Their sense of equality and human dignity is mainly limited to men of white skins. Even among these there are prejudices of which I as a Jew am clearly conscious; but they are unimportant in comparison with the attitude of the ''Whites'' toward their fellow-citizens of darker complexion, particularly toward Negroes. The

Credit: Photo by Percy W. Witherall-AIP.

Only on cold days did Einstein wear his wool hat.

more I feel an American, the more the situation pains me. I can escape the feeling of complicity in it only by speaking out . . . . I believe that whoever tries to think things through honestly will soon recognize how unworthy and even fatal is the traditional bias against Negroes.

What, however, can the man of good will do to combat this deeply rooted prejudice? He must have the courage to set an example by word and deed, and must watch lest his children become influenced by this racial bias.

I do not believe there is a way in which this deeply entrenched evil can be quickly healed. But until this goal is reached there is no greater satisfaction for a just and well-meaning person than the knowledge that he has devoted his best energies to the service of the good cause."[269]

Some of the legends built up through the years about Einstein are true, some false. Yes, he did give the answer to a math problem to a student over the phone. But the elated student later found that he would have to find the steps leading to the answer elsewhere. No, Einstein never failed math in school; he simply preferred to concentrate on physics. Yes, he used mostly bar soap with which to shave.

And when one of his assistants made a present to him of a supply of shaving cream, Einstein was delighted with the results. One could shave without scraping one's face. But when the cream ran out, he went back to scraping his face with the soap. And yes, it was always a battle to keep his hair trimmed. The sweater, pipe, and sandals simply made him feel more comfortable. And he kicked off his socks as often as he thought of it, they only get holes in them and have to be mended. He was never absent-minded. His mind was always alert and rapier quick. In the words of Tom Bucky, "He was very much on the ball."[270] He corresponded with the world's luminaries, but he never used engraved stationery; he bought his at the local five and dime.

A prodigious worker and prolific writer throughout his life, Einstein never quite attained the quiet and solitude he often protested he preferred above all things. He busied himself, if not with physics then in letter writing, signing petitions, speaking for and against causes he supported and denounced. He opposed capital punishment as well as the draft, and he sought to influence the political events of his time by championing the freedom of expression.

Looking over the model of the Albert Einstein Medical College of Yeshiva University. Left to right, Dr. Samuel Balkin, Einstein, Nathaniel Goldstein, Dr. Marcus D. Kogel.

Some of Einstein's warmest correspondences, never made public until this centennial year are the excerpts from letters gathered by Helen Dukas and Banesh Hoffmann (a former colleague), and placed into a book entitled, "Albert Einstein, The Human Side." Other of his writings, including essays on Education, Moral Decay, the Negro Question, Science and Religion, Towards a World Government, Open Letter to the General Assembly of the United Nations, Atomic War or Peace, Military Intrusion in Science, and The Goal of Human Existence can be found in the book "Out of My Later Years." A later publication, "Ideas and Opinions" by Einstein contains essays on Freedom, Religion, Politics, Government, Pacifism, the Jewish people, and Germany.

"Albert Einstein, Philosopher-Scientist" edited by Paul Schilpp, offers what comes closest to an autobiography, though Einstein begins, "Here I sit in order to write, at the age of 67, something like my own obituary." With brief references to his beginnings Einstein relates his assessment of contemporary physics as he experienced it. Also included are essays by Niels Bohr, Arnold Sommerfeld, Wolfgang Pauli, Max Born, and Max von Laue. "Einstein On Peace" painstakingly edited by Dr. Otto Nathan and Heinz Norden "is a printed record of his ceaseless efforts against militarism and war."

Einstein never did find a satisfactory method of unifying the electromagnetic and gravitational worlds. Factors then unknown to him but which were discovered after his death, such as the existence of a "strong nuclear force" and a "weak nuclear force" and such post-Einsteinian concepts as "supersymmetry" and "super-gravity" of course, had not been taken into consideration by Einstein. Today, however, work is being continued with *all* the *known* factors to attempt to complete the unified field theory.

Two matters to which Einstein had devoted a major part of his nonscientific life, world peace and the State of Israel, occupied his last days. On the initiative of Bertrand Russell, they collaborated on a strongly-worded, antiwar statement, addressed to the two nuclear powers. In their joint declaration they took the side of neither the communist bloc nor of the West; rather they pointed out to both that there can no victor in a war with thermonuclear weapons; that a simple outlawing of these weapons was not sufficient and could not be enforced anyhow. They called on the two adversaries to come to the realization that "all equally are in peril, and, if the peril is understood, there is hope that they may collectively avert it."[271] Since the destructiveness of these new bombs was as much as twenty-

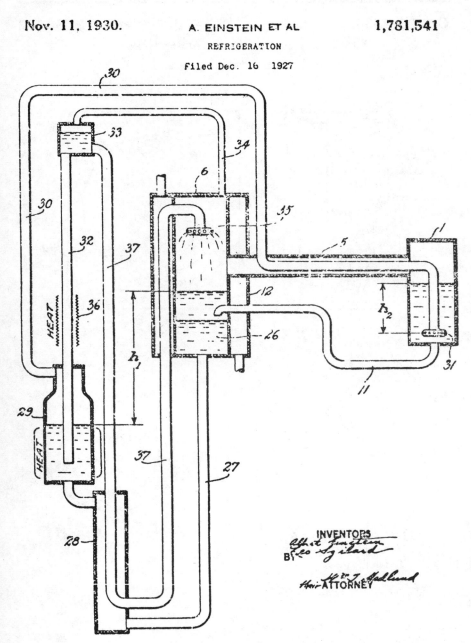

Refrigeration unit invented by Leo Szilard and Einstein, Berlin, 1927.

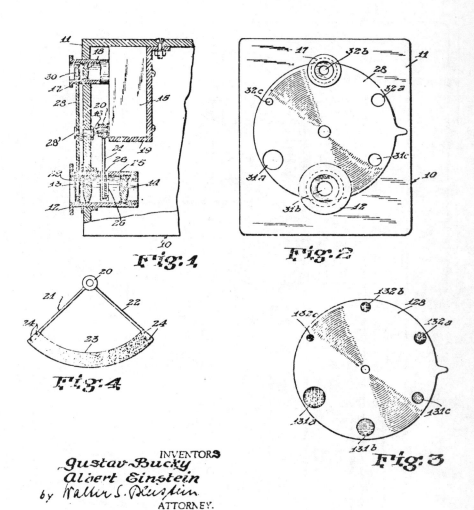

Oct. 27, 1936.   G. BUCKY ET AL   2,058,562

LIGHT INTENSITY SELF ADJUSTING CAMERA

Filed Dec. 11, 1935

INVENTORS
Gustav Bucky
Albert Einstein
by *Walter S. Blustein*
ATTORNEY.

Built in light meter for single lens reflex cameras, invented by Gustav Bucky and Einstein, 1935.

five hundred times the one dropped on Hiroshima, "A great war with nuclear weapons means, at the lowest possible estimate, appalling disaster, and, not improbably, extinction of all life on our planet."[272] The only option Russell and Einstein left open to mankind, to save itself, is the total abolition of war itself: "Their lies before us, if we choose, continual progress in happiness, knowledge and wisdom. Shall we, instead, choose death, because we cannot forget our quarrels? We appeal as human beings to human beings: Remember your humanity and forget the rest. If you can do so, the way lies open to a new paradise; if you cannot, there lies before you the risk of universal death."[273]

In the few days before his death, Einstein was busily writing the text of an address he was to make on radio and television celebrating the May anniversary of Israeli independence. He had written in part: "I speak to you today not as an American citizen and not as a Jew, but as a human being who seeks with the greatest seriousness to look at things objectively."[274] Instead of laying the blame for the Mideast conflict on the nations directly involved, he took the loftier view that saw the struggle as evidence of the balance of power game, with Israel and the Arab countries victims of East-West manipulations. And in an era of atomic weapons, a war in the Middle East could easily set the stage for a world conflagration. Once more and for an agonizing last time he appealed for the establishment of a world government and a supranational authority.

The message was never completed, for Einstein fell ill on April 13, 1955 and was removed to Princeton Hospital. Hans Albert was summoned from California and the Bucky's came in from New York. After a routine examination, the medical team recommended an operation to stop the suspected internal bleeding; but Einstein said no.

The old professor with the familiar halo of white hair and the old-world, bottlebrush moustache died quietly on April 18th. He had refused an operation that could possibly have prolonged his life a few more years. Evidently he felt he had staved off the call of the "Old One" long enough; perhaps he felt his work was finished. It may have been because, in the words of Alexander Moszkowski: "He never rids himself of the feeling that he is only paying a visit in the world."[275] In any event, perhaps the greatest mind in the twentieth century, the man who had propounded "one of the highest achievements of human thought,"[276] whose brilliant outpourings came closer than anyone's in history to formulating the equations upon which the geometry of the universe was based, was ready to go.

An autopsy revealed that Einstein died of a burst aorta; an operation would not have helped. His wish to be cremated was carried out. But before this procedure his brain was removed and set aside for study. Tentative findings indicate that the brain of Albert Einstein is no different than that of an ordinary human. The examination of the brain, however, is continuing and the final results are not in as of this writing. His remains were scattered in a nearby waterway.

Centennial Year Tribute by sculptor Robert Berks, commissioned by the National Academy of Sciences, Washington, D. C. 1979.

EPILOGUE

For centuries to come the name of Albert Einstein will be emblazoned as one of the few pioneers whose advanced thinking gave experimentalists a direction from which they have never veered and civilization a revealing view of the universe.

With newly developed space technology, methods now known will be used in future years to continue to test Einstein's gravitational theory. Our own solar system still offers the best and most convenient vehicle for that purpose. For instance, NASA has on its drawing boards the Solar Probe. And if the funds are approved the solar probe will become a reality in 1987. The solar probe would send an exploratory spacecraft to within two million miles of the sun to investigate regions near the sun's corona. The effect scientists most hope to find is the "gravitational red-shift," where Einstein had predicted that on a large mass, such as the sun, its gravitational effect would cause time to slow down. This effect, we recall, is the third Einstein prediction incorporated into his gravitational theory, and has always proved the most difficult to test.

In earlier years, scientists lacked the sophisticated equipment with which to make accurate measurements through the earth's atmosphere. But now, without earthly debris with which they were heretofore forced to contend, the scientists conducting "experimental relativity" might finally catch up to its theory. In the same probe, tests will also be conducted to attempt to verify the existence of "gravity waves," another Einstein prediction.

Several years ago, Robert F.C. Vessot and Martin W. Levine of the Harvard-Smithsonian Center for Astrophysics had performed a successful gravitational red-shift experiment. Vessot said, "With gravity waves we'll be looking at the reverberations of the origins of galaxies. They'll be the oldest thing we can look at besides the cosmic background radiation. It will enable us to go back to the dawn of creation."[277]

NOTES

1. *The Independent,* April 16, 1920.
2. Albert Einstein: *Relativity, The Special and General Theory* (afterward referred to as "Relativity"), p. 75.
3. *The Independent,* April 16, 1920.
4. Albert Einstein, with Lorentz, Weyl, Minkowski: *The Principle of Relativity,* p. 108.
5. Sir Arthur Eddington: *The Observatory,* December, 1919.
6. Ibid.
7. Philipp Frank, *Einstein, His Life and Times* (afterward referred to as "Frank") p. 3.
8. Ibid, p. 4.
9. Autobiographical notes in *Albert Einstein: Philosopher-Scientist,* Paul A. Schilpp, ed. (afterward referred to as "Schilpp"), p. 9.
10. Alexander Moszkowski: *Conversations With Einstein* (afterward referred to as "Moszkowski"), p. 221.
11. Lucius Bugbee: *Living Leaders Judged By Christian Standards* (afterward referred to as "Bugbee"), p. 14.
12. Einstein Archives.
13. Albert Einstein: *Ideas And Opinions* (afterward referred to as "I&O"), p. 22.
14. Albert Einstein: *Manifesto,* October 12, 1931. Einstein Archives.
15. I&O, p. 69.
16. Albert Einstein: *The World As I See It* (afterward referred to as "Twaisi"), p. 239.
17. Schilpp, p. 3.
18. Ibid, p. 9.
19. Ibid, p. 15.
20. Max Talmey: *The Relativity Theory Simplified and the Formative Years of its Inventor* (afterward referred to as "Talmey"), pp. 159–163.
21. Ibid, p. 164.
22. Schilpp, p. 5.
23. Ibid, p. 5.
24. Antonina Vallentin: *The Drama of Albert Einstein* (afterward referred to as "Vallentin"), p. 168.
25. Dr. Otto Nathan and Heinz Norden: *Einstein On Peace* (afterward referred to as "Nathan & Norden"), p. 406.
26. H. Gordon Garbedian: *Albert Einstein, Maker of Universes* (afterward referred to as "Garbedian"), p. 27.

27. Schilpp, p. 15.
28. Ibid, p. 21.
29. Einstein Archives.
30. Schilpp, p. 3.

31. Ibid, pp. 15–17.
32. Ibid, p. 17.
33. Ibid, p. 17.
34. Albert Einstein: *Out Of My Later Years,* (afterward referred to as Oomly), p. 34.
35. Frank, p. 23.
36. Albert Einstein: *On The Electrodynamics of Moving Bodies,* from *The Principle of Relativity,* p. 65.
37. David Reichenstein: *Albert Einstein, A Picture of His Life and His Conception of The World* (afterward referred to as "Reichenstein"), pp. 22–23.
38. Garbedian, p. 79.
39. Dr. Solomon Freehof: *Marx, Freud and Einstein* (afterward referred to as "Freehof"), p. 33.
40. Ibid, p. 34.

41. Bugbee, p. 46.
42. Relativity, pp. 9–10.
43. Max Born: *The Restless Universe,* pp. 38–39.
44. Hans Reichenbach: *Atom and Cosmos,* p. 139.
45. Samuel H. Guggenheimer: *The Einstein Theory Explained and Analyzed* (afterward referred to as "Guggenheimer") pp. 33–34.
46. Mario Palmieri, *Relativity, An Interpretation of Einstein's Theory,* p. 31.
47. Freehof, p. 35.
48. Jeremy Bernstein: *Einstein* (afterward referred to as "Bernstein"), p. 52.
49. Garbedian, p. 52.
50. Frank, p. 64.

51. Guggenheimer, p. 59.
52. Guggenheimer, pp. 59–60.
53. Albert Einstein: *Cosmic Religion,* pp. 52–53.
54. Albert Einstein: *Investigations On The Theory Of the Brownian Movement,* p. 2.
55. Bernstein, pp. 184–185.
56. Max Born: *Einstein's Statistical Theories,* from Schilpp, p. 166.
57. Martin J. Klein: *Max Born On His Vocation,* p. 361.
58. Schilpp, pp. 163–164.
59. F. Gaynore: *Max Planck-Scientific Biography and Other Papers.*
60. Freehof, p. 32.

61. Aaron B. Lerner: *Newton And Einstein;* quote from Isaac Newton.
62. Relativity, pp. 25–27.

63. Richard Keating and Joseph Hafele: Around-The-World Atomic Clocks, *Science,* July 14, 1972.
64. J.S. Ames: Einstein's Law of Gravitation, *Science,* March 12, 1920, p. 256.
65. Schilpp, p. 57.
66. Albert Einstein: *The Principle of Relativity,* p. 71.
67. Ibid., p. 71.
68. Leopold Infeld: *Albert Einstein: His Work And Its Influence On Our World,* p. 44.
69. Anton Reiser: *Albert Einstein, A Biographical Portrait,* p. 81.
70. Frank, p. 75.

71. Ibid, p. 76.
72. Hermann Minkowski: Space And Time, *The Principle of Relativity*, p. 75.
73. Charles Proteus Steinmetz: *Four Lectures on Relativity and Space,* p. 24.
74. Reichenstein, p. 24.
75. Ibid, pp. 47–48.
76. Frank, p. 78.
77. Ibid, p. 82.
78. Ibid, p. 80.
79. Albert Einstein: *The Principle of Relativity,* p. 99.
80. Ibid, p. 108.

81. I&O, p. 80.
82. Vallentin, p. 31.
83. I&O, p. 82.
84. Henrik A. Lorentz: *Problems of Modern Physics*. Lecture at the California Institute of Technology, 1922, pp. 220–221.
85. I&O, p. 83.
86. Marie Curie: *Pierre Curie,* p. 69.
87. Ibid, p. 69.
88. Marie Curie; ETH, November 11, 1911.
89. Henri Poincare; ETH, November 11, 1911.
90. Hans Albert Einstein and Bela Kornitzer: *Einstein is My Father, Ladies Home Journal,* pp. 134–136.

91. Garbedian, p. 108.
92. S.L.A. Marshall: *World War I,* p. 14.
93. Georg Nicolai: *The Biology of War,* p. xi.
94. Ibid, pp. xi-xiii.
95. Georg Nicolai and Albert Einstein: *Manifesto to Europeans,* pp. xiii–xix.
96. Vallentin, pp. 61–62.
97. Nathan & Norden, p. 13.
98. Ibid, p. 16.
99. Leopold Infeld: *Quest: The Evolution of a Scientist,* p. 219.
100. Martin J. Klein: *Paul Ehrenfest,* p. 303.

101. Nathan & Norden, p. 20.
102. Ibid, p. 18.
103. *Rijksmuseum Voor De Geschiedenis Der Natuurwetenschappen,* Leiden, Holland.
104. Harold Jacoby: The Gravitation Of Light, *Literary Digest,* December 27, 1919, p. 28.
105. *The Times,* London, December 13, 1919.
106. Ibid.
107. Ibid.
108. Leopold Infeld: *Albert Einstein: His Work and its Influence on our World,* p. 121.
109. Lyndon Bolton: Relativity, *Scientific American,* February 5, 1921, p. 106.
110. Albert Einstein: *Berliner Tageblatt.*

111. Frank, p. 172.
112. Vallentin, pp. 93–94.
113. Leopold Infeld: Portrait . . . Einstein, *American Scholar* (afterward referred to as "Portrait"), July, 1947, pp. 337–341.
114. Albert Einstein: The Gravitation of Light, *Literary Digest,* December 27, 1919, p. 29.
115. Albert Einstein: Professor Einstein at Home, *Literary Digest,* March 20, 1920, p. 73.
116. Chaim Weizmann: *Trial And Error* (afterward referred to as "Weizmann"), pp. 266–267.
117. Vallentin, p. 103.
118. Weizmann, p. 273.
119. Talmey, p. 174.
120. Vallentin, p. 106.

121. Charles Nordmann: L'Illustration, *With Einstein On The Battlefields, Living Age,* June 3, 1922 (afterward referred to as "Nordmann"), p. 591.
122. Nathan & Norden, p. 588.
123. Nordmann, p. 588.
124. Ibid, p. 591.
125. Ibid, p. 591.
126. Ibid, p. 592.
127. Nathan & Norden, p. 49.
128. Ibid, p. 50.
129. Moszkowski, p. 5.
130. Reichenstein, pp. 66–67.

131. Nathan & Norden, p. 56.
132. Nathan & Norden, p. 75, *New York Times,* May 17, 1925.
133. Albert Einstein: *About Zionism* (afterward referred to as "Zionism"), p. 42.
134. Ibid, p. 44.
135. Ibid, p. 33.

136. Ibid, p. 79.
137. Ibid, p. 76.
138. Albert Einstein; Einstein Archives.
139. Twaisi, p. 21.
140. Arthur Eddington: *The Nature of the Physical World,* p. 2.

141. I&O, pp. 79–80.
142. Vallentin, p. 159.
143. Albert Einstein; Einstein Archives.
144. Zionism, pp. 79–80.
145. Vallentin, pp. 196–197.
146. Vallentin, p. 199.
147. Albert Einstein: *New York Times,* December 3, 1930.
148. Vallentin, p. 102.
149. Reichenstein, pp. 110–111.
150. Albert Einstein; Einstein Archives.

151. "We May Not 'Get' Relativity, But We Like Einstein," *Literary Digest,* December 27, 1930, p. 29.
152. Albert Einstein; Einstein Archives.
153. Garbedian, p. 245.
154. Albert Einstein; Einstein Archives.
155. Albert Einstein: *The Fight Against War* (afterward referred to as Tfaw), p. 35.
156. Albert Einstein: Einstein Archives.
157. Ibid.
158. Albert Einstein: Professor Einstein At The California Institute of Technology, *Science,* April 10, 1931, p. 379.
159. Nathan & Norden, p. 122.
160. Tfaw, p. 40.

161. Ibid, p. 40.
162. Ibid, p. 37.
163. Twaisi, p. 243.
164. Tfaw, pp. 43–44.
165. Albert Einstein: Gravitational and Electromagnetic Fields, *Science,* October 30, 1931, pp. 438–439.
166. Nathan & Norden, p. 156.
167. Tfaw, p. 59.
168. Albert Einstein; Einstein Archives.
169. Twaisi, p. 63.
170. Abraham Flexner: *I Remember* (afterward referred to as "Flexner"), p. 362.

171. Tfaw, p. 61.
172. Note deleted.
173. Sigmund Freud, Albert Einstein: *Why War?*, Nathan & Norden, pp. 188–200.
174. Ibid.
175. Ibid.

176. Flexner, p. 383.
177. Ibid, p. 383.
178. Vallentin, p. 202.
179. Ibid, p. 203.
180. Frank, p. 226.

181. I&O, p. 19.
182. Garbedian, pp. 276–277.
183. Albert Grzesinski: *Inside Germany* (afterward referred to as "Grzesinski"), p. 168.
184. Oomly, p. 215.
185. Frank, p. 226.
186. Albert Einstein, *New York World Telegram,* March 11, 1933.
187. Albert Einstein, *New York Times,* March 17, 1933.
188. Ibid.
189. Grzesinski, p. 197.
190. Ibid, p. 215.

191. Ibid, p. 184.
192. Ibid, p. 189.
193. Albert Einstein, *New York Times,* March 17, 1933.
194. I&O, p. 203.
195. Vallentin, p. 221.
196. Morris Goran: *The Story of Fritz Haber,* p. 161.
197. Weizmann, p. 352.
198. Ibid, p. 352.
199. Ibid, p. 352.
200. Ibid, p. 353.

201. Ibid, p. 354.
202. Ibid, p. 354.
203. I&O, p. 203.
204. Ibid, p. 205.
205. Ibid, pp. 205–207.
206. Nathan & Norden, p. 217.
207. Ibid, p. 220.
208. Frank, p. 232.
209. Ibid, p. 232.
210. Vallentin, p. 231.

211. Ibid, p. 222.
212. Nathan & Norden, p. 230.
213. Ibid, p. 231.
214. Albert Einstein, *New York World Telegram,* September 19, 1933.
215. Oomly, pp. 148–151.
216. Vallentin, p. 221.

217. Dr. Thomas L. Bucky interview (afterward referred to as "Bucky"), July 1977.
218. Grzesinski, p. 253.
219. William L. Shirer: *Berlin Diary* (afterward referred to as "Shirer"), p. 37.
220. Max Gallo: *The Night Of The Long Knives,* p. 10.

221. Ernest Rutherford, *New York Herald Tribune,* September 12, 1933.
222. Karl T. Compton, *New York Times,* March 30, 1934.
223. Shirer, p. 26.
224. Ibid, p. 35.
225. Ibid, pp. 52–53.
226. Nathan & Norden, p. 268.
227. Portrait, p. 338.
228. Albert Einstein; Born Letters.
229. Portrait, p. 338.
230. Bucky.

231. Sendel Grynszpan: *Eichmann Trial,* Jerusalem, 1961.
232. David H. Buffum: *American Consul in Leipzig, Nazi Conspiracy and Aggression,* Office of the U.S. Chief of Counsel for Prosecution of Axis Criminality. United States Government Printing Office, Washington, DC, 1946, Vol. VII, pp. 1037–41.
233. Franklin D. Roosevelt: *National Archives,* Roosevelt Library, Hyde Park, N.Y.
234. Bucky.
235. Albert Einstein, Eugene Wigner, Leo Szilard: *National Archives,* Roosevelt Library, Hyde Park, N.Y.
236. Albert Einstein, *New York Times,* June 23, 1946.
237. Nathan & Norden, p. 368.
238. Walter Clay Loudermilk: *Palestine, Land of Promise,* pp. 9-10.
239. Albert Einstein, Hearings before the Anglo-American Committee of Inquiry on Palestine, Washington, DC, January 11, 1946.
240. Zionism, p. 41.

241. Ibid, p. 42.
242. Ibid, p. 52.
243. Dr. Israel Goldstein, *Brandeis University,* pp. 27–29.
244. Ibid, p. 36.
245. Ibid, p. 95.
246. Ibid, p. 9.
247. Magnes-Weizmann–Einstein Controversy, Herbert Parzen.
248. Albert Einstein: Open Letter to the General Assembly of the United Nations, *United Nations World,* October, 1947, p. 13.
249. Ibid, p. 13.
250. Ibid, p. 13.

251. Ibid, p. 14.

252. Ibid, p. 14.
253. Oomly, p. 162.
254. Ibid, pp. 170–171.
255. Ibid, p. 175.
256. *Albert Schweitzer Archive* (Alsace, France; by permission of Rhena Schweitzer-Miller (afterward referred to as "Schweitzer").
257. Albert Einstein, quote from *Albert Schweitzer,* a Biography, by George Marshall and David Poling, pp. 240–241.
258. Ibid, pp. 241–242.
259. Schweitzer, p. 287.
260. I&O, p. 160.

261. Ibid, p. 160.
262. Ibid, p. 160.
263. Ibid, p. 161.
264. *New York Post,* February 2, 1950.
265. Nathan & Norden, pp. 546–547.
266. Ibid, p. 572.
267. Ibid, p. 573.
268. I&O, pp. 165–166.
269. Oomly, pp. 132–134.
270. Bucky.

271. Nathan & Norden, pp. 632–633.
272. *New York Times,* July 10, 1955.
273. Nathan & Norden, p. 633.
274. Ibid, p. 639.
275. Moszkowski, p. 241.
276. Sir Joseph Thompson, President of The Royal Society: The Deflection of Light by Gravitation and the Einstein Theory of Relativity, *Scientific Monthly,* January, 1920.
277. *Science News*, Vol. 116, No. 8, August 25, 1979, by Marcia F. Bartusiak.

BIBLIOGRAPHY

AMES, J.S. "Einstein's Law of Gravitation," March 12, 1920.

ANTHONY, H.F. "Sir Isaac Newton," London, 1960.

BARNETT, Lincoln. "The Universe and Dr. Einstein," New York, 1948.

BERNSTEIN, Jeremy. "Einstein," New York 1973.

BORN, Max. "Restless Universe," 1951.

BORN, Max. "Einstein's Statistical Theories," Albert Einstein, Philosopher-Scientist, 1949.

BRONOWSKI, Jacob. "Einstein's Influence," Nation, March 17, 1956.

BUCHANAN, L.B. "Einstein For The Man In The Street," 1920.

BUCKY, Dr. Thomas L. Interview July, 1977.

BUFFUM, David H. American Consul in Leipzig: *Nazi Conspiracy and Aggressions,* Office of the U.S. Chief of Counsel for Prosecution of Axis Criminality; United States Printing Office, Washington, DC, 1946, Vol. VII pp. 1037–41.

BUGBEE, Lucius. "Living Leaders Judged By Christian Standards," Nashville, 1923.

CAHN, William. "Einstein, A Pictorial Biography," New York, 1955.

CLARK, Ronald, W. "Einstein, The Life And Times," New York, 1971.

COFFMAN, Edward, M. "The War To End All Wars," Oxford, 1968.

CUNY, Hilaire. "Albert Einstein, The Man And His Theories," Greenwich, 1962.

CURIE, Eve. "Madame Curie," New York, 1937.

CURIE, Marie. "Pierre Curie," New York 1923.

EDDINGTON, Sir Arthur. "The Nature of The Physical World," Cambridge 1930.

EINSTEIN, Albert. "Ether and the Theory of Relativity," lecture at the University of Leiden, Holland, May 5, 1920.

_____. "Cosmic Religion," New York, 1931.

_____. "Ideas and Opinions," New York, 1954.

_____. "Investigations on the Theory of the Brownian Movement," London, 1930.

_____. "About Zionism," London, 1930.

_____. "Principle of Relativity," with Lorentz, Weyl, Minkowski, London, 1923.

_____. "The Fight Against War," New York, 1933.

_____. "What I Believe," Forum, October, 1930.

_____. "Manifesto to Europeans," with Georg Nicolai, Berlin, 1914.

_____. "Why War," with Sigmund Freud, Berlin, 1932.

_____. "The Evolution of Physics," with Leopold Infeld, New York, 1938.

_____. "Relativity: The Special and General Theory, New York, 1952.

_____. "Out Of My Later Years," New York, 1950.

317

————. "Open Letter to the General Assembly of the United Nations," October, 1947.

————. "Autobiographical Notes," 1949.

EINSTEIN, Hans Albert. "Einstein Is My Father," with Bela Kornitzer, Ladies Home Journal, April, 1951.

FANNING, A.E. "Planets, Stars & Galaxies," New York, 1963.

FEINBERG, J.G. "The Story of Atomic Theory and Atomic Energy," New York, 1960.

FERRIS, Timothy. "The Red Limit," New York, 1977.

FEUER, Lewis, S. "Einstein And The Generations of Science," New York, 1974.

FLEXNER, Abraham. "I Remember," New York, 1940.

FRANK, Philipp. "Einstein, His Life and Times," New York, 1947.

FREEHOF, Dr. Solomon. "Marx, Freud and Einstein," Chicago, 1933.

GALLO, Max. "The Night of the Long Knives," New York, 1972.

GARBEDIAN, H. Gordon. "Albert Einstein, Maker of Universes," New York, 1939.

GARDNER, Martin. "Relativity For The Million," New York, 1962.

GAYNORE, F. "Max Planck-Scientific Biography."

GOLDSTEIN, Israel. "Brandeis University," New York, 1951.

GORAN, Morris. "The Story of Fritz Haber," Norman, Oklahoma, 1967.

GRYNSZPAN, Sendel. "Testimony at Eichmann Trial," Jerusalem, Yad Vashem Archives, April 25, 1961.

GRZESINSKI, Albert. "Inside Germany," New York, 1939.

GUGGENHEIMER, Samuel. "The Einstein Theory Explained and Analyzed," New York, 1925.

HAFELE, Joseph and Richard KEATING. "Around-the-World Atomic Clocks," American Association for the Advancement of Science, 1972.

HEATHCOTE, Neils, H. deV. "Nobel Prize Winners In Physics,"

HENDERSON, Archibald. "Contemporary Immortals," London, 1930.

HERZL, Theodore. "Zionist Writings," New York, 1973.

HOFFMANN, Banesh. "Albert Einstein, Creator And Rebel," New York, 1972.

HOFFMANN, Banesh. "The Strange Story Of The Quantum," New York, 1947.

HOFFMANN, Banesh and Helen DUKAS. "Albert Einstein, The Human Side," Princeton, 1979.

INFELD, Leopold. "Quest: The Evolution of a Scientist," New York, 1941.

————. "Albert Einstein: His Work And Its Influence On Our World," New York, 1950.

————. "Portrait . . . . Einstein," American Scholar, July, 1947.

JASTROW, Robert. "Red Giants And White Dwarfs," New York, 1967.

JUNGK, Robert. "Brighter Than A Thousand Suns," Switzerland, 1956.

KLEIN, Martin J. "Paul Ehrenfest," New York, 1970.

    "Max Born On His Vocation," Washington, DC, 1947.

LANCZOS, Cornelius. "Albert Einstein And The Cosmic World Order," London, 1965.

LAURENCE, William, L. "Men And Atoms," New York, 1946.

LERNER, Aaron B. "Einstein & Newton," Minneapolis, 1973.

LORENTZ, Henrik Antoon. "Theory of Electrons," a course of lectures at Columbia University, March–April, 1906.

_____. "Problems of Modern Physics," California Institute of Technology, 1922.

MAC DONALD, Charles, B. and Anthony Cave BROWN. "The Secret History Of The Atomic Bomb," New York, 1977.

MARDER, L. "Time And The Space Traveler," Pennsylvania.

MARSHALL, S.L.A. "World War I," New York, 1964.

MC ADAM, D.J. "Einstein's Relativity: A Criticism," New York, 1922.

MICHELMORE, Peter. "Einstein, Profile Of The Man," New York, 1962.

MINKOWSKI, Hermann. "Space and Time," The Principle of Relativity, Cologne, Germany, 1908.

MOSZKOWSKI, Alexander. "Conversations With Einstein," Oxford, 1921.

MOTZ & BOORSE, "The World Of The Atom."

NATHAN, Dr. Otto and Heinz NORDEN. "Einstein On Peace," New York, 1960.

NICOLSON, Ian. "Astronomy," New York, 1971.

NORDMANN, Charles. "Einstein and the Universe," New York, 1922.

_____. "With Einstein On The Battlefields," from L'Illustration, April 15, 1922.

PALMIERI, Mario. "Relativity: An interpretation of Einstein's Theory," Los Angeles, 1931.

PARZEN, Herbert. "Magnes-Weizmann-Einstein Controversy."

PLANCK, Max. "Eighth lecture on Theoretical Physics, Columbia University, 1909.

POLING, David and George MARSHALL. "Albert Schweitzer: A Biography," New York, 1975.

REICHENBACH, Hans. "Atom and Cosmos," New York, 1933.

REICHENSTEIN, David. "Albert Einstein: A Picture of his Life and his Conception of the World," Prague, 1933.

REISER, Anton. "Albert Einstein: A Biographical Portrait," New York, 1930.

ROLLAND, Romain. "Above The Battle," Switzerland, 1915.

RUSSELL, Bertrand. "ABC of Relativity," 1925.

SANFORD, Hugh W. "A Major Premise Of Albert Einstein," Knoxville, 1950.

SHAPLEY, Harlow. "Through Rugged Ways To The Stars," New York, 1969.

SHIRER, William L. "Berlin Diary," New York, 1941.

SNOW, C.P. "On Albert Einstein," New York, 1967.

STEINMETZ, Charles Proteus. "Four Lectures on Relativity and Space," Toronto, 1923.

TALMEY, Max. "The Relativity Theory Simplified and the Formative Period of its Inventor," New York, 1922.

THALMANN, Rita and Emanuel FEINERMANN. "Crystal Night," Paris, 1972.

THOMSON, George Malcolm. "The Twelve Days,"

TUCHMAN, Barbara. "Bible And Sword," New York, 1956.

VALLENTIN, Antonina. "The Drama of Albert Einstein," New York, 1954.

VECHIERELLO, Reverend Hubert. "Einstein And Relativity-LeMaitre And The Expanding Universe," Paterson, New Jersey, 1934.
WEIZMANN, Chaim. "Trial and Error," Philadelphia, 1949.
WHITROW, G.J. "Einstein, The Man And His Achievement," London, 1967.
WILKS, Willard, E. "The New Wilderness," New York, 1963.
WISE, William. "Albert Einstein, Citizen Of The World," New York, 1960.

REFERENCE PERIODICALS

America
American Heritage
American Image
American Mercury
American Scholar
Astronomy
Atlantic Monthly
Aviation Week
Bulletin of Atomic Scientists
Catholic World
Christian Century
Colliers
Commentary
Commonweal
Current History, New York Times
Fortune
Forum
Harper's
Independent
Jewish Telegraphic Agency
Ladies Home Journal
Literary Digest
Living Age
Look
Nation

National Review
New Republic
Newsweek
New Yorker
New York Times
Outlook
Popular Mechanics
Popular Science
Readers Digest
Saturday Evening Post
Saturday Review of Literature
School and Society
Science
Science Digest
Science News
Science News Letter
Scientific American
Scientific Monthly
Sky and Telescope
Smithsonian Report
United Nations Review
Vital Speeches of the Day
Wilson Bulletin for Librarians
Worlds Book

ACKNOWLEDGEMENTS

A particular note of appreciation to Rabbi H. Leonard and Priscilla Poller. It was in the warm atmosphere of their home that the seed was planted.

Edward J. BANDER, New York University Law Library, Suffolk University Law Library, and longtime friend.

Paula BAXTER, American Institute of Physics.

Dr. Thomas L. BUCKY, personal friend of Albert Einstein.

Elizabeth M. COX, Yerkes Observatory, Williams Bay, Wisconsin.

Peter DEWS, American Institute of Physics.

Helen DUKAS, Institute For Advanced Study, Princeton, New Jersey, Secretary to Albert Einstein. Trustee of Einstein Estate.

John DUTTON, World Federation of Scientific Workers, London.

G. J. ELTRINGHAM, Deputy Registrar, University of Nottingham, Nottingham, England.

Barbara ENNIS, Director of Freedom of Information Staff, Department of State, Washington, DC.

F. E. EVANS, Science Research Council, Royal Greenwich Observatory, East Sussex, England.

Rosina FIGGIS, London Express News.

Deborah FRANKLIN, Jewish Film Archives, Jerusalem, Israel.

Milton O. GUSTAFSON, General Services Administration, Washington, DC.

Dr. Israel GUTMAN, Holocaust Research Center, Jerusalem, Israel.

F.A. HANDLER, University of Texas Department of Physics, Austin.

Adina HARAN, The Central Zionist Archives, Jerusalem.

Richard KEATING, U.S. Naval Observatory, Washington, DC.

Inge KISSENICH, German Information Office, New York.

Dr. Roland KLEMIG, Staatsbibliothek, Berlin, Germany.

Mrs. E. LAKE, Librarian, Royal Astronomical Society, London.

Chevalier A. de Selliers de MORANVILLE, Le President, Le Musee De La Dynastie, Brussels, Belgium.

E. MYNN, Photographic Library, The Times, London.

Mireille NAHMAN, Paris.

Dr. Otto NATHAN, Trustee of the Einstein Estate.

Tanya OSTER, American Institute of Physics.

Dennis E. OVERBYE, Sky and Telescope, Cambridge, Ma.
Bob and Sandy ROSS, The Albert Schweitzer Friendship House, Great Barrington, Ma.
Rhena SCHWEITZER-MILLER, Atlanta, Georgia.
Mary Lea SHANE, Lick Observatory, Santa Cruz, California.
Irwin I. SHAPIRO, Massachusetts Institute of Technology, Cambridge, Ma.
Ali SILVER, Schweitzer Archiv, Gunsbach, Alsace, France.
M. H. SJOLLEMA, Rijksmuseum Voor De Geschiedenis Der Natuurwetenschappen, Leiden, Holland.
W. N. SLADE, New Scientist, London.
Philip SNOWDON, The Sunday Express, London.
Institut de SOLVAY, Brussels.
Dr. SPECKER, Stadtarchiv, Ulm, Germany.
J. SPEIGHT, The Institute of Electrical Engineers, London.
I. STEENWERTH, Fritz Haber Institut der Max Planck Gesellschaft, Berlin.
Esther TOGMAN, Zionist Archives, New York.
Joan WARNOW, American Institute of Physics.
Sven WELANDER, United Nations Library, Geneva, Switzerland.
Eliane YOUNG, Office of Consulate General of Belgium, New York.
I. ZANDELL, Nobel Foundation, Stockholm, Sweden.

The personnel at the Library of Congress, Washington, DC.

The personnel at Bobst Library, Larchmont Library, Mamaroneck Free Library, White Plains Library, New York City Public Library (main Branch).

Others who helped are, Alice Einstein, Charles Feman, Donn Fine, Florence Hannon, Bernie Liebler, Paul Martel, Marjorie Meyer, Wendy Miller, Pauline Ostrow, Frank Richter, Sam Schmidt, Leonard Swern, Eunice Thibodeau, Jim Youngman.

The Drama of Albert Einstein by Antonina Vallentin. Used with permission of Doubleday & Company.

Around-The-World Atomic Clocks by Joseph Hafele and Richard Keating. Science Vol. 177 pp. 160–170, 14 July 1972. Used with permission of the American Association for the Advancement of Science.

Einstein by Jeremy Bernstein © 1973, Viking Penguin Inc.

The Nature of the Physical World by Arthur Eddington 1928. Used with permission of the Cambridge University Press.

Einstein And His Influence On Our World by Leopold Infeld. Used with permission of Chas. Scribner's Sons.

About Zionism by Albert Einstein. © by Macmillian Publishing Company Inc.

Einstein His Life And Times by Philipp Frank. Translated by George Rosen, edited and revised by Schuichi Kusaka. © 1947 Alfred A. Knopf.

Theory Of The Brownian Movement by Albert Einstein. Translated by A.D. Cowper, edited with notes by R. Furth. Originally published in 1926 by Methuen and Company Ltd. Published by Dover Publications, Inc. 1956.

The Principle Of Relativity by Albert Einstein, Henrik Lorentz, Hermann Weyl and Hermann Minkowski. Translated by W.Perrett and G. B. Jeffrey, with notes by A. Sommerfeld. Originally published by Methuen and Company Ltd. in 1923. Published by Dover Publications, Inc. 1952.

Pierre Curie by Marie Curie. Translated by Charlotte and Vernon Kellogg. Originally published by The Macmillan Company in 1923. Published by Dover Publications, Inc. 1963.

Restless Universe by Max Born, 1951.

Inside Germany by Albert C. Grzesinski, translated by Alexander S. Lipschitz. Copyright © 1939, by E.P. Dutton & Co., Inc. Reprinted by permission.

The American Scholar, Volume 16, Number 3, Summer, 1947. Copyright © 1947 by the United Chapters of Phi Beta Kappa. By permission of the publishers.

INDEX